T0301356

Knowledge Management in Developing
Economies

Knowledge Management in Developing Economies

A Cross-Cultural and Institutional Approach

Edited by

Kate Hutchings

*Associate Professor, Department of Management,
Monash University, Australia*

Kavoos Mohannak

*Lecturer, School of Management, Queensland University
of Technology, Australia*

Edward Elgar

Cheltenham, UK • Northampton, MA, USA

Published by
Edward Elgar Publishing Limited
Glensanda House
Montpellier Parade
Cheltenham
Glos GL50 1UA
UK

Edward Elgar Publishing, Inc.
William Pratt House
9 Dewey Court
Northampton
Massachusetts 01060
USA

A catalogue record for this book
is available from the British Library

Library of Congress Cataloguing in Publication Data

Knowledge management in developing economies : a cross-cultural and
institutional approach / edited by Kate Hutchings, Kavoos Mohannak.
     p. cm.
   Includes bibliographical references and index.
   1. Knowledge management—Developing countries. 2. Knowledge
management—Cross-cultural studies. I. Hutchings, Kate. II. Mohannak,
Kavoos.
   HD30.2.K63675 2007
   658.4'038—dc22

                                                             2006028681

ISBN 978 1 84542 786 3

Printed and bound in Great Britain by MPG Books Ltd, Bodmin, Cornwall

Contents

Contributors

Simon Best (PhD) is a Small Business Management Consultant and principal of Access Business Consultants. Simon has owned and operated several small businesses before setting up Access Business Consultants. He is interested in globalisation and its effects on small businesses. Currently Simon is working with a number of clients in Bangladesh, Vietnam and Egypt who are seeking to take advantage of the benefits globalisation has brought to small businesses. Simon is also employed at Queensland University of Technology as a sessional lecturer in Management. Simon's research interests are in entrepreneurship, business improvisation and cultural effects on businesses. He recently completed his PhD through Swinburne University of Technology, Melbourne. E-mail: spdbest@acenet.net.au

Mehraz Boolaky (PhD) is an Associate Professor in the Faculty of Law and Management, University of Mauritius. He was previously Dean in the Faculty of Law and Management, University of Mauritius. Dr Boolaky held senior management positions in the private sector for more than 14 years before joining the University of Mauritius in 1993. He has taught in Malaysia, France, Madagascar, Reunion, Morocco and the Seychelles. He is currently on leave from the University of Mauritius and attached to the Al Akhawayn University in Morocco. He has provided consultancy in various areas of Management including training and development, recruitment and selection exercises, marketing and strategic planning. He has presented several papers at international conferences. His current research interests are in entrepreneurship, knowledge management, organisational restructuring, customer relationship management, marketing and strategic management. E-mail: M.Boolaky@aui.ma; mboolaky@uom.ac.mu

Luis Felipe Calderón-Moncloa (DEA, U. Nice, France) is an Associate Professor in the Graduate Business School, ESAN University, Lima, Peru. He has also been a management consultant for the last 24 years and has published regularly in the most prestigious financial newspapers and journals in Peru. He has taught in Estonia, Serbia, Austria, Dubai, Paraguay, Bolivia and Guatemala and he has been a Visiting Professor in France. He has published two books and, amongst others, in *Revista de Empresa* from IE, Madrid, Spain. His current research interests include intercultural management, intercultural knowledge management and intercultural negotiations. E-mail: Lcalderon@esan.edu.pe

Te Fu Chen is a Lecturer in the Department of International Trade, Cheng Shiu University, Taiwan and is enrolled as a PhD candidate at UWS. He previously worked at the Ton Da Computer and Information Co. Ltd as a CEO, and prior to that he was a consultant to the high-tech industry and SMEs. He was Head of School in Computing & IT of a senior high school in Hsin Chu Scientific and Technological Park in Taiwan. He has published over 45 papers for international conferences and journals about knowledge management, knowledge-based innovation, e-business, e-commerce and supply chain management for high-tech industries and SMEs. His current research interests include knowledge management in Taiwan, knowledge-based innovation for high-tech industry and SMEs, integrated models for e-business and m-business, and innovation supply chains. E-mail: phd2003@hotmail.com

Gerhard Fink is Jean Monnet Professor for applied micro-economics in European integration and Director of the doctoral program at Wirtschaftsuniversität Wien. He was Chairman of the Business Faculty at Wirtschaftsuniversität Wien during 2001–02 and Director of the Institute for European Affairs (Jean Monnet Centre of Excellence) during 1997–2003. In the past, he also taught at the Johns Hopkins University Bologna Centre and at universities in Munich, Trieste, Linz, Vienna and Krems. During 1973–90 he was affiliated with the Vienna Institute for Comparative Studies (WIIW, Director during 1984–90). He is certified as a business consultant by the Austrian Chamber of Commerce. Professor Fink has published about 180 publications in learned journals and authored or (co-)edited about 15 books. He is co-editor of a Special Issue of the *Academy of Management Executive* on the global transfer of management knowledge (2005). He speaks German and English, and has a working knowledge of Russian, Italian and French. E-mail: gerhard.fink@wu-wien.ac.at

Mridula Gungaphul (MBA) is a Senior Lecturer in Marketing and Management in the Faculty of Law and Management, University of Mauritius. She joined the University in 1999 after having spent three years in managerial positions in the private sector. She is currently registered for an MPhil/PhD in Management in the field of Entrepreneurship at the University of Mauritius. She has participated in several international conferences. Her areas of research are in SMEs, entrepreneurship and marketing. E-mail: m.gungaphul@uom.ac.mu

Nigel Holden (PhD, Manchester Business School, 1986) has held professorial appointments in Denmark and Germany and is currently Professor of

Comparative and International Management at Nottingham Business School, UK. His fields of publication embrace cross-cultural management, knowledge management, international marketing, management change in Russia, marketing in Japan and intercultural business communication. He has co-authored management books on Japan (1994) and Russia (1997), and his *Cross-Cultural Management: A Knowledge Management Perspective* (2002) was published in Russian and Chinese in 2005 and 2006 respectively. He was co-editor with Gerhard Fink of a Special Issue of (a) the *Academy of Management Executive* on the global transfer of management knowledge (2005) and (b) the *Journal of Managerial Psychology* on the absorption and application of management knowledge (2005). He is Queensland University of Technology Visiting Professor at the Vienna University of Economics and Business Administration and has given over 100 invited lectures and keynote addresses to academic and professional audiences in several European countries, Japan, Taiwan, the USA and Russia. In addition to his native English, he speaks German and Russian and has a working knowledge of several other languages. E-mail: nigel.holden@ntu.ac.uk

Kate Hutchings (PhD, UQ) is an Associate Professor in the Department of Management, Monash University, Australia. She was previously employed at the Queensland University of Technology and prior to that at the University of Queensland. She has taught in China and Malaysia as well as having held visiting positions at Rutgers, Copenhagen Business School and CERAM. She has co-authored or co-edited three books and, amongst others, her research has appeared in *Asia Pacific Journal of Management*, *Human Resource Management Journal*, *International Journal of Human Resource Management*, *Journal of Management Studies*, *Journal of Organisational Change Management* and *Thunderbird International Business Review*. Her current research interests include human resource management in China, expatriate management, intercultural knowledge sharing and intercultural networking. E-mail: kate.hutchings@buseco.monash.edu.au

Rajni Kakkar is one of the founders and the Vice President (Business Development) of Canam Consultants Ltd. Rajni has developed the company into India's second largest resettlement solutions business with over 30 offices throughout India. She also developed *Destinations Abroad*, a magazine distributed throughout South East Asia. After completing her Bachelor degree in political science, Rajni completed a Masters in Public Administration. Prior to starting Canam Consultants Ltd, Rajni worked as a volunteer examining rights abuses in Nagaland and Manipur. Rajni is also active in a charitable organisation that sponsors education for underprivileged children. Her research interests focus on business development.

Renata Kaminska-Labbé is a Professor in Management at CERAM Sophia Antipolis European School of Business, France, where she also directs the continuing education programme for mid-career professionals. She is a Visiting Professor at Kozminski School of Entrepreneurship and Management in Warsaw and at Krakow University of Economics. She studied in Poland, Canada and France, and holds a Doctorate in Management from the University of Nice. Her current research interests include knowledge management and transfer of competencies, specifically in transitional economies. She also works on organisational dynamics, with research on co-evolution of decisional structures and environmental factors. E-mail: renata.labbe@ceram.fr

Maren Lehmann (Dr Phil) qualified in print studies and design, pedagogy and sociology at the University of Art and Design Burg Giebichenstein, Halle, the Martin-Luther-University Halle-Wittenberg and Bielefeld University, respectively, and obtained a diploma in pedagogy and her doctorate in sociology (on inclusion and exclusion in religious observations) at the University of Halle-Wittenberg. She was a researcher in the departments of sociology and business administration at the Martin-Luther-University Halle-Wittenberg and in the department of media studies at the Bauhaus-University Weimar. She was a guest Lecturer at universities in Halle, Leipzig, Weimar and Vienna. She is currently preparing her post-doctoral dissertation (on careers as organisational calculations with individuals) in the Department of Fundamental Studies at the University Witten/Herdecke. Her fields of publication embrace system theory and second order cybernetics, sociological studies on individualism, life-course and career, and design theories. In addition to her native German, she speaks English and Russian. Website: www.maren-lehmann.de. E-mail: DompfarramtMerseburg@t-online.de

Snejina Michailova is Professor of International Business at the University of Auckland Business School, New Zealand (PhD degree from Copenhagen Business School, Denmark). Her research interests are in international management (focus on cross-cultural management), knowledge management (focus on knowledge sharing) and emerging economies (focus on Russia and China). Much of her research has bridged these three areas in different constellations. Her work has appeared in, among others, *The Academy of Management Executive*, *California Management Review*, *Journal of Management Studies*, *Management Learning*, *Journal of World Business*, *Organisational Dynamics* and *International Management*. Snejina Michailova is Editor Europe of the *Journal of World Business*. E-mail: s.michailova@auckland.ac.nz

Kavoos Mohannak (PhD, Monash) is a Lecturer in the School of Management, Faculty of Business, Queensland University of Technology,

Australia. He previously worked as a postdoctoral research fellow at the Centre for Asia Pacific Social Transformation Studies at the University of Wollongong. He also studied, worked and taught at the International University of Japan for several years. Currently he teaches technology, innovation and knowledge management at Queensland University of Technology. His research focuses on management of technology and knowledge from the perspective of government policy, innovation and knowledge management in SMEs, R&D networks and regional clusters. In recent years, he has completed major research projects on R&D and innovation in the biotechnology industry and has studied Australian ICT and manufacturing clusters in various regions of Australia, which led to publication of a book. E-mail: k.mohannak@qut.edu.au

J.C. Spender (PhD) is trained as a nuclear engineer and has worked on the UK nuclear submarine programme. He then worked for IBM (UK) and Slater-Walker Securities before entering the PhD programme at Manchester Business School. His thesis won the Academy of Management A.T. Kearney Prize and was subsequently published as *Industry Recipes* (Blackwell, 1989). He served on the faculty at City University, UCLA, Glasgow University, and Rutgers before becoming Dean of the School of Business and Technology at FIT/SUNY in Manhattan. He is now retired but continues to write, consult, teach and research around the world. E-mail: jcspender@yahoo.com

Catherine Thomas is a Professor in Management at the University of Metz, France and a member of the RODIGE team of GREDEG (Groupe de Recherche en Droit, Economie et Gestion, UMR 6227, CNRS) research laboratory. Her current research interests include knowledge management and, more precisely, knowledge codification and the conception of ICT solutions in a use-oriented, co-constructionist perspective. She has coordinated an inter-disciplinary project 'Knowledge Management Platform' with the objective to develop and implement a competence-based website for a network of firms and research institutions in the telecommunications industry. Currently she also pilots a RODIGE research group working on the Dynamics of Knowledge and Competencies. E-mail: thomas@idefi.cnrs.fr

David Weir (MA, Oxon, Dip.PSA Oxon, CCIIM) is Professor of Management at CERAM Sophia Antipolis in France and Visiting Professor in Management Development at Lancaster University and Bristol Business School. He was previously Director of the Bradford University School of Management and inaugural Professor of Organisational Behaviour at Glasgow University. He is Emeritus Professor of the University of Northumbria. He has been involved in business as a company Director and is active as a business and management development consultant in the MENA region, Europe and Latin America. He undertook a British Council project on Management Education in Mauritius, leading to the setting up of the first MBA programme in Mauritius, and has remained closely involved with Higher Education in Mauritius. He teaches on the Knowledge Management cluster of the Theseus MBA. He inaugurated and led the Arab Management Conference for many years. He is author and editor of 12 books and many academic papers, including several chapters in the *Encyclopaedia of Business and Management* on the Arab World, Jordan, Algeria and the Gulf States. He is currently completing a book on management in the Arab World to be published by Edward Elgar. E-mail: David.Weir@Ceram.fr

Acknowledgements

Completing this book would not have been possible without the assistance of many people. We gratefully acknowledge the contributing authors for their expertise in their specialist areas and commitment to meeting required deadlines. We give our heartfelt thanks to our families and friends for their continued support and encouragement for this book and our associated research endeavours. We are also very appreciative of the Edward Elgar publishing house for their belief in the value of this book and encouragement and advice. We particularly acknowledge the efforts of Francine O'Sullivan of Edward Elgar Publishing for her support throughout the editorial process. We also sincerely thank Suyi Lim of Monash University for her meticulous assistance in copy editing.

PART ONE

Theoretical developments in intercultural and inter-institutional knowledge management

1. Introducing knowledge management in developing economies

Kate Hutchings and Kavoos Mohannak

BACKGROUND AND RATIONALE

From the late 1980s, researchers began to emphasise the need for organisations to enhance their learning or be 'learning organisations' (Roth and Senge, 1996; Senge, 1989; Senge and Fulmer, 1993). Since the seminal article by Cangelosi and Dill (1965), organisational learning has been described at three different levels: individual, group and organisation. While many organisational learning theorists have argued for the existence of learning at these levels, some researchers, especially academics in the field of international management, have extended the framework to include learning at the intra-organisational level (see, for example, Miller, 1996). Another large corpus of work grew from the learning organisation and focused around the concept of knowledge management (KM). Defined as intentional efforts to increase, share and improve knowledge usage as intellectual capital, KM has been asserted, by leading organisational scholars, as essential for organisational competitiveness (Drucker et al., 1997; Von Krogh, 1998). Boisot (1998) has suggested knowledge assets are only just being regarded as economic goods in their own right and argues that a core competence is the fruit of an organisational learning process, and that, as it gets used repeatedly in a variety of circumstances, it deepens and the benefits to the organisation are enhanced.

KM theorists also argue that knowledge is the pre-eminent resource of the firm (Davenport and Prusak, 1997; Grant, 1996; Spender, 1996) and that the primary rationale for the firm is the creation and application of knowledge (Bierly and Chakrabarti, 1996; Conner and Prahalad, 1996). Among the questions addressed in this body of literature are: What knowledge exists in organisations? Who holds that knowledge? How can we capture and/or share the knowledge? However, initial research and practice in the field focused on knowledge transfer, with academicians and practitioners identifying the necessity for international businesses to transfer distinctive knowledge to their subsidiaries to build their own competitive advantage and provide knowledge to the subsidiary employees and foreign business partners. Yet, while *knowledge transfer* is largely a one-way process that maximises learning for subsidiary employees, the more optimal *knowledge sharing* focuses on a two-way process, in which each party has access to skills and competencies of their partners and suggests an equally beneficial flow of information (Kogut and Zander, 1992).

In the mid 1990s, Nonaka and Takeuchi (1995) developed a knowledge matrix (referred to as SECI) in which they classified knowledge as either *explicit* or *tacit*, and either *individual* or *collective*. Cabrera and Cabrera (2002) explain that while explicit knowledge refers to information as it is communicated, tacit knowledge refers to more innate, hard-to-communicate skills, know-how or practical knowledge. Weir and Hutchings (2005) argue that, for Nonaka and Takeuchi (1995), human knowledge is created and expanded through the social interaction between tacit knowledge and explicit knowledge and importantly an organisation cannot create knowledge on its own; knowledge creation is dependent upon the initiative of individuals and the interaction that takes place within the group (Nonaka and Takeuchi, 1995; Nonaka, 1998). As Weir and Hutchings (2005) interpret the work of Nonaka and Takeuchi, they acknowledge that while knowledge may be held by one person, it can also be embedded in the interactions amongst a group of people and the value of knowledge grows as it is shared. The work of Nonaka and Takeuchi has been regarded as seminal work in the discipline of KM and has received substantive international reference and commendation.

Yet, Glisby and Holden (2003) have suggested that what is assumed about KM in a Western industrialised context or in a Japanese context (on which the work of Nonaka and Takeuchi is based) may not necessarily be translated to other cultural settings where much more knowledge is tacit. Further, an increasing number of researchers are questioning the very belief in the assumption of the existence of intra-organisational knowledge sharing. Hutchings (2005) has indeed purported that an important limitation on the capacity of international organisations to achieve international competitiveness has been problems not only with cross-cultural communication, but also an inability to harness cross-cultural knowledge sharing and management learning through an inability to tap into tacit knowledge.

Recent research on intercultural KM has advocated that a key problem with much of the KM research and literature is that it has been largely viewed through a Western or industrialised nation lens and, accordingly, such findings may not be interculturally applicable. Weir and Hutchings (2005) suggest that managers and management alike are cultural products and the behaviour and attitudes of managers and employees are rooted in specific cultural contexts. As such, they suggest that knowledge cannot be understood outside the cultural parameters in which it emerges and develops. Sbarcea (2001) has maintained that KM outside the industrialised world is not as 'natural' nor as self-evident as they argue it is usually presented in mainstream KM literature. Accordingly, Hutchings and Michailova (2003) state that it is important to realise that in developing economies, people may not share the knowledge they possess with others or tap into the collective corporate knowledge base as readily as people in the Western world. Nonaka (1998) proffers that efficient organisational knowledge sharing depends on the willingness of individuals to identify the knowledge they possess and share that knowledge if, and when, required. However, Husted and Michailova (2002) emphasise that such willingness to share knowledge is affected by knowledge being asymmetrically distributed in organisations. Moreover, Demirbag and Weir (2004) argue that knowledge is experience, which has been codified and then transformed into processes and procedures which are implemented. In such contexts, tacit knowledge may be as significant as explicit formal communications.

Zhu (2004, p. 67) also questions the perceived universalism of KM in arguing that there should be the development of an 'interactionist strategy of constructing, connecting and sharing cross-cultural contexts'. Building on Chen's East–West schema, which he claims provides insufficient discrimination about KM between and within these regions, Zhu studied American, Chinese, European and Japanese approaches to KM. While suggesting there are convergences between the KM styles employed in these regions, such as the application of Brown's 'knowledge ecology' (Brown and Duguid, 1991; Cook and Brown, 1999) to China (Zhu, 2001) and to Nonaka and Takeuchi's (1995) Japanese style of knowledge creation, he argues still for varieties and divergence.

Both Glisby and Holden (2003) and Holden (2002) have called for understanding of how knowledge is constructed and constituted outside of the industrialised world, from which most KM research has surfaced. They suggest that literature on KM in a cross-cultural context is almost non-existent (for interesting exceptions in addition to some of those mentioned here, see also Edwards and Kidd, 2003; Kidd, 1998). While academic literature on intercultural KM is growing, and there have been a few recent books on cross-cultural KM (Gupta and Sharma, 2004; Pauleen, forthcoming) we do concur that most books in this field address KM from a Western perspective (Dixon, 2000; Leonard, 1995; Nonaka, 1998; O'Dell and Grayson, 1998; Von Krogh et al., 2000). There is still a dearth of understanding of how KM is constructed across a range of intercultural contexts and, moreover, how the cultural interplay with pre-existing and rapidly changing institutions affects KM processes.

We contend that KM is embedded in cultural understanding, and institutional determinants and knowledge processes cannot be examined in isolation from locally situated meaning that arises from a range of cultural and institutional influences, which can be key drivers or inhibitors of knowledge sharing. Thus far, there has been a limited amount of research that examines the interface between specific national cultural features and KM approaches. There is limited research that directly examines the interplay of culture and institutions in their impacts on KM in the developing economies. Moreover, while there is substantive literature that provides prescriptions for achieving KM within Western organisations in Western nations, there is limited dialogue on how to engender KM in international joint ventures and wholly owned foreign enterprises in developing economies. Indeed, achieving intercultural trust and tapping into tacit knowledge that leads to intra-organisational knowledge sharing is a time consuming and complex process for international organisations, and yet it is an issue which has not been sufficiently addressed in accepted models of KM.

As intercultural researchers, we have long been involved in research collaboration across national and organisational boundaries and have for some years been exploring aspects of intercultural KM. The genesis of this book came from our recognition, through our own research, that, although there is a growing body of international journals including articles addressing KM in an intercultural context, there is a need to collate extant intercultural KM research into a central reference point. In so doing, this book provides a framework of intercultural KM cognition. Moreover, extant research has suggested that there is a distinct gap between what international managers in subsidiary operations in developing economies are doing to grow KM organisational cultures and what are the KM attitudes and behaviours of local employees and business partners in these host nations. Therefore, our intention was also to design a book that would have practical application and relevance for those working in, or interested in establishing, international businesses. In designing the focus and selecting the contributions to this book, we were cognisant of the need to explore not only the cultural and institutional factors that can assist or hinder KM within developing economies, but also to provide recommendations for international managers about how to work with existing KM practices.

CONTRIBUTORS

In selecting contributions that would cover a range of developing economies with a vast medley of cultures and institutions, it was also our deliberate intention that, in the spirit of embracing diversity, the chapter authors should be given considerable academic autonomy and integrity in the writing of their respective chapters. The authors were given a general chapter structure to follow and a requirement that that they include implications for management. Beyond this, though, we were keen to embrace a diversity of views and approaches, ranging from contributions that followed a standard academic empirical research methodology, through very theoretical approaches, to chapters written in a fairly speculative fashion. Moreover, in undertaking to present a diverse range of contributions which explore differing aspects of culture and institutions across all four corners of the globe, we also sought to include a diverse range of nationalities amongst our contributors, including Western recognised experts in KM and cross-cultural research, as well as new researchers who hail from the nations which they research. While most of the contributors are presently employed as academicians at universities throughout the world, all have, at one time or another, been business managers or consultants, and to this end are well placed to address managerial implications of intercultural and inter-institutional KM.

STRUCTURE OF THE BOOK

The book is divided into five parts. Part One introduces the significance of developing theoretical and practical understanding of KM in the developing economies and provides an overview of extant literature and research in KM generally and in the developing economies specifically. Part Two explores KM in the transition economies of Central and Eastern Europe, Poland, Russia and China, and examines the impact on KM of the interplay between culture and institutions in the Communist and post-Communist eras. Part Three addresses KM in the world's economic powerhouse of Asia with reference to Taiwan, a nation that is in the final stage of economic development, and India, a rapidly developing nation that some scholars suggest will be Asia's next China. Part Four explores much less researched areas of the world with the focus shifting to Africa, the Middle East and Latin America, with the writers examining how knowledge sharing is impacted by modernisation and Westernisation and engagement with traditional approaches to networks and trust. Finally, in Part Five, we conclude the book by summarising key themes developed throughout the chapters and provide a framework for understanding aspects of KM in an intercultural and inter-institutional context.

While Chapter 1 provides a rationale for this book's exploration of aspects of KM in an intercultural and inter-institutional context, in Chapter 2, J.C. Spender undertakes a critique of KM in which he questions whether the whole interest in KM is over-hyped, is declining, or ever offered anything really new. Through an in-depth exploration of KM literature, both classical and recent, Spender draws some conclusions but presents more questions for readers in arguing that there is a wide gulf between knowledge-as-practice and knowledge-as-meaning. While arguing that bounded knowledge is extended by imagination, he cautions that when we submit knowledge to analysis we also constrain it, and the ability to undertake sophisticated KM analysis is no less important in the developing world than it is in the developed.

In Chapter 3, the first chapter devoted to exploration of KM in a specific region of the developing world, Gerhard Fink, Nigel Holden and Maren Lehmann undertake an historical assessment of KM in Central and Eastern Europe. They suggest that there was, and continues to be, a 'socialist-style of KM' premised on crucial distinctions between public and private, family and work, reliable and unreliable people. They maintain that, in such a system, communication channels were reduced to tacit knowledge transfer embedded in the official political language in which transfer could only occur for those who knew the context. They further suggest that translating modern concepts of management and human resource management has been problematic for reasons such as language and interpretation as well as a legacy of a climate lacking in trust.

In Chapter 4, Renata Kaminska-Labbé and Catherine Thomas examine KM and competence renewal in Poland, with specific reference to the experience of three Polish organisations and their strategic adaptation during economic transition in the post-socialist era. They discuss the complexities involved in building new competencies and the influence of the legislative environment as well as political, social and economic change. They suggest that the case study organisations reveal that in a post-rupture deconstructionist context, strategic renewal requires new regulatory processes with greatly modified structures; lessons which they maintain can be applied to other societies equally beset by rapid environmental changes.

In Chapter 5, Kate Hutchings and Snejina Michailova discuss knowledge sharing in Russia and China through an exploration of the impact of cultural traditions and Communist influences. They argue that, contrary to earlier research suggesting that people in transition economies such as Russia and China have a propensity not to share knowledge, Russians and Chinese are actually more inclined to share knowledge than people in Western, industrialised countries, but that this willingness to share knowledge is highly influenced by group membership. Moreover, they maintain that the extent to which knowledge sharing is impeded or facilitated in Russia and China is determined by an interplay of both cultural and institutional factors.

In Chapter 6, Te Fu Chen examines KM in Taiwan and argues that against a backdrop of declining industries, increasing unemployment and movement of work and organisations to China, a focus on knowledge, information and the management of knowledge is in the ascendant. Chen discusses the development of Taiwanese multinationals in the small–medium enterprise sector and how they have relied on external knowledge development.

Importantly he highlights the Taiwanese government's commitment to emphasising innovation and how organisations are being encouraged to distribute and construct knowledge for the new knowledge worker economy.

In Chapter 7, Simon Best and Rajni Kakkar explore the Indian approach to KM. They argue that in analysing KM in the Indian context, consideration needs to be given not only to legal, political and bureaucratic systems and processes, but also to a recognition of cultural impacts in a country that has been described as the most culturally diverse in the world. In particular, Best and Kakkar argue that in this highly populated nation that has variations across religion, caste, language and region, subtleties and variants of behaviour linked to these cultural differences dramatically impact on the sharing or managing of knowledge and information on an individual level. Moreover, they suggest that cultural differences can be extremely emotive at times in a way that profoundly affects the knowledge sharing process.

In Chapter 8, Mehraz Boolaky, Mridula Gungaphul and David Weir locate their research of KM in Africa in the specific environment of Mauritius and explore the development of this small island state as a potential future knowledge hub. They examine how this ethnically diverse yet socially cohesive nation has actually achieved widespread sharing and understanding of social goals, supported by the inflow of foreigners and lessons learnt from them, a shared civic vision and an entrepreneurial culture. They argue that Mauritius directly and indirectly has created an environment conducive for knowledge development because of its emphasis on lifelong learning and other human resource development initiatives and growing the information technology sector. Yet, while other nations and regions examined in this volume grapple with how to achieve greater sharing of existing knowledge, Mauritius is focused on growing knowledge and faces emerging problems of a widening knowledge gap and how to sift, screen, sort, absorb and understand new information flows.

In Chapter 9, David Weir considers the role of knowledge growth and KM against a background of varying levels of modernisation in the Middle East and North Africa. As well as discussing such issues as the influence of Islam and family business, Weir explores economic and infrastructural issues hindering knowledge growth in some parts of the region in opposition to rapid industrialisation in other parts. Importantly, Weir explores traditional cultural practices which may hinder sharing of knowledge between the Middle East and North Africa and the international businesses dominated by the West, as well as the need to move away from constraining Western-focused views on the KM discourse.

In Chapter 10, Luis Felipe Calderón-Moncloa suggests that (as is the case in many regions of the developing world), trying to establish a generic pattern for how knowledge is shared and disseminated in Latin America is a highly difficult task, given the vast diversity and complexity of Latin American societies according to their disparate history, social evolution and present socio-economic situation. Nonetheless, he does identify factors which he considers to be core to management in Latin America and which have important ramifications for KM. He refers to 'mafia' values and organisational feudalism or the existence of in-groups, which has important implications for a distance between managerial theory and practice. Moreover he argues that an anti-empowerment culture and a focus on hiding mistakes contribute to a lack of knowledge sharing. Yet, he also proffers that what can be disadvantages can also be real advantages, as the tacit use of knowledge can be transformed where trust is maximised, and the informality that characterises Latin American organisations can be utilised to create highly adaptive organisations.

Finally, in Chapter 11, Kavoos Mohannak and Kate Hutchings present a summary of key themes addressed throughout the book and develop a framework for interpreting KM in developing economies as based on the nations and regions explored in this volume.

REFERENCES

Bierly, P. and A. Chakrabarti (1996), 'Generic Knowledge Strategies in the US Pharmaceutical Industry', *Strategic Management Journal*, **17**, 123–35.
Boisot, M. (1998), *Knowledge Assets: Securing Competitive Advantage in the Information Economy*, Oxford: Oxford University Press.
Brown, J.S. and P. Duguid (1991), 'Organisational Learning and Communities of Practice: Toward a Unified View of Working, Learning and Innovation', *Organisation Science*, **2**, 40–57.
Cabrera, A. and E.F. Cabrera (2002), 'Knowledge Sharing Dilemmas', *Organisation Studies*, **23**(5), 687–710.
Cangelosi, V. and W. Dill (1965), 'Organisational Learning: Observations toward a Theory', *Administrative Sciences Quarterly*, **10**(2), 175–203.
Conner, K. and C. Prahalad (1996), 'A Resource-based Theory of the Firm: Knowledge versus Opportunism', *Organisation Science*, **7**(5), 477–501.
Cook, S.D.N. and J.S. Brown (1999), 'Bridging Epistemologies: The Generative Dance between Organisational Knowledge and Organisational Knowing', *Organisation Science*, **10**(4), 381–400.
Davenport, T. and L. Prusak (1997), *Information Ecology: Mastering the Information and Knowledge Environment*, Oxford: Oxford University Press.
Demirbag, M. and D. Weir (2004), 'Enterprise Trust and Commitment in International Joint Ventures: An Approach through Knowledge Management', paper presented at the Academy of Management Conference, New Orleans.
Dixon, N. (2000), *Common Knowledge: How Companies Thrive by Sharing what They Know*, Boston, MA: Harvard Business School Press.
Drucker, P.F., E. Dyson, C. Handy, P. Saffo and P.M. Senge (1997), 'Looking Ahead: Implications of the Present', *Harvard Business Review*, **75**(5), 18–19.

Edwards, J.S. and J.B. Kidd (2003), 'Knowledge Management Sans Frontieres', *Journal of the Operational Research Society*, **564**, 130–39.

Glisby, M. and N. Holden (2003), 'Contextual Constraints in Knowledge Management Theory: The Cultural Embeddedness of Nonaka's Knowledge-creating Company', *Knowledge and Process Management*, **10**(1), 29–36.

Grant, R.M. (1996), 'Prospecting in Dynamically Competitive Environments: Organisational Capability as Knowledge Integration', *Organisation Science*, **7**(4), 375–88.

Gupta, J. and S. Sharma (eds) (2004), *Creating Knowledge Based Organisations*, Hershey, PA: Idea Group.

Holden, N.J. (2002), *Cross-cultural Management: A Knowledge Management Perspective*, Harlow: Financial Times/Prentice Hall.

Husted, K. and S. Michailova (2002), 'Diagnosing and Fighting Knowledge-sharing Hostility', *Organisational Dynamics*, **31**(1), 60–73.

Hutchings, K. (2005), 'Examining the Impacts of Institutional Change on Knowledge Sharing and Management Learning in China: Some Challenges for International Managers', *Thunderbird International Business Review*, **47**(4), 447–68.

Hutchings, K. and S. Michailova (2003), *Facilitating Knowledge Sharing in Russian and Chinese Subsidiaries: The Importance of Groups and Personal Networks*, Centre for Knowledge Governance Working Paper 2003-9; Copenhagen: Copenhagen Business School.

Kidd, J.B. (1998), 'Knowledge Creation in Japanese Manufacturing Companies in Italy', *Management Learning*, **29**(2), 131–46.

Kogut, B. and U. Zander (1992), 'Knowledge of the Firm, Combinative Capabilities and the Replication of Technology', *Organisation Science*, **3**(3), 383–97.

Leonard, D. (1995), *Wellsprings of Knowledge*, Boston, MA: Harvard Business School Press.

Miller, D. (1996), 'A Preliminary Typology of Organisational Learning: Synthesising the Literature', *Journal of Management*, **22**(3), 485–505.

Nonaka, I. (1998), *Harvard Business Review on Knowledge Management*, Boston, MA: Harvard Business School Press.

Nonaka, I. and H. Takeuchi (1995), *The Knowledge Creating Company*, Oxford: Oxford University Press.

O'Dell, C. and C.J. Grayson (1998), *If Only We Knew what We Know: The Transfer of Internal Knowledge and Best Practice*, New York: Free Press.

Pauleen, D. (ed.) (forthcoming), *Cross Cultural Perspectives on Knowledge Management*, London: Libraries Unlimited.

Roth, G.L. and P.M. Senge (1996), 'From Theory to Practice: Research Territory, Processes and Structure at an Organisational Learning Centre', *Journal of Organisational Change*, **9**(1), 92–103.

Sbarcea, K. (2001), 'The Mystery of Knowledge Management', *New Zealand Management*, **48**(19), 33–6.

Senge, P.M. (1989), *Organisational Learning: A New Challenge for Systems Dynamics*, Working Paper D-4023, Cambridge, MA: Sloan School of Management, MIT.

Senge, P.M. and R.M. Fulmer (1993), 'Simulations, Systems Thinking and Anticipatory Learning', *The Journal of Management Development*, **12**(6), 21–33.

Spender, J.-C. (1996), 'Making Knowledge the Basis of a Dynamic Theory of the Firm', *Strategic Management Journal*, **17**, 45–62.

Von Krogh, G. (1998), 'Care in Knowledge Creation', *California Management Review*, **40**(3), 133–53.
Von Krogh, G., K. Ichijo and I. Nonaka (2000), *Enabling Knowledge Creation*, New York: Oxford University Press.
Weir, D. and K. Hutchings (2005), 'Cultural Embeddedness of Knowledge Sharing in China and the Arab World', *Knowledge and Process Management*, **12**(2), 89–98.
Zhu, Z. (2001), 'What is to be Managed: Knowledge, Knowing or Knower and Does it Matter?', in Z. Wang, Y. Nakamori, J. Gu and Y. Dang (eds), *Proceedings of the International Symposium on Knowledge and Systems Science*, Dalian, China: Dalian University of Technology, pp. 29–45.
Zhu, Z. (2004), 'Knowledge Management: Towards a Universal Concept or Cross-cultural Contexts?', *Knowledge Management Research and Practice*, **2**(2), 67–79.

2. Social institutions and knowledge management

J.C. Spender

INTRODUCTION

Knowledge management (KM) sees itself as a new theoretical field equipping us for the Information Age. Knowledge, we are told, has become the most strategic of corporate assets, and managers need new techniques and sensitivities to succeed in this new environment (Boisot, 1998; Lubit, 2001). Prusak (2001), intimately involved in the growth of the field, argues the impetus comes from three trends: (a) powerful new information technologies, (b) globalisation of the world's trade and its major companies; and (c) increasing attention to the economic implications of learning-by-doing and intellectual property management.

There may be more to this story than these KM boosters suggest, for knowledge has always been crucial to commerce, politics, romance and warfare alike: Bacon famously remarked 'knowledge is power' in 1597. While we obviously have new technologies with the capacity to capture, move, analyse, store and deliver data like never before, it is not clear how this might affect today's developed and developing economies. We are on a technological trajectory but unclear about where it is leading – to a land of health and plenty perhaps, or the disappearance of privacy and community, to a utopia or a dystopia? Looking at global flagship companies like Microsoft, Dell, Amazon and eBay, we see new commercial opportunities and business models capturing the rocketing global business and household spending on computing and communications. These opportunities are as present in the developing economies as they are in the developed world. Whether the penetration of personal computers in the society is high or low, these changes affect us all as governments and businesses computerise, as we use mobile phones, as the landfill content is changing greatly, and as data is collected and moved in ways that make bureaucracies vastly more powerful. If the Stasi had been computerised, the history of Europe might well have been different. While these opportunities are omnipresent, they are seldom the same in the developed and developing nations, though we hear India's richest man is, like

Bill Gates, a software entrepreneur. We know the initiatives that eventually take hold reflect in some important way the social and commercial contexts of the places in which they are advanced, so the technical question is how these contexts bear on the strategic deployment of KM.

The KM industry is doing its utmost to exploit this demand. There are new data collection, data management and KM tools, a brisk new business in KM consulting, and a rising proportion of organisations have set up KM projects (Cabrera and Cabrera, 2002). There is also much confusion and debate about what KM is and where it is going (Alvesson and Kärreman, 2001; Davenport, 1997; Fahey and Prusak, 1998; Gupta et al., 2000; Lucier and Torsilieri, 2001; Marren, 2003; McAfee, 2003; Renzl et al., 2006; Spender, 2005; Storey and Barnett, 2000; Sutton, 2001). Indeed there may be a growing sense that the KM phenomenon is already in decline, over-hyped and having failed to deliver anything significantly new or different. Much of what passes as KM is no more than the kinds of systems analysis, work study, and human capital accounting, and so on, that have been common since the 1960s. Much KM consulting is no more than the computerising and re-labelling of existing products and services. One of the most popular KM initiatives, which is capturing the knowledge of departing professionals so as to retain it for the company, is just a return to the 1980s expert system agenda.

To clarify what is going on, we need to dig into the basic concepts comprising the KM discourse and identify its novelty, if any. In particular we need to know whether this Information Age is simply a matter of knowledge quantity – in the sense of our having and using more data and information than ever before; or if there is a Parkinson's Law of Information operating – with the knowledge expanding to fill the computing capacity available; or if it is a question of better quality information – in the sense of greater timeliness and accuracy. When do these improvements in quantity or quality amount to anything of strategic significance and what, in consequence, is the likely future of KM?

The chapter considers the KM discourse's concepts first. I argue that KM's main novelty lies in shifting our attention from knowledge assets to knowledge absences, and this calls the imagination into play to supplement our reasoning. I move on to consider social institutions as important constraints over the application of managerial imagination. Finally, I consider how such institutions come into being, concluding with some discussion of the differences between developed and developing societies.

CONCEPTS

Knowledge

First I look at knowledge itself, and only then at the notion of managing it.

There is much confusion here so I assume we can never really know what we mean by knowledge. It has puzzled the finest minds for millennia and we are not likely to overturn this history by loud trumpeting of knowledge's new strategic importance. Instead I shall change the question and offer a new typology of knowledge as data, or meaning, or practice. Each of these is knowable, and together they may give us a handle on what knowledge might then mean. There are profound methodological issues here for we shift from trying to define knowledge, surely a fruitless endeavour given the definition must also include itself, to learning something about knowledge by comparing these sub-categories. We might then understand how social institutions shape each type of knowledge.

As the chapter unfolds, I shift the emphasis from the conventional view, that KM is about techniques for managing existing knowledge assets, and bring knowledge generation onto the centre stage. I argue that management theory has done little to help practising managers with managing the creation of knowledge, despite our enthusiastic rhetoric about learning organisations (Cohen and Sproull, 1996; Easterby-Smith and Lyles, 2003). As we consider how organisations might learn and what this might mean, and what organisations need to learn about, their institutional context becomes more important to the analysis. It turns out that KM's real novelty lies in its attention to the management of uncertainty rather than to what is known. Economics famously assumes managers have complete knowledge, and management theory has been all too happy to follow this lead, in spite of widespread criticism that it makes the analysis irrelevant to managers immersed in uncertainty. This silence about uncertainty may be breaking down as we learn that the Information Age may have less to do with computers than with the increasing pace of organisational and economic life. As a result, academics and business people need more and more information to avoid being over-run.

Knowledge is a tricky concept. KM literature divides sharply between writers who take the notion for granted and see no problems with it, and those who appreciate that a great deal turns on their view of the serious problems that lie within it. One of the most important consequences of this new interest in knowledge is that it has raised the level of our epistemological discourse, helping us address management issues that have been tacitly ignored for decades. The most important is how managers and theorists should deal with bounded rationality and uncertainty. In the half century since Simon (1997) presented organisational theorists with this challenge, we have made little progress and it is still not clear we really understand what he was getting at. The downside of looking into KM is that we must do some epistemologising, but it will be on the light side. Those interested in a managerial treatment of the deeper philosophical issues can do no better than review the work of

Tsoukas and his colleagues (Tsoukas, 2005; Tsoukas and Mylonopoulos, 2004; Tsoukas and Vladimirou, 2001) or the summary edited by Choo and Bontis (2002).

This high quality philosophical work contrasts with that of Ackoff (1989) whose DIKW (data, information, knowledge and wisdom) typology has been excessively influential in the KM field. Ackoff argues that data is raw, it 'just is', while information is data imbued with meaning. Knowledge is information drawn together into 'something useful', while wisdom is knowledge brought into relationship with the moral dimensions of the human condition. Implied is a spectrum from raw sense-data to comprehension and control, and ultimately to understanding the good life. Missing is any sense of what this spectrum requires of us, the knowers, given that our knowledge is within us, in our minds, and not at all in the same place as the objects in the world that we might know about. We can puzzle over the steps along this spectrum, such as the difference between data and information, and ask how we actually go about attaching meaning to sense-data. These questions do not seem to concern Ackoff because he takes a 'naive realist' position that assumes whatever we know is a more or less correct representation of what we are sensing out there in the world of reality. This comfortable lay view has penetrated much of the KM literature, being a handy way of looking at the physical sciences and how we manipulate the physical world in our interest.

Unfortunately it is an exceedingly limited and limiting view. In particular it prevents us from dealing with the most obvious fact of social life, that each of us has our own views about the world, perhaps because of our differing cultures, or our personal idiosyncrasies, or our professional training. A great deal of management is about dealing with these disagreements day-to-day, whether they are within the organisation, or between organisations, or between nations. Managers paint themselves into a very small corner when they presume these disagreements are simply matters of fact, and that fully informed of the facts we are all going to agree. Presuming this pushes the strategic questions about our differing values, interests and utilities out of the analysis. Indeed, we cannot get to these issues from the naive realist position which thereby seems (a) uninformed in its neglect of the history of Western philosophy, and (b) disabling in leaving one unaware of the nature and extent of the managerial role and its contribution to organisational life.

Data and Meaning

The KM discourse has certainly made us look more carefully at these matters, and we can begin with a focus on the difference between data and meaning. Data is a signal, a unit of sense-data, while meaning is the cognitive framework in which we interpret that signal and connect it to our lives. We might say a number like 43 is just that, a number that means nothing beyond arithmetic until we know, for example, that it is an indication of how fast we are travelling in a speed-restricted zone, or the number of people coming to the party we are driving to, or the age of the person whose birthday is being celebrated. Some use the term 'lenses' to describe our different perceptions of the world around us. Meaning is about our lenses and not about the sense-data we process through them.

Managing knowledge means nothing if we do not know what knowledge is, and as we parse it into data and meaning we see it means quite different things. It carries different implications depending on whether we are managing data or meaning. The attention being paid, quite properly, to computers, communication systems and information technology within the KM field shows the strategic importance of managing data and illustrates the impact of today's technologies on organisations, for they are massive generators and consumers of data. IBM tells us that by 2010, the codified body of human knowledge will be doubling every 11 hours (citing Bontis and Fitz-enz, 2002). For example, managers know the cash requirements of a complex organisation are minimised when cash is managed centrally. Managing working capital becomes a more effective portfolio project and the firm's financial efficiency is maximised. But when departments do not have cash on hand, and must submit formal requests for funds for small items, it may make everyday operations awkward – recall a crown was lost for the want of a nail. Modern computing can solve these problems and help firms improve their cash management and reduce their working capital requirements significantly. Many other internal resource and inventory management processes have also been improved. Coordinated real-time planning enables the firm's individual units to optimise their operations and respond better to market changes. Improved data collection, now commonplace in retailing, enables firms to manage the distribution of goods and services better, adapting quickly while minimising inventory. New data about markets, customers' tastes and behaviour, mass-customisation and 'customer relationship management', and so forth, greatly improves the business's effectiveness and return on investment.

All of this merges into an important story about how things have been affected by the Internet, data collection, data-mining and the multiplicity of ways in which better communications can affect the organisation's operation. This matters at least as much in developing countries. But is it KM? Or rather, is there anything new here that is a conceptual break with the techniques of 1960s' electronic data processing and would warrant using this new KM label? There are many new statistical and data handling techniques, such as relational databases, search engines, or the 3D virtual data rooms used increasingly in the oil and gas exploration industry, and they are all useful, but do we need the term knowledge? Is data not adequate? Would it not be clearer to speak of 'data', a term we understand, rather than 'knowledge', which remains deeply obscure?

Thinking of the meaning of lenses or the cognitive framework that brings data into a relationship with us and our goals, and making it 'meaningful', points immediately to difficulties with communicating meaning. We can transmit data, but meaning? Think of encryption; with a key in hand, we encrypt the message for transmission, and away it goes. But now the recipient needs the key to decrypt and read the message, or else it remains 'meaningless'. This seems clear. But how do we transmit the key? We cannot encrypt it without another key, and so on. Eventually a key has to be communicated 'in the clear'. The point here is not to suggest that public key encryption trivialises this problem. In fact, it makes it more complicated as the example points to the basic epistemological difference between the message and the key, between data and its meaning.

Managing meaning is not at all the same thing as managing data. We can write a message that we think explains meaning and send it, but does this do the trick? Most organisations recognise the difficulty with getting everyone 'on board', to share the corporate meaning system. Many KM projects are about getting people to share meaning systems and data, and most focus on motivating individuals to release the knowledge in their possession. But how do the people with whom this knowledge is shared know what it means? There are difficulties here (Hislop, 2002). For instance the idea of absorptive capacity is that we can only learn by leveraging what we already know, so how are we to make sense of unfamiliar meaning? We can draw on a vast amount of theoretical and empirical work on organisational development and communications theory, but this literature avoids the term knowledge and is not normally considered to lie within KM, and there is little to be gained by adding the K-word to its vocabulary.

The important thing to appreciate about meaning is that it only begins to be relevant as we question naive realism; for realism presumes that the meaning of things is determined by reality. But if things are not what they appear to be, how do we ever get to know what they are? This is one question philosophers want to puzzle out. But it is difficult to make sense of their answers until we get clearer about their problem, which is about the balance between reality and perception. Realists think of knowledge as the essence of the thing observed; there is no problem with meaning for that is grounded in the thing's essence. What is known is independent of us and has no relationship to our perceptions. But if we appreciate that we only know through our species-specific senses and powers of perception, as Kant told us, we can never completely separate what we see from how we see it. Whatever we might mean by knowledge is then some mixture or amalgam of the thing known and the person doing the knowing, seeming to lie somewhere between objectivity and subjectivity. Complete objectivity is then beyond us, while complete subjectivity severs the link with the thing known. From the knowledge manager's point of view, it is not necessary to follow these philosophical debates in depth, only to see that meaning is something that is not in the message but is created by us, the recipients. Every meaningful message presumes some prior lens or meaning – or absorptive capacity – already in place. It is only a short step from here to see that meaning is evidence of our imagination, without which we only process things rationally and do not create anything.

This becomes clearer when we look at the philosophy of language and its three broad justifications for the assertion that a message means this rather than that; things theories, idea theories, and practice theories (Stainton, 2000). The first is an appeal to the thing in itself, to its essence, what we have called realism. The second boils down to an appeal to another person or authority, such as a social institution. The third leads us to practice, to argue that what things mean is determined by what works. This justification or warranting debate is evidence of our struggle with the consequences of admitting both uncertainty and the human imagination into the analysis. On the one hand we are pushed to doubt, to appreciating we can never know the essence of things, and to realise we might be mistaken. On the other, we discover our imagination can create meanings where none existed. It can connect the dots, as we say nowadays. Our acceptance of uncertainty about the ways things are creates a need for us to use our imaginations – uncertainty and imagination are direct correlates.

Ultimately this chapter is about shaping or managing the human imagination. This is such a devastatingly powerful apparatus that it needs strong constraint if we are to avoid solipsism or anarchic relativism, the position that knowledge can be whatever we care to think it is simply because we think it. The three warrants are about constraining the human imagination so we might speak meaningfully of knowledge after we admit imagination. The first warrant appeals to non-philosophers comfortable with realism, even critical realism, and shades off into the temporary-ness of Popperian positivism (Popper, 2002). The second category is Kuhnian, interpretive, and has many different themes. It is becoming familiar through social constructionism: the idea that knowledge is ultimately legitimated by the knower's society (Fuller, 2003; Gergen, 1995; Kuhn, 1970). The third category is often presented as Wittgenstein's maxim that if one wants to understand meaning, one should look to the way things are used (Ayer, 1985; Wittgenstein, 1972). This brush with epistemology shows us KM moves on from being a simple relabelling of a normal science like systems analysis and communications theory, as it engages the uncertainties that provoke these categories and so begins to deal with the most fundamental problems with how we – and managers – know.

INSTITUTIONAL CONSTRAINTS

Social Institutions

In this section, I focus initially on the second category of warrants and look at the way social institutions constrain the imagination, which is the principal subject of this chapter. We know from Hofstede's work that a culture is not just a set of lenses, it is also a set of constraints over how we deal with what seems to be impossible or difficult to process through our existing schema (Hofstede, 1984; Jaju et al., 2002). That our social institutions are the socially generated responses to the uncertainties we face is explicit in the work of North (1990, 1991). He sees them as systems of informal constraints, such as sanctions, taboos, customs, traditions and codes of conduct, and formal rules, such as constitutions, laws and property rights. We put these in place to deal with our divergent competitive impulses and thus create order and reduce uncertainty in exchange. In the economic domain, they define the choice set available to the actors together with their corresponding transactions and production costs. North tells us institutions are emergent and evolve incrementally, providing us with a measure of how history changes and a connection between the past, the present and the future. They also act as systems of incentives for shaping the direction of social evolution (North, 1991, p. 97). They are necessary for social order under the circumstances of uncertainty which would otherwise lead to many types of social disorder, for instance, the wealthier taking advantage of the poorer or those with knowledge advantages abusing those without. In this sense, social institutions are the glue that holds a society together so that it becomes meaningful to talk of society.

North's view contrasts with Williamson's which is less concerned with holding society together under uncertainty and is more focused on the economic efficiency of economic systems (Williamson, 1975, 1987). Williamson sees markets and franchising, for example, as social institutions that are efficient to the extent they assist the economy towards an optimum distribution of resources. As an economic historian, North's complaint is that Williamson's analysis is abstract and universal, and much more needs to be understood about how societies, and their institutions and histories, differ. North sees the relationship between the division of labour and social institutions as the key to the analysis. As the division of labour proceeds, the society's knowledge deepens but its knowledge differences become greater and communications and agreement more problematic, so threatening its integrity. North's argument is that social institutions need to grow along with this specialisation if society is to hold together, and since its trajectory is shaped by the institutional apparatus already present, history becomes path-dependent.

Of particular relevance is the shift from kinship as a means of managing the uncertainties of trade, employing family members to reduce the probability of theft and so on, and towards impersonal rule systems backed by the power of the State. In Commons' institutional theory, social institutions are the means by which the State's power penetrates the everyday processes of exchange and contract (Commons, 1924, 1931). In particular Commons argues a transaction cannot be abstracted from the social and legal context in which it takes place. Greif's (2006) analysis goes further in contrasting the notions of institutions as systems of functional rules, increasing socio-economic efficiency, against institutions as systems of stable behaviour. Also a historian, contrasting economic growth in Europe and the Middle East, and observing institutional differences, Greif pays particular attention to the abandonment of kinship and the development of an impersonal legal apparatus. He contrasts behaviour commanded by the State, with threatened sanctions, and what he calls the 'private order' or the self-organising processes that arises among motivated individuals. His argument is that the history of social institutions cannot be understood if the analysis presupposes the existence of the State, for that itself is one type of private order, and presuming leads us to ignore the imaginings and creativity of the citizens who created it.

The main thrust of these arguments is that we cannot engage the uncertainty of everyday existence and examine the KM processes needed to resolve it by abstracting State, organisations, markets and their constituting transactions from their specific background or infrastructure of social institutions. These directly constrain the managers' imagination. Obviously the possible legitimate forms of the corporation are constrained by corporate law (Hansmann et al., 2006). Likewise the possibilities for trade are limited by what consumers desire in this particular community or marketplace. The likelihood of entrepreneurial activity is limited by the prevailing cultural attitudes towards trade versus class and religion. These three institutional contexts – corporate law, market demand and cultural attitudes towards trade – are typical of the constraints over the managerial imagination that are the target of this chapter. All this seems pretty obvious, yet we still find writers looking for a context-free theory of the firm and its management.

Personal and Physical Constraints

In addition to social institutions, there are also personal constraints over the entrepreneurial imagination as it fills the epistemological space created by uncertainty. Greif (2006) deals with these as he considers motivation. If we think through how social institutions constrain the socio-economic actor's imagination, we have to ponder the degree to which these individuals also take part in the creation of these same institutions. We must also consider if the constraints are absolute and determining, permitting no variation, or are just one of many influences over the actor's choices and creations. The institutional apparatus of the organisation, its system of rules, as well as its corporate culture, are penetrated by other influences such as the actor's class and ethnic identity, religious affiliation, moral and ethical attributes, and so on. Social institutions interpenetrate each other because of the prevalent and ambiguous uncertainties of life. There is no a priori way of establishing that a situation should be framed as political, or religious, or economic, or as a matter of institutional loyalty or an opportunity for personal advancement. Institutional analysis defeats its own intentions if we presume any one social institution is necessarily more important than every other. In this sense, institutional analysis is profoundly empirical, recognising that our knowledge of the world is bounded and fragmented.

The emphasis shifts from presuming or hoping for a complete under-standing of the world onto the creativity of the actor who makes sense of the limited knowledge available. Here Greif makes a connection with the long discussion of methodological individualism (MI) which argues socio-economic theorising must be grounded in observable individual behaviour, in this case the actor's creativity. He says his analysis is 'neo-institutionalist' in pursuing the micro-foundations of socio-economic activity (Greif, 2006, p. 8n). The MI tradition has been popularised in the work of Hayek and the other libertarians anxious to deny organisations and institutions their own agenetic identity, that is, to avoid treating them as socio-economic actors that can stand apart from the individuals who constitute them (Felin and Foss, forthcoming). Thus Simon is often quoted as telling us only individuals can know, organisations cannot (Simon, 1996). Of course, his use of the term 'know' muddies things up and it would have been clearer if Simon had told us only individuals can imagine and create meaning, organisations cannot. Writers such as Nelson and Winter (1982) would disagree as they believe that organisational routines are meaning systems that are held within and constitute the firm. Likewise the bureaucratic tradition leads us to think of organisations as systems of rules, and these too can be seen as meaning systems or strategic lenses inherent in the organisation. Organisations can clearly 'know' the data they possess and would seem to be able to contain and project systems of meaning. Indeed KM projects designed to capture and retain professional knowledge presume the knowledge which individuals possess can be transferred to the organisation rather than merely to other individuals through a process of apprenticeship.

Grief's (2006) notion of institutions is finely balanced between the exogenous stable rule systems presumed by writers like Scott or DiMaggio and Powell, and endogenous self-organising constraints over personal behaviour. He makes an important methodological point that leads him to regard the case method as the most appropriate to the study of these issues. Institutions cannot be regarded as static monolithic entities unaffected by those individual actors who 'play against the rules'. At the same time, institutions achieve a degree of distance from those actors as Durkheimian 'social facts'. Consequently institutions are best studied in a dialectical manner, evolving between the external constraints on one side and the individual's imagination on the other. Neither a theory-driven deductive method, nor an inductive approach which stands on unambiguous empirical identification and classifies institutions based on their observable features, can work. Greif argues the analysis should be evolutionary, historical, sociological and closely intertwined with narrative and language itself as an evolving social institution.

In the sections above, I suggest that imagination is a defining personal and human characteristic constrained by those impersonalities of the social context that appear as social facts, stabilities and solidities. While the balance is dialectical, the imagination itself is not. Neither institutions nor organisations nor collectives have imagination, only living species do. There is a side argument here about autopoiesis as a biological theory of living systems that has persuaded some to treat social systems as living (Maturana and Varela, 1980). Maturana, the father of autopoietic theory, insists this is a category error and that only biological entities can be autopoietic. Thus creativity or agency is their demarcating characteristic. It is also crucial to differentiate between data, which organisations and computers can both possess, and meaning, which is a consequence of our imaginative agency alone and must be projected into the processing system, like a computer program, by us. Thus a knowledge-oriented analysis drives a wedge between (a) moving existing knowledge around, the main agenda when knowledge is regarded as data, and (b) creating knowledge, the key to any treatment of uncertainty and meaning.

Institutions, considered broadly, are evidence of a creative actor's long-term multi-period interaction with creative others, and institutionalisation is about having an ongoing sense of order in these interactions. Selznick (1957) remarks that this only happens if the agents to the functional process 'infuse it with meaning', and creates a sense of order and continuity that carries over to other interactions. But this continuity is never so great that the individual's agency and choosing are eliminated, for uncertainty is ever present. Even if the situation seems identical, it cannot be; we never step into the same river twice. Within the organisation itself, an institution of formal and informal rules and practices, individuals are also influenced by external institutions, their class and ethnic identity, family and professional affiliations, as well as by what seems to be internal moral and ethical constraints. No one of these constraints dominates the others, for the world is replete with surprise and is forever uncertain. This is painting a complex, shifting, post-modern picture of the context in which we enact our agency, leading us away from seeking fixed, deterministic, or causal models with predictive power. Ultimately the multiplicity and ambiguity of our institutional structures present us with uncertainties, whose resolution becomes our agentic identity as we make the choices that precede our reasoned actions.

Though I have edged away from realism for the purpose of highlighting the creative demands of making sense of uncertain situations, I do not deny that reality seems to exist in the sense that it too places constraints over our imagination. We cannot make pigs fly, no matter how creatively we dream. Perhaps the principal difference between dreaming and being agentic in the world is to experience the constraints of reality. More generally, we know physical constraints in terms of the Second Law of Thermodynamics, the speed of light, the physical constants and so forth. Summarising, in the sections above I imply three universes of constraint – physical, social and personal – and this does a little more than restate Barnard's analysis of the executive function as the creative activity of synthesising these three sub-systems into the organisation itself (Barnard, 1968).

Industry Recipes

Empirical research into the shaping and constraining of senior managers' choices reveals a previously unremarked social institution, the 'industry recipe' (Spender, 1989). Loosely speaking, this is the lens that sees the industry as a community of creative actors brought to the world. It can be understood best as a preliminary synthesis of the physical, social and personal universes noted above. While some see the industry recipe as a purely cognitive frame, I argue it carries much information as practice, evidencing the trilogy of knowledge-as-data, knowledge-as-meaning and knowledge-as-practice.

The research method behind industry recipes was conversational, straight-forward discussion along the lines that any consultant might adopt when beginning an assignment; talking with the client to get a sense of the issues, history, personalities, concerns, constraints and possibilities. Instead of asking direct questions or using a structured questionnaire, the responding managers were asked to talk about what they saw themselves doing, that is to talk about their contribution to the organisation, who reported to them and what these subordinates were supposed to be doing, and so forth. While seemingly straightforward, this is actually a verbal projection technique which produces recorded conversations. These can be listened to over and over again, inductively, with a sense of the vocabulary being adopted and, most importantly, the constructs behind what was being said. This is an ethnographic search for the meanings adopted or generated by these managers, that is, a method for collecting quantitative data about this or that manager, firm, or event.

My research hypothesis was that the top managers' meaning systems would not be company-specific, as many organisational culture and entrepreneurship theorists presume, given their assumption that firms and their histories are unique. Nor would the meaning system be universal, as neo-classical microeconomics presumes with its monocular focus on profit maximisation. Nor would they be culture- or society-specific, as North and other institutional or social constructivist theorists presume. My central notion was that there would be a relationship between the way managers identify their industry and the way they think, talk and act. By 'industry', I do not mean whatever a standard industrial classification code identifies, rather I used industry in the way industry analysts and Wall Street professionals do as they talk about sectors and industries such as 'entertainment' or 'telecommunications', implying a network of mutually dependent social, economic, technological, marketing and consumer activities. Thus 'winter sports industry' might embrace resort management, skiwear, airlines, snowmaking equipment, snowboards, ski-wax, and so on. There is some tautology here, of course, and the empirical research was designed to tease apart the circularity by investigating how the meaning structures of three particular industry recipes were constituted. The underlying theory of cognition and action was drawn from 'personal construct theory', an operationalisation of bounded rationality and sense-making as Weick uses the term (Kelly, 1955; Weick, 1995).

My analysis shows: (a) that each recipe or managerial meaning system can be captured with around a dozen distinct categories or dimensions of influence, and that these are axiomatic to the industry's strategic discourse, (b) that the recipes of different industries are wholly dissimilar, and (c) that a recipe captures the major characteristics of a firm's environment and identity. Most notable is the difficulty of predicting what dimensions and issues will seem to be uppermost to the senior managers. *Ex-post*, after the interviews, the dimensions revealed make sense in terms of a normal economic analysis; concerns with market behaviour, technological change, degree of competition, and so forth. But *ex ante*, the dimensions that the managers selected were uncertain – and that is the whole point. They could have chosen otherwise and have created quite different ways of looking at their situation. The notion that their view is determined by the context and circumstances misses the fundamental point – that this causal chain is rendered uncertain by the mediating effect of the imagination. For instance I researched small-scale iron-founding, an industry that was experiencing extreme competitive pressure from customers, suppliers, new entrants and substitutes alike (Porter, 1980). But Porter's categories are abstractions, disconnected from the specific systems of institutional constraints and identity that comprise the reality of the industry's context.

At the same time, in the manner of institutional empiricism, we discover the individual firms' creativity becomes manifest at the collective industry level, as a recipe of shared knowledge, or rather a widely shared system of both meaning and practice for the firms comprising the industry. In the iron-foundry case, the first two constructs listed relate to the industry's perceived dynamics (Spender, 1989, p. 124). Some protective institutional features or structures had arisen, long-term trust or ownership relationships, so the next construct dealt with whether the firm was within these or not. At the same time the industry is highly granular, with niche markets resulting from specialisation and much division of labour and product knowledge. So the next constructs dealt with the labour market, given the work is labour and skill intensive, and whether the firm had a workforce able to use new technologies to open up new protected niches. The final constructs dealt with the firm's potential quasi-monopoly and trust relationships with its customers, and ultimately whether the senior management was planning to exit the industry, as many did.

We review these constructs not to convey the richness and complexity of the iron-foundry industry's or individual manager's view of the world, as that would require much more work, but merely to indicate how the view might be built up or analysed. The crucial point is that each construct reflects a different line of institutional influence or constraint over the management's strategic imagination. Having made a selection of dimensions, managerial sense-making brings the disparate constructs into the coherent relationship that we might call the industry's identity. The knowledge added is evidence of managerial agency and illustrates the tacit dimension of this theory of the firm.

A distinction between the tacit and explicit types of knowledge is the hallmark of the bulk of the KM discourse and, as we know, is normally drawn from Polanyi (1962). One of the reasons why the KM field is so fragmented is that we are unable to define this pivotal term securely and unambiguously. Gourlay's penetrating analysis shows that there are three distinct kinds of definition (Gourlay, 2004). It should not surprise us that they correspond with the three warrants for meaning discussed earlier in the chapter. The most common usage is realist, so tacit knowledge is defined as explicit knowledge that has not yet been properly codified (Boisot, 1998). The second most common usage relates to knowledge-as-practice, the tacit element being the skilfulness we demonstrate in our practice but which we cannot readily express in our language – hence the maxim 'we know more than we can tell'.

The third, by far the most important but least recognised definition, is that the tacit dimension of what we know is about the way we direct our attention, and select cues and data. Many KM writers tell us the difference between the expert and the novice cyclist is a matter of skill, and that the expert cannot explain this skill to the novice. This messes things up because it conflates the kinetic knowing we see in ballet, where the dancer's knowledge is embodied, and the very different knowledge-of-experience tied up with the way we manage our attention. While Simon has helped us argue rationality is bounded, he also pointed out that attention is our scarcest resource (Simon, 1991). The expert and the novice bicycle riders are getting the same physiological data on balance, arm position, centre of gravity, momentum, and so forth. But the novice is unable to select successfully which cues to attend to and which to ignore, and so is surprised and falls off. The expert, selecting correctly, finds balance and soon reduces its maintenance to a process of 'automatic' attention, requiring no conscious effort and leading to a state of 'flow' (Czikszentmihalyi, 1988). Such direction and selective attention are the core of the industry recipe as an industry-specific social institution that goes some way to resolve the uncertainties of the firms' context and identity.

CONCLUSIONS

This quick overview of industry recipes helps draw the threads together into this chapter's conclusions about (a) how managers deal with uncertainty, (b) how those uncertainties might be described, and (c) how they are shaped by social institutions. Thus far my argument is that the uncertainties are best understood as knowledge absences, the deficiencies that arrest logical analysis. They are manifest in the manager's limited and fragmented knowledge of the situation, and especially in the inconsistencies of perception between these fragments. Forced by circumstance to take explainable action, managers arrive at a point where they must apply their judgement to make up for or resolve these uncertainties. Their choices are then no longer driven solely by data, but as much by their imagination and the meaning they construct in that uncertain context. Many social institutions have a part in shaping the creativity the managers bring to this imagination. The industry recipe can be both seen as data, identifying the circumstances' specifics, but also as a selection apparatus, a set of industry conventions about what needs to be paid attention to. It massively reduces the variety that would otherwise bear on the imagination. What is selected becomes manageable, and in this sense our institutions are only as complex as our imaginations can handle.

We could stop at this point, given that the industry recipe is easy to research empirically. Then, like much of institutional theory, this empirical basis could be taken as a grounding against which we can research or explain the management's strategy-making process, suggesting a highly context-specific theory of the firm, just as empirical descriptions of cultures ground cultural analysis without an overarching deductive theory. There are two obvious problems with this. One is that the analysis is retrospective, a static snapshot of a process of change that we have not even framed, let alone revealed. There is no dynamic, no theory of imagining or learning. Secondly I have skipped the most puzzling aspect of the process – which is how the disparate and mutually exclusive elements of a recipe are imagined into something that approaches a workable rationality for strategic action. I say approach because it is clear from the empirical research that the pattern of meaning the managers construct will not be free from contradiction. Just as normal science puts up with anomalies and gaps, so do managers.

There is an important clue here. One of the lessons we learn from Polanyi, whose work is best seen as a polemic against the abstract notions of scientific thought championed by the positivist philosophers of science, is that the working frameworks that shape scientific practice cannot ever be detached from the physical, social and personal contexts and experiences of that practice. Polanyi introduces tacitness to show how all our knowledge remains situated and shaped by our experience of our practice. This takes us back to the distinction at the start of the chapter between knowledge-as-data, knowledge-as-meaning and knowledge-as-practice. Talk of practice is neither mumbo-jumbo nor obscurantism, it is simply difficult to theorise (for example Bourdieu, 1990; Turner, 1994). But it is the way we experience the world in its immediate present-ness and, as such, is the absolute foundation of all our knowledge. We inherit a tendency to overlook practice in our theory because we are persuaded that, given full knowledge, our decisions are purely rational, logical, objective, abstracted and de-contextualised, and that practice is no more than their enactment. But were this correct we would have no need for social institutions, just as Simon argued there would be no need for administration or managers if we were all rational. By extension we might argue, along with Williamson, that there would be no need for organisations either for markets would then be all we need for one person to exchange the fruits of their labour with another. The world of full knowledge is unlike the real one in which managers exist, immersed in uncertainty. Thus we have evolved a vast array of institutions to help keep uncertainty's destructive influences at bay, so that we are not always at each other's throats in a Hobbesian struggle to get our next meal.

The key to this chapter, then, is practice, for it underpins our knowledge typology. But the gulf between knowledge-as-practice, that sense of competence in dealing with the present-ness of context to which Polanyi draws our attention, and knowledge-as-meaning, evident in the cognitive frameworks we use to make sense of our sense-data, is deep. Here we are in the midst of a philosophical struggle between neo-Platonists, who think that it is in our power to know the essences of the world because we are part of it, and the Kantian interpretivists who argue our knowledge is in our heads and forever in a universe quite different from the reality we inhabit. It is not important to take a position on this, but it is vital to see that without our imaginations, we cannot negotiate either universe without already possessing complete knowledge. So long as we agree that our knowledge is bounded, we need an imagination, and so long as we admit imagination to the analysis, it must be constrained. Our social institutions do this.

Finally, when it comes to comparing the developed and developing nations, there is nothing impractical or over-complicated about these issues. Developing societies are no less complicated than developed ones. On the contrary, both Commons' and Greif's approaches to institutional analysis stress the increasing bureaucratisation and institutionalisation of developing societies, for the very purpose of both permitting and constraining change in human society. On the one hand, institutions create space for the freedoms which permit the imagination freer play, allow for new meanings and practices and so press forward the division of labour. This, as Smith reminded us, determines the extent of the market. On the other hand, institutions create the complexities of contemporary society in which individual freedoms are both offered and protected from the imaginings of others. The bottom line is that developing societies have just as much at stake as the developed societies in applying the lessons of a sophisticated KM analysis (Spender, 1993).

REFERENCES

Ackoff, R.L. (1989), 'From Data to Wisdom', *Journal of Applied Systems Analysis*, **16**, 3–9.
Alvesson, M. and D. Kärreman (2001), 'Odd Couple: Making Sense of the Curious Concept of Knowledge Management', *Journal of Management Studies*, **38**(7), 995–1018.
Ayer, A.J. (1985), *Wittgenstein*, New York: Random House.
Barnard, C.I. (1968), *The Functions of the Executive*, Cambridge, MA: Harvard University Press.
Boisot, M. (1998), *Knowledge Assets: Securing Competitive Advantage in the Information Economy*, Oxford: Oxford University Press.
Bontis, N. and J. Fitz-enz (2002), 'Intellectual Capital ROI: A Causal Map of Human Capital Antecedents and Consequents', *Journal of Intellectual Capital*, **3**(3), 223–47.
Bourdieu, P. (1990), *The Logic of Practice*, Stanford, CA: Stanford University Press.
Cabrera, A. and E.F. Cabrera (2002), 'Knowledge-sharing Dilemmas', *Organisation Studies*, **23**(5), 687–710.

Choo, C.W. and N. Bontis (2002), *The Strategic Management of Intellectual Capital and Organisational Knowledge*, New York: Oxford University Press.
Cohen, M.D. and L.S. Sproull (1996), *Organisational Learning*, Thousand Oaks, CA: Sage Publications.
Commons, J.R. (1924), *The Legal Foundations of Capitalism*, New York: Macmillan.
Commons, J.R. (1931), 'Institutional Economics', *American Economic Review*, **21**, 648–57.
Czikszentmihalyi, M. (1988), 'Optimal Experience: Psychological Studies of Flow in Consciousness', in M. Czikszentmihalyi and I.S. Czikszentmihalyi (eds), *Psychological Studies of Flow in Consciousness*, Cambridge: Cambridge University Press, pp. 15–35.
Davenport, T.H. (1997), 'Ten Principles of Knowledge Management and Four Case Studies', *Knowledge and Process Management*, **4**(3), 187–208.
Easterby-Smith, M. and M.A. Lyles (2003), *The Blackwell Handbook of Organisational Learning and Knowledge Management*, Malden, MA: Blackwell.
Fahey, L. and L. Prusak (1998), 'The Eleven Deadliest Sins of Knowledge Management', *California Management Review*, **40**(3), 265–76.
Felin, T. and N.J. Foss (forthcoming), 'Strategic Organisation: A Field in Search of Micro-foundations', *Strategic Organisation*.
Fuller, S. (2003), *Kuhn vs Popper: The Struggle for the Soul of Science*, Cambridge: Icon Books.
Gergen, K.J. (1995), 'Social Construction and the Educational Process', in L.P. Steffe and J. Gale (eds), *Constructivism in Education*, Hillsdale, NJ: Lawrence Erlbaum Associates, pp. 17–39.
Gourlay, S. (2004), 'Knowing as Semiosis: Steps towards a Reconceptualisation of Tacit Knowledge', in H. Tsoukas and N. Mylonopoulos (eds), *Organisations as Knowledge Systems*, Basingstoke, Hampshire: Palgrave Macmillan, pp. 86–105.
Greif, A. (2006), *Institutions and the Path to the Modern Economy: Lessons from Medieval Trade*, New York: Cambridge University Press.
Gupta, B., S.I. Lakshmi and J.E. Aronson (2000), 'Knowledge Management: Practices and Challenges', *Industrial Management and Data Systems*, **100**(1), 17–21.
Hansmann, H., R. Kraakman and R. Squire (2006), *Law and the Rise of the Firm*, Working Paper 57/2006; New Haven, CT: Yale Law School, co-published by Cambridge, MA: Harvard Law School.
Hislop, D. (2002), 'Mission Impossible? Communicating and Sharing Knowledge via Information Technology', *Journal of Information Technology*, **17**(3), 165–77.
Hofstede, D.H. (1984), *Culture's Consequences: International Differences in Work-related Values*, Newbury Park, CA: Sage Publications.
Jaju, A., H. Kwak and G.M. Zinkhan (2002), 'Learning Styles of Undergraduate Business Students: A Cross-cultural Comparison between the US, India, and Korea', *Marketing Education Review*, **12**(2), 49–60.
Kelly, G.A. (1955), *The Psychology of Personal Constructs*, New York: W.W. Norton.
Kuhn, T.S. (1970), *The Structure of Scientific Revolutions*, Chicago, IL: University of Chicago Press.
Lubit, R. (2001), 'Tacit Knowledge and Knowledge Management: The Keys to Sustainable Competitive Advantage', *Organisational Dynamics*, **29**(3), 164–78.
Lucier, C.E. and J.D. Torsilieri (2001), 'Can Knowledge Management Deliver Bottom-line Results?' in N. Ikujiro and D. Teece (eds), *Managing Industrial Knowledge: Creation, Transfer, and Utilisation*, London: Sage, pp. 231–43.

Marren, P. (2003), 'Where Did All the Knowledge Go?' *Journal of Business Strategy*, **24**(3), 5–7.

Maturana, H.R. and F.J. Varela (1980), *Autopoiesis and Cognition: The Realisation of the Living*, Dordrecht, Holland: D. Reidel.

McAfee, A. (2003), 'When Too Much IT Knowledge is a Dangerous Thing' *MIT Sloan Management Review*, **44**(2), 83–9.

Nelson, R.R. and S.W. Winter (1982), *An Evolutionary Theory of Economic Change*, Cambridge, MA: Belknap Press.

North, D.C. (1990), *Institutions, Institutional Change, and Economic Performance*, Cambridge: Cambridge University Press.

North, D.C. (1991), 'Institutions', *Journal of Economic Perspectives*, **5**(1), 97–112.

Polanyi, M. (1962), *Personal Knowledge: Towards a Post-Critical Philosophy*, Chicago, IL: University of Chicago Press.

Popper, K.R. (2002), *Conjectures and Refutations: The Growth of Scientific Knowledge*, London: Routledge.

Porter, M.E. (1980), *Competitive Strategy: Techniques for Analysing Industries and Competitors*, New York: Free Press.

Prusak, L. (2001), 'Where Did Knowledge Management Come From?', *IBM Systems Journal*, **40**(4), 1002–6.

Renzl, B., K. Matzler and H. Hinterhuber (2006), *The Future of Knowledge Management*, Basingstoke, Hampshire: Palgrave Macmillan.

Selznick, P. (1957), *Leadership in Administration: A Sociological Interpretation*, New York: Harper and Row.

Simon, H.A. (1991), 'Bounded Rationality and Organisational Learning', *Organisation Science*, **2**(1), 125–34.

Simon, H.A. (1996), 'Bounded Rationality and Organisational Learning', in M.D. Cohen and L. Sproull (eds), *Organisational Learning*, Thousand Oaks, CA: Sage, pp. 175–87.

Simon, H.A. (1997), *Administrative Behaviour: A Study of Decision-Making Processes in Administrative Organisation*, New York: Free Press.

Spender, J.C. (1989), *Industry Recipes: The Nature and Sources of Managerial Judgment*, Oxford: Blackwell.

Spender, J.C. (1993), 'Transferring Management Techniques to Eastern Europe: An Institutional Critique', *International Journal of Organisational Analysis*, **1**(3), 237–54.

Spender, J.C. (2005), 'An Overview: What's New and Important about Knowledge Management? Building New Bridges between Managers and Academics', in S. Little and T. Ray (eds), *Managing Knowledge: An Essential Reader*, London: Sage, pp. 127–54.

Stainton, R.J. (2000), *Perspectives in the Philosophy of Language: A Concise Anthology*, Peterborough, Canada: Broadview Press.

Storey, J. and E. Barnett (2000), 'Knowledge Management Initiatives: Learning from Failure', *Journal of Knowledge Management*, **4**(2), 145–56.

Sutton, D. (2001), 'What is Knowledge and Can it be Managed?', *European Journal of Information Systems*, **10**(2), 80–88.

Tsoukas, H. (2005), *Complex Knowledge: Studies in Organisational Epistemology*, Oxford: Oxford University Press.

Tsoukas, H. and N. Mylonopoulos (2004), *Organisations as Knowledge Systems: Knowledge, Learning and Dynamic Capabilities*, Basingstoke, Hampshire: Palgrave Macmillan.

Tsoukas, H and E. Vladimirou (2001), 'What is Organisational Knowledge?', *Journal of Management Studies*, **38**(7), 973–93.

Turner, S. (1994), *The Social Theory of Practices: Tradition, Tacit Knowledge, and Presuppositions*, Chicago, IL: University of Chicago Press.

Weick, K.E. (1995), *Sensemaking in Organisations*, Thousand Oaks, CA: Sage Publications.

Williamson, O.E. (1975), *Markets and Hierarchies: Analysis and Antitrust Implications*, New York: Free Press.

Williamson, O.E. (1987), *The Economic Institutions of Capitalism: Firms, Markets, Relational Contracting*, New York: The Free Press.

Wittgenstein, L. (1972), *On Certainty*, New York: Harper and Row.

PART TWO

Knowledge management in the transition
economies

3. Survival by subversion in former socialist economies: tacit knowledge exchange at the workplace

Gerhard Fink, Nigel Holden and Maren Lehmann

INTRODUCTION

In the socialist era following the Second World War, there were, despite prevailing perceptions to the contrary, marked differences in general governance and even quality of life among the countries of East and Central Europe as well as the Soviet Union itself. Poland was unique in being a 'supercharged Catholic country' (Davies, 1986, p. 11). In no socialist country was there a ruling family comparable to the Ceauşescu's in Romania (Gallagher, 1995), whilst Tito's Yugoslavia was a communist system pragmatically designed to neutralise the dominance of two key national groups, that is Serbs and Croats (Glenny, 1992). The Soviet Union itself was a centralised Eurasian empire, in which Russian national consciousness embed communism with 'a demotic quality, a defensiveness, and an earth-boundedness which still have strong echoes today' (Hosking, 1992, p.17). For all these dramatic disparities bequeathed by history, all the communist countries were run by totalitarian parties and implemented a highly centralised system of economic management. There was nowhere the state apparatus could not reach (Deletant, 1995). Our chapter is premised on the assumption that all citizens of socialist countries – whether Czechs, Poles, Russians or Kazakhs – led lives in full consciousness of the implacably intrusive nature of the state. It is this general experience, that is past but not forgotten, to which we apply the understandings of knowledge management (KM). But more than that: our approach helps us to explain why KM in today's post-socialist countries is not straightforward in theory or practice.

In many ways, the general Western view of life under socialist regimes was dominated by prevailing images of the ubiquity of the secret police, but it was also distorted by a failure of imagination to grasp that ordinary people in the countries concerned led lives that kept the intrusions of the State at bay. It is the major thesis of this chapter that the workplace was paradoxically the locale of this rarely recognised form of subtle dissent. This conviction raises important issues about what we can regard as normal behaviour in socialist regimes and the cultural standards that are associated with it. One feature of this normal behaviour is that people for reasons of survival and self-protection exchanged a considerable amount of tacit knowledge with each other.[1]

In standard KM theory, tacit knowledge is private, context-specific, and thus hard to formalise, communicate and codify (Nonaka and Takeuchi, 1995). In the business context, this knowledge belongs to the domain of what is not noticed. It therefore often remains elusive and is readily lost. It is as if corporations do not place high value on it. But in a socialist environment, tacit knowledge had high value indeed; it was a resource for deflecting unwelcome intrusions by the State. In some cases it was, literally, a pathway to survival. Tacit knowledge in the form of informed whispers from *trusted* acquaintances prepared people for unforeseen situations in which they could avoid or forestall a false denunciation about their commitment to the ideals of socialism, an encounter with someone expert in delation, or an interview with the secret police *for any reason*.

This tacit knowledge contrasted with the overly explicit nature of knowledge promulgated by the State. This knowledge was risky. It could often incriminate. So people avoided it, preferring to circulate tacit knowledge. But such knowledge was also not without risks and, perhaps surprisingly, it could easily involve economic calculations that excluded the State. Consider the role of the black markets which were in fact a significant feature of the economy in each socialist country. The people's desire for nylons, jeans, toiletries and consumer electronics was met by a market economy system, which operated independently of the planned economy and which procured such items from Western Europe, the USA and Japan. Precisely when and how these 'unplanned' items might make a discreet appearance belonged squarely to the sphere of tacit knowledge, which lay beyond the reach of the State. This rampant activity, which might even involve hard currency in transactions, constituted the anti-socialist crime of 'speculation': that is in essence, selling things at a profit.

One needed special skills to survive in socialist societies (that applied to the mighty too). In the case of the workers, they protected their survival know-how by adroit subversion of official orders by simultaneous outward affirmation and inner rejection. This survival by subversion creates a special cultural standard,[2] which is to be found in rigidly controlled organisations and societies. It operates like this: workers show the expected unconditional loyalty to their political leaders. But this is purely superficial, as the 'rules' of survival require the workers to protect their integrity as individuals independent of the stifling control of the regime. This is what Hahn (2004,

p. 60) means when he talks about workers having a 'life underneath'. 'Ordinary' workers survived by applying tacit knowledge in ways which are from a Western perspective most unusual. In essence, workers based tacit knowledge on interactions with their equally oppressed fellow workers, whom they could trust (that is, trust not to report their private misgivings about the regime to the authorities). Indeed this tacit knowledge may be seen as a form of ironic managing of the balancing act between outward conformity and the striving for inner independence (see Rorty, 1989). Naturally, the authorities were aware of the charade played by the 'loyal' workers, whose behaviour was perforce a permanent source of suspicion. We should note in passing that this use of tacit knowledge in former communist countries is strikingly similar to Nonaka and Takeuchi's (1995) concept of socialisation, which is also trust-dependent.

By applying terms like 'tacit' and 'explicit' to socialist society and emphasising the role of trust in the transfer of tacit knowledge, we come to the proposition that it is possible to study life in socialist regimes from the KM perspective. However, in order to put these points into preliminary perspective, we need to examine the nature of the socialist system. We can then fruitfully apply modern concepts of KM to throw unusual light on socialism and practice. That in turn will enable us to develop insights into post-socialist societies, which are having variable success in transforming themselves into market economies.

In order to apprehend the significance of that assertion, we go back to history, and include some notes on irony and trust. Next, we try to shape a short description of the workplace in socialist economies, and finally we draw some conclusions on observations in the current transition processes.

KNOWLEDGE MANAGEMENT IN FORMER SOCIALIST ECONOMIES

The concept of KM is not one that is readily associated with behaviour in the former socialist countries. Yet we, the three co-authors, believe that a KM approach can shed new light on understanding aspects of behaviour in the socialist workplace. This chapter distils our respective knowledge and experience of socialist countries which go back to the 1960s. Our knowledge ranges from sociology, political economy and linguistics with special reference to East/Central Europe and USSR/Russia; our experience embraces residence as a citizen (Lehmann), language student and later businessman (Holden), and research into economics and management (Fink). Between us over the years we have, as academic researchers, written more than 250 contributions ranging from books, book chapters, official reports and monographs. In recent times two of us have made notable contributions to the field of global transfer of management knowledge (Fink and Holden, 2002, 2005a, 2005b). Our chapter then is an attempt to fuse together many significant themes and reconstitute them in order to let emerge a new picture of organisational life under socialism.

This chapter is based on different sources of knowledge accumulated over many years: our own research on communist countries in Europe since the late 1960s, well documented in a few hundred publications by the authors; personal experiences of all three authors in either having been a citizen of former socialist countries or having gained insights as visiting scholars; having had hundreds of interactions with scholars and inhabitants of the countries concerned, at workplaces, international conferences and in public spheres; and having had training and education in socialist ideology, political and economic thought, and dialectic materialism. In this section, we provide insights about the emergence of particular cultural standards as a consequence of ideological thought and political action.

ORGANISATIONS IN THE SOCIALIST SYSTEM: THE ROLE OF THE CADRE

As the industrial revolution became established in Europe and with it the setting up of manufacturing concerns and financial institutions, the term 'organisation', which formerly did not refer to the structures of the new commercial enterprises, was re-invented. Before, 'organisation' (just like 'system') was understood as a state of order. In the context of the industrial enterprise this understanding was supplemented by a notion, which describes a social practice of controlling the unruly masses of the proletariat in industrial enterprises. This practice of social control persisted under the name 'bureaucracy'. After this shift in meaning, organisation now means a summary of all measures taken when individuals and their ways of life are disciplined. Consequently, organisationally controlled lives are perceived as 'work', that term being understood as the opposite of 'real life', which never can be controlled. The 'work–life' distinction persisted throughout the entire era of socialism.

It is evident from the preceding discussion that the workers, on whose very behalf the socialist state had been brought into existence, could not be trusted by the authorities. They were, as we noted earlier, permanently under suspicion of wrecking or even wanting to wreck the entire system. In order to ensure that workers were under constant pressure to conform, a method of control was introduced which was called 'socialist discipline'. The socialist discipline was a state of mind the authorities enforced, by threatening to use all means of enforcement at its disposal. At the workplace a special kind of socialist discipline was deployed. This went by the name of cadre.

Originally, the cadre was an invention of military politics in eighteenth-century France. It labelled a core staff of armed forces, especially the republican army. Later, the term was transferred to the sphere of state administration and signified the core staff of bureaucracy, trained in elite schools. Supposing the proletarians were the leading class of society, Lenin copied this tradition and supplemented it with the American practice of management, especially Taylor's 'scientific management'. After all, as Skidelsky (1995, p. 26) has sharply observed, Lenin 'saw the State as the agent of big business'. Taylor divided organisational staff into those who work physically (for Lenin: the proletarians, the mass resource) and those who work intellectually (for Lenin: the suspicious individuals). Consistent with his own ideology, Lenin had to create both a sort of intellectual worker who could be perceived as a proletarian (a mere element of a mass substratum) and a sort of physical worker who could be perceived as an intellectual or at least as someone who is able to follow the ideology (presented as a 'scientific' programme) for rational reasons (for further discussion, see Service, 2000; Shub, 1966). That is why each personal file in socialism was called a 'cadre file'. In the Soviet Union, the cadres were to be found in each and every kind of organisation to ensure that the will of the State prevailed. When the Soviet occupation of East and Central Europe began in 1945, the notion of 'cadre' was reintroduced in other languages of socialist countries as if being of Russian descent.

Lenin, of course, copied the nineteenth-century traditional concept of masses of industrial workers being controlled by industrial organisation, but he extended it to a concept of labour that included all intellectual work as well. The intellectuals who could not be easily described in terms of masses and classes were described as organisational staff; in practice most were engineers. In his thinking Lenin was influenced by German notions of bureaucracy and even American methods of management. He saw the latter not so much as an expression of capitalist exploitation (as many might expect), but as a necessary means of control. Lenin, like Taylor, whom he admired, was suspicious of workers and their potential power to disrupt *any* economic system. For Lenin, politics and economy merged into one, and so did society and organisation. To resolve all the inherent contradictions, Lenin developed a concept of the State led by one party, the Communist Party, to which everything and everyone were subordinate. Influenced by Weber's concept of bureaucracy[3] and Taylor's notions of organisation,[4] Lenin saw that there was a need to supervise the State's arrangements and activities by loyal enforcers, namely the cadres.[5] Part of their role was to root out the negative influence of 'disruptive elements'; individuals who did not conform to the requirements of compliance.

In the socialist era, millions of people worked under the direct control of cadres whose task was to secure the best performance from workers to ensure that production and other targets were met. Individuals, whether disruptive elements or not, realised that to survive under close surveillance was to do what is ordered – to do everything correctly, to meet the plan, and so on. A man or woman who presented himself or herself as a reliable worker who did precisely as ordered without any doubt or question, made no difference to a planning organisation: he or she seemed to be a perfect tool, just like organisation itself. But this was an illusion; it was a front stage game played against a hidden backstage (see Goffman, 1996, pp. 99ff.; see also 23ff. for the notion of chosen façades).

In this charade, the aim of individuals was to protect themselves from degradation and humiliation. They gave themselves sustenance through informal knowledge-sharing with other individuals they could trust. But, paradoxically, this communication stratagem involved another troublesome consequence for the authorities. Workers were not just exchanging information on how to avert censure by the authorities; they were in effect using coded language to discuss their entire lives under socialism. In this sense they brought the enacted experience of socialist society into the workplace and in ways that potentially undermined the authorities. Given that vast amounts of subversive tacit knowledge were shared by workers in the workplace, we can note an irony of socialism: that the workers were to all intents and purposes what we might call 'tacit knowledge managers', in contrast to the cadres who were enforcers of explicit knowledge. In this charade, people used 'work' and not 'organisation' as their favourite joker in the socialist economic game. They played a complex, dangerous game with communication stratagems, which could be neither completely appropriated nor perfectly controlled by the totalitarian party. This is the essence of the people's twist (Baecker, 2002; Fink and Lehmann, 2006).

Irony and Trust at the Workplace

Accordingly, and paradoxically, the authorities assumed that people were less suspicious at the workplace, where their association with other people could be controlled and monitored. Privacy seemed to be much more suspicious. Outside the workplace people formed other associations, often based on genuine friendship or shared interest in activities such as sport, music or literature. People were aware that their activities outside the workplace were more difficult for the State to monitor except with huge armies of informers. They discovered that they enjoyed more freedom at the workplace provided that they associated with people they could trust: that is to say, trust them not to betray them to the authorities for any alleged transgression. That is one side.

The other is that if the suspicion emanated from a closed shop model (you could trust those who are included but you should mistrust those who are excluded), the culture of suspicion also contaminated private life. Whilst there were no 'cadres' in private kitchens, at barbecues and wedding parties, their mode of control was always present, because it was the other side of that life. Everybody could be a snooper, but in private life this problem could not be pushed aside as was done at the workplace. At the place of work there had to be communication to ensure that decisions were implemented, work was allocated, and harangues to the workers to achieve and more importantly over-achieve production targets were acted upon. In the socialist context communication was crucial, because it acted as a form of work linking decisions to implementation. The more sophisticated the operation, the more communication: but the more communication, the more opportunities *to learn how to avoid being suspicious*.

It follows from this that workers played a game: they outwardly con-formed, professed commitment and loyalty in order to avoid retribution. To paraphrase McCarthy and co-authors (2005), everybody – not just 'managers' – had to be 'masters of circumventing rules and directives' and generally work in underhand ways (see also Puffer et al., 2000). As long as workers did what the State required of them at the place of work, they could not be easily held to be disruptive. Thus cadres turned a blind eye: this was the essence of the paradoxical form of freedom at the socialist workplace. People had a fall-back position there; but they did not have one at home. Thus, the special socialist politics of fear always threatens privacy, not work. Hence the authorities controlled private life more tightly than life at the workplace. This state of affairs meant that at the workplace the cadres were less omnipotent than we might think today. Cadres could only operate explicit networks but the workers had the tacit ones, which was, paradoxically, the source of their survival power. This explains why in socialist societies, the workplace was a place of comparative freedom.

To summarise: we may say that trust in socialism was based on the perception that everybody – or virtually everybody – led a double life and engaged in survival by subversion. The result was a special kind of social inclusiveness. Insiders knew it, strangers could not perceive it, cadres suspected it, everybody who wanted to be included tried to learn it. So it was that the workplace evolved as a kind of marketplace for a great exchange of trust-based tacit knowledge. This translation of the workplace into an invisible trust-based marketplace for knowledge-sharing for survival was the subtle irony of socialism, and it entailed danger for everyone – even for secret policemen, who much preferred not to have to catch alleged subverters of socialism at the sacrosanct workplace.

SOCIALIST-STYLE KNOWLEDGE MANAGEMENT

Two considerations follow from this. One is obvious, the other less so. The first concerns the nature of work attitudes at the socialist workplace; the second concerns what we might call 'socialist-style KM'. As we have noted, the authorities in socialist countries had a fear of individuals, who were seen as disruptive, uncontrollable and unreliable. Hence workers learnt that the important thing was not to stick out or become unwittingly conspicuous to the authorities, who were always on the outlook for scapegoats to protect their own positions. But note: these tactics of evasion for personal survival had to be learnt at the workplace. One tactic, and its legacy still exists today in former socialist countries, is to avoid knowing anything, even by accident, which could prove to be disadvantageous.

This brings us to a consideration of 'socialist-style KM'. As we have noted, socialist society observed various crucial distinctions between public and private, family and work, reliable and unreliable people. We suggested that personal survival depended on a game of survival that was outwardly conformist, but was often subversive: 'the people's twist'. To operate in these conditions, one needed knowledge of a special kind. It was tacit knowledge that had nothing to do with creativity to improve a work process in the normal sense of the expression. It was tacit knowledge that took many forms, but it was in essence the knowledge of how to communicate in official 'party' language to transmit private information and how to screen, filter and employ publicly available explicit knowledge for private use.

Thus there was tacit–tacit transfer at the workplace among friends, and there was also explicit–tacit transfer of knowledge made publicly available, but at the workplace there was no tacit–explicit conversion from workers to supervisors, and there was no explicit–explicit transfer from workers to supervisors. In short, the workplace was a knowledge-creating domain, to which the Nonaka and Takeuchi (1995) model applies, but only very selectively. Seen from this perspective, the socialist system was one in which communication channels were reduced to tacit knowledge transfer embedded in the official political language, which acted as a vehicle for knowledge transfer only to those who knew the context. Those who knew the context could internalise new tacit knowledge; those who did not know were excluded from the communication channels. Survival was only possible by subversion, whereby the socialist economy established itself as a system in which cadres and workers engaged in mutual undermining of each other's efforts for mutual survival. In the end the system imploded on itself, exhausted.

ISSUES OF TRANSITION TO MARKET ECONOMY

In light of the previous section, it is obvious that the modes of communication which persisted throughout the communist era could not be sustained. They had to be adapted to the requirements of firms and corporations acting in a market economy context.

Given the complexities of subversive survival, it should not be surprising that there were – and indeed still are – substantial obstacles to effecting a smooth change process. As Skidelsky (1995, p. xii) has observed: 'there was no ready-made world-order into which the post-Communist societies could slot … nor was there a single Western model of success'. Not only that, the gulf between the post-socialism world and 'the West' has manifested itself in ways which were largely unanticipated. A case in point concerns the translation of Western management textbooks as well as business guidelines and decision procedures into the languages of former socialist countries. It has often proved extremely difficult and occasionally virtually impossible, to produce accurate translations. A survey of translations of Western management texts into Russian, for example, has identified the following causes for mistranslations of case studies concerning three major European corporations. It should be borne in mind that the highlighted difficulties of transferring Western management terminology affect all languages of former socialist countries:

- Complete misunderstanding of a term in the original (for example: mapping translated into *kartografiya*; learning history into history of learning; sense-making into understanding; assumptions into axioms).
- Absence of a close lexical equivalent in Russian (examples concern the verb 'to facilitate' and the nouns 'excellence' and 'vision').
- Use of circumlocutions and/or free translations, which do not convey the meaning of the original (for example: the mission statements and other promotional material from Novo Nordisk and Sulzer Infra).
- Creation of loanwords based on the English originals which in russified form would be not readily understood (for example: *fasilitatsiya*).

Reviewing the last 20 years, it is possible to identify classes of Western management terminology that have proved difficult to translate into Russian (Fink and Lehmann, 2006):

1. Figurative language
    Terms like 'benchmarking', 'the bottom line' and 'sticking to the knitting' defy literal translation. They become circumlocutions, which reflect the core idea in neutral language.
2. Terminology that refers to 'soft management'
    Modern management uses a vast range of words to cover aspects of communication and motivation (currently fashionable are words like 'team-player', 'coach', 'mentor', 'facilitate', 'empower', 'vision', 'mission', and so on). Many words of this class are virtually untranslatable (except by wordy circumlocutions). Native words, which might be used for literal translation, are completely inappropriate. For example, the standard Russian word for 'empower' confines its semantic area to high politics, whereas *nastavnik*, meaning 'mentor', is very much someone who is going to guide you to a more upright and ascetically conditioned life.
3. Terms used in models
    Terms in models are often a kind of shorthand for a weighty or complex notion. A good example concerns the Hofstedian notion of 'power distance'. Pshenichnivoka (2003) has attested four different translations of this term into Russian, all of them unsatisfactory when back-translated into English. A fifth variation is in the word 'assumptions', where two separate Russian words are used to translate the word in models. Terms are often figurative, as are 'cash cow' and 'dog' in the Boston Consulting Group's growth-strategy matrix. They too prove exceptionally difficult to render into Russian. Models are widely used in management education and research. A survey of Russian-language versions of Western management would very likely reveal substantial variation in the translations of terms used in models. Iconic terms like 'cash cow' or 'power distance' can be taken to be the tip of the iceberg.
4. Terminology that refers to aspects of organisational life, which were radically different in Soviet society
    Two obvious areas are human resource management and marketing, for which entirely new areas of vocabulary are being created based on foreign loanwords, especially from (American) English, and reconstituted native word-stock. The absorption of these special functional languages – and the attitudes that go with them – will take many years, perhaps decades, to be accomplished.

Beyond the purely linguistic aspects, the transition to the market economy involves countries of Central and Eastern Europe (CEE); societies in a major knowledge transfer process at governmental, institutional (organisational) and personal levels of interactions with the West as the direct or indirect source of knowledge. In the case of business, the process entails strategic changes from the corporate cultures of old-style socialist enterprises (which we have described) to new ones in tune with the behaviour of market economies (May et al., 2005). A key method facilitating this particular kind of 're-engineering' is mergers and acquisitions. Privatisations, which do not always involve foreign partners, are also driven by a perceived need for market orientation. Evidence suggests that the new knowledge does not replace the old knowledge. This means that a new knowledge system is evolving, which is better understood as a hybrid system, instead of a transitional one. This evolution of knowledge systems occurs in companies located in CEE countries, including Russia. Let us add substance to these observations by studying an acquisition by a foreign corporation.

This process is usually initiated by headquarters of foreign corporations which want to transfer management techniques or management know-how to the subsidiary or a joint venture. The manoeuvrings of the acquiring corporation often induce culture shock at the local end, which usually leads to resistance and passivity at all organisational levels (Fink and Feichtinger, 1998; Fink and Holden, 2002, 2005a, 2005b; Hurt and Hurt, 2005; Javidan et al., 2005; Lunnan et al., 2005; May et al., 2005; Napier, 2005).

Since an elementary cause of the collective culture shock is collective lack of orientation or even disorientation (Fink and Feichtinger, 1998; Fink and Holden, 2002), several sets of issues aggravate the related problems:

- Prospective receivers of 'new and valuable knowledge' are incapable of making sense of verbal and non-verbal communication. Given the modes of communication as they were developed at the workplace during communist times, any explicit form of communication provided by new supervisors (Western managers) is suspected of carrying a much more important tacit component – in other words, a hidden agenda – which needs to be known before anyone dares take any action.
- The (Western) senders consider their knowledge as useful, sometimes even infallible. The fact that receivers do not understand this knowledge or are not willing to adopt it as the suppliers of new knowledge think they should (maybe people reproduce their backstage politics) constitutes a shock – an often-unanticipated shock – to the senders, too.
- Power games aggravate the issues: more often than not Western managers react unwillingly and arrogantly to the perceived rejection of 'their superior knowledge', they are inclined to consider the refusing receivers as simpletons, malcontents, moaners and whiners.
- Deliberately misleading communication by those who pursue specific personal or group interests aggravates the collective culture shock.

All of these factors must be seen against the complex historical, cultural and geopolitical context in which the former socialist countries are found and from which they cannot fully escape. We may see them as markets or transitional economies. But we should not forget that the entire region, which spreads from the geographical centre of Europe in the west to Vladivostok in the east, is one in which millions have been victims of forced migrations, interethnic violence, religious intolerance, political persecution and genocidal war. They have also seen their countries disappear and borders change. History is ever-present and memories long, whilst the communist experiment still conditions mentalities (and even creates nostalgia). Firms that wish to be seen as enlightened insiders and not mere economic invaders must take into account this context. It helps to explain why knowledge transfer is such an arduous process and encounters resistance.

Experience shows that the observed hesitancy to act or outright resistance begins to fade after about 18 months to two years. Local staff begin to take the initiative. This makes it possible to generate a 'common space' for knowledge transfer between the acquiring corporation and local staff (Fink and Holden, 2005a; Hurt and Hurt, 2005; Lunnan et al., 2005) or the local staff are generating their own subsystem in the 'global setting' of their firm (Paik and Choi, 2005).

However, in several instances these hybrid cultures are not stable. They will be finally dominated by a new local corporate culture seemingly closer to the headquarters culture (Hurt and Hurt, 2005; Lunnan et al., 2005). In other instances, when the corporation explicitly decides to leave the local culture untouched and establishes the cultural crossing at the headquarters (Koivisto, 1999), the local corporate culture will prevail. This is definitely the case if supplier–customer relations are at the core of cross-cultural interaction (Glisby and Holden, 2005). Importantly, seven to ten years are required for the processes we have described to resolve themselves (Fink and Holden, 2002; Hurt and Hurt, 2005; Napier, 2005).

DISCUSSION

We noted how under socialism, the people's twist involved irony at the workplace. This problem is reproduced in the present post-communist era when management is nothing more than a replacement of control instances. If the West assumes (like the communists before them) they have the right answers for the individual, people will use the ancient ways of survival. When the communists took over power, they introduced a new socio-economic and politico-cultural discourse. Presenting management methods as undoubtedly the right programmes to impose the new thinking, the West somehow does the same because it (unintentionally or not) copies the socialist ideology of 'scientific knowledge'. Socialist thinking has not disappeared without a trace: indeed entire sections of the populations miss some aspects of socialist life, not least the low prices. In Eastern Germany, 'Ostalgie' has become a branch not only of the German entertainment industry, it is widely – more or less successfully – used in marketing and advertising to create a special internal market for 'our original products', of course referring to 'our original way of life'. Western firms, which for example are implementing management by objectives, are in fact introducing much more rigid and effective management control systems than the so called 'planned economy' ever had.

Just as people under communism needed survival strategies, so do people coping with the turmoil of transition and the market economy system, with its perceived unpleasant competitiveness and uncivilised social behaviour. Is it any wonder then that Western management textbooks contain concepts which so often cannot readily be found in the local language? And is it any wonder then that people follow the Western style ironically, 'playing the game as if it makes sense'?

This chapter is conceptualised as a retrospective study. From the perspective of rigorous methods, this certainly would constitute a weakness because to those who believe in questionnaires, the insights derived in this chapter may seem difficult to validate and replicate. However, there are no alternatives. In communist times, it was extremely difficult to conduct interviews or impossible to send out questionnaires to workers in socialist countries (see Lawrence and Vlachoutsicos, 1990; Michailova, 1996; Michailova and Liuhto, 2000). But times have passed and changed. People (individuals, workers, managers) reconstruct their social realities to gain a new basis for survival in a new, yet transitory, system: the system of and in economic transition from plan to market. Again, it would be difficult to formulate questions which would render 'unbiased and true' responses. The 'socially desirable', for example from the perspective of Western managers active in the East European economies, would largely differ from the 'actual' behaviour as perceived by the workers who over the last 15 years may have lost their jobs several times.

Thus, the retrospective method of comparative study of texts seemingly is the only available method to gains insights into that past yet not remote period, which still has an impact on the present forms of communication, action and interaction. Roth (2004) and Desai (2005) both direct an impressive retrospective project on 'everyday culture in socialism'. Although these authors use a completely different point of departure, we find that our analysis resonates with their insights, which suggests that our knowledge management perspective on life at the workplace in socialism is not without validity.

CONCLUSIONS

The study of socialist societies has been dominated by economists and political scientists. What we are suggesting is that there is scope for a sociological theoretical approach, which highlights a 'cultural–organisational' concept of behavioural attitudes at the workplace in socialist economies. We have argued that loyalty was more important than efficiency and that there was a collective connivance involving both cadres and workers to maintain this particular status quo. The workers operated their people's twist. The cadres reacted by not imposing excessive demands on their subordinates, as this might lead to disruptive behaviour which the cadres to their potential detriment could not control. It was a game of skill and cunning, fraught with danger for both sides. For their part, the workers made it all more tolerable by gaining a certain freedom at the workplace to develop friendships with their fellows and create powerful bonds of solidarity in the face of ever-present retribution.

The most striking feature of our analysis has been to apply concepts of knowledge management to our understandings of workplace relationships in socialist societies. In the socialist world, tacit knowledge was generated as a counterpoise to explicit knowledge as a means of self-protection. But it also served to undermine the cadres. All in all we may conclude that the experiences of millions who lived under the conditions of socialism, suggest a wholly unknown conception of the term 'knowledge worker' and a very specific perception of what 'tacit' knowledge is about.

MANAGERIAL IMPLICATIONS

Our analysis both corroborates and extends the existing literature on the challenges of transferring foreign management knowledge to former socialist countries (for example Hurt and Hurt, 2005; Kuznetsov and Yakavenka, 2005; May et al., 2005). It provides an explanation as to why cross-cultural relationships can be marked by wariness and mistrust. Managers who engage in cross-cultural knowledge transfer should:

- Anticipate that knowledge changes its meaning when travelling: for example, through the lack of equivalent terms in other languages or insufficient understanding of post-socialist contexts.
- Accept that former socialist countries are still experiencing a collective culture shock, which contributes to forms of resistance about absorbing and implementing foreign know-how.
- Learn to become enlightened insiders by initiatives to promote 'reverse learning' from local managers and staff and to integrate the mindset and worldviews of headquarters staff so that they and colleagues from CEE

countries: (a) develop understanding of each other's working contexts from where 'new' knowledge is emerging, which should be absorbed locally; and (b) create an atmosphere conducive to knowledge transfer.

- Develop themselves as culturally perceptive knowledge transmitters and identify others who could act as cross-cultural interfaces between the headquarters culture and the local culture, thus maintaining rich communication channels.
- Induce expatriate managers at all levels to build trust and socialise with local managers and subordinates and enable socialising of headquarters nationals with host country nationals (inpatriates) at headquarters.

NOTES

We wish to thank Elisabeth Beer for support in finalising this chapter according to the publisher's and editors' guidelines.

1. The notions 'tacit' and 'explicit' refer back to Michael Polanyi (1966). This distinction had gained particular importance, since Nonaka and Takeuchi (1995) built their model of knowledge creation (SECI: socialisation, externalisation, combination, internalisation) on that distinction.
2. 'By cultural standards we understand all kinds of perceiving, thinking, judging, and acting, which in a given culture are considered by the vast majority of the individuals for themselves and others as normal, self-evident, typical, and obligatory' (Thomas, 1993, p. 381, translation by G. Fink).
3. Max Weber's notion of 'bureaucracy' probably is the most important and best-known part of his sociology of rule and power which is included in his great treatise on economy and society (Weber, 1980). Weber's critical description of bureaucracy (focusing the problems of administration and professionalism) should be seen in the context of his analysis of the rise of modern capitalism because he expected a tight connection between bureaucratic professionalism and Protestant ascetic ethics (Weber, 1988).
4. We refer to Fredrik Winslow Taylor (1911) as the inventor and promoter of 'scientific management', taking 'organisation' in a strict instrumental sense for a steering technology, which Lenin admired and copied. The interesting point is that Lenin tried to adopt both the German administration tradition and the American management models.
5. Vladimir Ilyich Lenin's cadre politics, which is better known from Stalin's perverse continuing, tried to include 'the masses' in a general organisational plan of increasing the efficiency of both men and machines. The selection of the very best (that is, the fittest in the context of the plan) was only the second step; the first was the observation of individuals as technologically functioning elements. 'Cadres' are those who 'work' then (Best, 2005; Lehmann, 2003a, 2003b; Lenin, 1979).

REFERENCES

Baecker, D. (2002), 'Lenin's Twist, or the R-Factor of Communication/Lenin's Void: Toward a Kenogrammar of Management', *Soziale Systeme*, **8**(1), 88–100.
Best, H. (2005), 'Cadres into Managers: Structural Changes of East German Economic Elites Before and After Reunification', *Historical Social Research/Historische Sozialforschung*, **30**(2), 6–24.

Davies, N. (1986), *Heart of Europe: A Short History of Poland*, Oxford: Oxford University Press.

Deletant, D. (1995), *Ceauşescu and the Securitate: Coercion and Dissent in Romania, 1965–1989*, London: Hurst and Company.

Desai, P. (2005), 'Russian Retrospectives on Reform from Yeltsin to Putin', *Journal of Economic Perspectives*, **19**(1), 87–106.

Fink, G. and C. Feichtinger (1998), 'The Collective Culture Shock in Transition Countries: Theoretical and Empirical Implications', *Leadership & Organisation Development Journal*, **19**(6), 302–9.

Fink, G. and N. Holden (2002), 'Collective Culture Shock: Contrastive Reactions to Radical Systemic Change', IEF Working Paper 45; Vienna, Austria: University of Economics and Business Administration Vienna.

Fink, G. and N. Holden (2005a), 'Introduction: The Global Transfer of Management Knowledge', *The Academy of Management Executive*, **19**(2), 5–8.

Fink, G. and N. Holden (2005b), 'Guest Editorial: Absorption and Application of Management Knowledge', *Journal of Managerial Psychology*, **20**(7), 560–65.

Fink, G. and M. Lehmann (2006), 'People's Twist: The Cultural Standard of "Loyalty" and Performance in Former "Socialist Economies"', in D. Pauleen (ed.), *Cross-Cultural Perspectives on Knowledge Management*, London: Libraries Unlimited Publishing.

Gallagher, T. (1995), *Romania after Ceauşescu*, Edinburgh: Edinburgh University Press.

Glenny, M. (1992), *The Fall of Yugoslavia: The Third Balkan War*, London: Penguin Books.

Glisby, M. and N. Holden (2005), 'Applying Knowledge Management Concepts to the Supply Chain: How a Danish Firm Achieved a Remarkable Breakthrough in Japan', *The Academy of Management Executive*, **19**(2), 85–9.

Goffman, E. (1996), *Wir alle spielen Theater: Die Selbstdarstellung im Alltag*, Aus dem Amerikanischen von Peter Weber-Schäfer, 5. Aufl, München/Zürich: Piper. (*The Presentation of Self in Everyday Life*, New York: Doubleday & Co., Inc. 1959.)

Hahn, A. (2004), 'Wohl dem, der eine Narbe hat. Identitäten und ihre soziale Konstruktion', in Peter von Moos (ed.), *Unverwechselbarkeit. Persönliche Identität und Identifikation in der vormodernen Gesellschaft*, Köln/Weimar/Wien: Böhlau Verlag, pp. 43–62.

Hosking, G. (1992), *A History of the Soviet Union 1917–1991*, London: Fontana Press.

Hurt, M. and Hurt, S. (2005), 'Transfer of Managerial Practices by French Food Retailers to Operations in Poland', *The Academy of Management Executive*, **19**(2), 36–49.

Javidan, M., G.K. Stahl, F. Brodbeck and C.P.M. Wilderom (2005), 'Cross-border Transfer of Knowledge: Cultural Lessons from Project GLOBE', *The Academy of Management Executive*, **19**(2), 59–76.

Koivisto, J.V. (1999), 'The Concept of Cultural Crossing as a Tool for Analysing Cross-cultural Organisations', Department of Intercultural Communication and Management, Copenhagen Business School, CBS Occasional Paper, February 1999.

Kuznetsov, A. and H. Yakavenka (2005), 'Barriers to the Absorption of Management Knowledge in Belarus', *Journal of Managerial Psychology*, **20**(7), 566–77.

Lawrence, P. and C. Vlachoutsicos (1990), *Behind Factory Walls: Decision Making in Soviet and US Enterprises*, Boston, MA: Harvard Business School Press.

Lehmann, M. (2003a), 'Don't Forget to Observe: The Organisation and the Cadre', paper presented at the Opening of Systems Theory Conference, Copenhagen.

Lehmann, M. (2003b), 'Cadres and High Potentials', paper presented at the 6th Chemnitz East Forum, Chemnitz.

Lenin, V.I. (1979), 'Lieber weniger, aber besser', in *Ausgewählte Werke in drei Bänden* (III), Institut für Marxismus-Leninismus beim ZK der KpdSU, Berlin: Dietz, pp. 876–90.

Lunnan, R., J.E.B. Lervik, L.E.M. Traavik, S.M. Nilsen, R.P. Amdam and B.W. Hennestad (2005), 'Cultural Counterpoints, Global Transfer of Management Practices across Nations and MNC Subcultures', *The Academy of Management Executive*, **19**(2), 77–80.

May, R.C., S.M. Puffer and D.J. McCarthy (2005), 'Transferring Management Knowledge to Russia: A Culturally Based Approach', *The Academy of Management Executive*, **19**(2), 24–35.

McCarthy, D., S. Puffer, O. Vikhanski and A. Naumov (2005), 'Russian Managers in the New Europe: Need for a New Management Style', *Organisational Dynamics*, **34**(3), 197–201.

Michailova, S. (1996), 'Approaching the Macro–Micro Interface in Transitional Societies: Evidence from Bulgaria', *Journal for East European Management Studies*, **1**(1), 43–70.

Michailova, S. and K. Liuhto (2000), 'Organisation and Management Research in Transition Economies: Towards Improved Research Methodologies, *Journal of East–West Business*, **6**(3), 7–46.

Napier, N.K. (2005), 'Knowledge Transfer in Vietnam: Starts, Stops, and Loops', *Journal of Managerial Psychology*, **20**(7), 621–36.

Nonaka, I. and H. Takeuchi (1995), *The Knowledge-creating Company*, New York: Oxford University Press.

Paik, Y. and D.Y. Choi (2005), 'The Shortcomings of a Standardised Global Knowledge Management System: The Case Study of Accenture', *The Academy of Management Executive*, **19**(2), 81–4.

Polanyi, M. (1966), *The Tacit Dimension,* Garden City, NY: Doubleday & Co.

Pshenichnikova, I. (2003), 'The Challenges of Socialisation in Business Education: The Case of the School of Management', 22 May 2006 *http://condor.depaul.edu/~rrotenbe/aeer/v21n2/Pshenichnikova.pdf*

Puffer, S.M., D.J. McCarthy and A.I. Naumov (2000), *The Russian Capitalist Experiment: From State-owned Organisations to Entrepreneurships*, Cheltenham, UK and Northampton, MA, USA: Edward Elgar.

Rorty, R. (1989), *Contingency, Irony, and Solidarity*, Cambridge: Cambridge University Press.

Roth, K. (ed.) (2004), *Arbeit im Sozialismus – Arbeit im Postsozialismus*, Münster: LIT Verlag.

Service, R. (2000), *Lenin: A Biography*, London: Macmillan.

Shub, D. (1966), *Lenin: A Biography*, Harmondsworth: Penguin.

Skidelsky, R. (1995), *The World after Communism: A Polemic for our Times*, London: Macmillan.

Taylor, F.W. (1911), *The Principles of Scientific Management*, New York: Dover.

Thomas, A. (ed.) (1993), *Kulturvergleichende Psychologie, Eine Einführung*, Göttingen: Hogrefe Verlag für Psychologie.

Weber, M. (1980), 'Soziologie der Herrschaft', *Wirtschaft und Gesellschaft. Grundriss der verstehenden Soziologie*, Hrsg. von Johannes Winckelmann, Studienausgabe, 5. ed., Tübingen: Mohr.

Weber, M. (1988), 'Die protestantische Ethik und der Geist des Kapitalismus', *Gesammelte Aufsätze zur Religionssoziologie I*, 9. ed., Tübingen: UTB, pp. 17–206.

4. Fostering learning to build new competencies in times of deconstruction: lessons from Polish ex-socialist firms

**Renata Kaminska-Labbé and
Catherine Thomas**

INTRODUCTION

The abolition of the centralised economic system in Eastern European countries was an unprecedented situation in which firms, markets, social and institutional systems had to be completely reconstructed. The specificity of Poland in comparison to its Eastern European neighbours concerning the choice of a transition programme resides in two principal elements: the influence of the Catholic Church and the role played by trade unions. Indeed, during the entire post-war period, the Roman Catholic Church constituted the only true and active opposition to the political system in place, openly manifesting its support for values such as equality and freedom. Poland was the first country of the socialist block to legalise the existence of the trade unions, which had until then operated illegally. In 1980, the first union, 'Solidarity', was founded leading to a wave of important social movements throughout the country. Having grown beyond proportions acceptable to the central authorities, these movements were brutally interrupted in December 1981 with the introduction of Marshal Law during which most of the union activists were imprisoned or forced to dissimulate their activity.

In 1982, at the end of this politically and socially turbulent period, the government introduced a new economic reform based on three principal elements: autonomy, self-financing and self-management. At the same time, legislation was modified and trade unions were once more legalised, obtaining considerable power, particularly through their participation in the firm Workers' Councils.

After 1989, the first Polish non-communist democratically-elected government opted for the introduction of a radical reform programme, known as 'shock therapy'. This programme consisted of three major elements: stabilisation, liberalisation and privatisation (Sachs, 1992).

The first decade of transition can be divided into three distinctive periods (Sudol, 1996). The main events of the first period (1989–90) included: freeing prices, slashing subsidies, tightening monetary policy to bring down inflation and introducing competition by opening up to international trade. The Zloty was devaluated sharply and made convertible. During the second period (1991–95), major changes concerned the institutional environment (reform of the banking system, creation of financial markets, and so on), improvement of quality of local products and environmental protection. The year 1995 marked the end of economic recession and the beginning of profits for State-owned firms. In the third period (1996–99), the political pressure to increase local firms' export capacities was increased.

Specific institutional arrangements which emerged in Poland after 1989 both enabled and restricted strategic and organisational options (Lewin and Volberda, 1999). Faced with increasingly intense international competition local firms had to rapidly adapt to the radical change in the external environment and renew their competencies. In this chapter, we propose to analyse the relationship between learning mechanisms and processes by which new organisational competencies were built in former State-owned firms. Two main stages of competence renewal have been identified. First, 'stabilisation' involves the elaboration of a social compromise making the radical change more comprehensible and acceptable. Second, 'competence building' involves creation of new knowledge and know-how necessary for strategy implementation.

The main conclusion drawn in this research is that the regulation capacity is a mediating variable of the emergence and development of learning capabilities. The understanding of this phenomenon is important for international managers wishing to acquire Polish firms as means of diversifying their business activity to Eastern Europe. Some general lessons can also be drawn in relation to competence renewal in all post-rupture contexts.

The chapter is organised into three distinct parts. First, a conceptual framework of competence building is presented. It highlights the role of learning in the development of dynamic capabilities. Second, the research design is briefly described. It is based on the longitudinal case study of strategic adaptation of three ex-socialist Polish firms during the economic transition. Third, the results of the empirical research are exposed and discussed.

KNOWLEDGE MANAGEMENT IN POLAND: STRENGTHENING LEARNING TO BUILD NEW COMPETENCIES IN TIMES OF ENVIRONMENTAL TURBULENCE

According to the resource-based view theory, firms can be conceptualised as systems of tangible and intangible resources (Barney, 1991; Penrose, 1959; Wernerfelt, 1984). Performance is therefore regarded as the result of the firm's inimitable idiosyncratic resource system and its capability to combine resources in order to build and leverage competencies (Hamel and Prahalad, 1994; Sanchez et al., 1996).

Competence Building

Competencies are deployed in the three domains: production systems, access to new markets and product differentiation (Hamel, 1994). Two of the main characteristics of centralised systems were the primacy of production over commercial functions and a high degree of specialisation, most of the time in a single technological base. This explains the fact that in planned economies firms developed significant industrial know-how. But their productive systems never really corresponded to the international standards of quality and environmental protection; neither did they offer comparable results in terms of productivity.

However, some of the firms underwent important modernisation pro-grammes prior to 1989 and therefore were in possession of quasi-modern productive systems at the beginning of the transition. An interesting question arises then: would these firms be pre-adapted to the emerging market economy? If yes, what role did this pre-adaptation play in the competence renewal process?

Before the rupture, markets and distribution networks were organised by the respective ministries. As a consequence, none of the firms had competencies relative to market access. However, at the beginning local firms clearly had an advantage over the Western firms in terms of understanding cultural contexts and commercial practices in the Eastern block. Therefore, focus on rapidly building these competencies rather than trying to develop the Western markets would appear as an efficient strategy of future development since the first option would definitely be more difficult and costly.

Many different factors influence the evolution and accumulation of competencies. The role of history and path-dependence appears to be particularly critical (Nelson and Winter, 1982; Penrose, 1959; Sanchez et al., 1996). However, competencies must be viewed in dynamic terms and therefore be governed by dynamic capabilities (Lewis and Gregory, 1996).

Indeed, history and path-dependence constrain the process of competence building which can be a disadvantage in high-velocity markets. In these markets, dynamic capabilities by which managers reconfigure and build competencies become essential (Eisenhardt and Martin, 2000). Competitiveness depends on a firm's aptitude to create one or several relatively large technological bases from which it can extend its activities in an uncertain and turbulent environment.

Nelson and Winter (1982) describe capabilities as routines which reduce both the possibility of change and the role of managerial intentionality. More recently, Sanchez et al. (1996) define capabilities as the ability to organise firm resources. Similarly to Teece et al. (1997) and Eisenhardt and Martin (2000), we define dynamic capabilities as 'the firm's processes that use resources – specifically the processes to integrate, reconfigure, gain and release resources – to match and even create market change'. According to Eisenhardt and Martin (2000), dynamic capabilities correspond to four specific and identifiable processes: strategic decision making, resource recombination, new resources acquisition and knowledge management. Dynamic capabilities exhibit common features across firms (Eisenhardt and Martin, 2000) and translate what may be called 'best practice'.

Development of Dynamic Capabilities and Learning

The evolution of dynamic capabilities depends on two principal factors: the firm's learning mechanisms and the degree of market dynamism (Eisenhardt and Martin 2000). In moderately dynamic markets, effective dynamic capabilities are embedded in cumulative, existing knowledge and are based on efficient processes that are predictable and relatively stable. The authors underline that in this perspective, dynamic capabilities exhibit the properties suggested by traditional research where effective routines are efficient and robust processes (Cyert and March, 1963; Nelson and Winter, 1982). In this case, the nature of learning is self-reinforcing and results in a tendency to strengthen the same distinctive competence, leading to niche specialisation (Levinthal and March, 1993). This mechanism called 'traps of distinctive competence' is self-destructing in dynamic environments (ibid.).

Indeed, in high-velocity markets, dynamic capabilities rely much more on rapidly created situation-specific new knowledge. They are simple, experiential and iterative processes which consist of a few rules specifying boundary conditions on the actions of managers or indicate priorities (Eisenhardt and Martin, 2000). Here markets exploration is predominant and the major difficulty resides in the necessity to avoid exploration traps. Sometimes the dynamic of failure pushes the firms to engage in excessive innovation, change and experimentation (Levinthal and March, 1993) where unsuccessful new technologies and products are repeatedly replaced by other unsuccessful ones.

The Role of Regulation Process in Learning

Learning mechanisms depend on the nature of the external environment and may rely more or less on existing knowledge. They also depend on the firm's organisation principles and on its social interaction. Levinthal and March (1993) highlight that organisations use rules, procedures and standard practices to ensure the transfer of individual experiences to the rest of the organisation. Durand (2000) makes a more general statement that a coordinated deployment of resources is more than a set of organisational processes and includes the organisational culture and strategy. Even in the context of a changing knowledge environment, where the challenge is to create new knowledge configurations based on absorption of different types of new component knowledge, this ability called 'absorptive capacity' presents distinctly organisational aspects (Cohen and Levinthal, 1990; Van den Bosch et al., 1999). We suggest that these organisational and social aspects be explained through the analysis of the firm's regulation process.

Many authors (Favereau, 1997; Giddens, 1987; Hatchuel, 1997; Reynaud, B., 1997; Reynaud, J.D., 1993, 1999) consider rules as central in the constitution of collective entities. Rules include conventions, norms and routines and appear to be a mediating variable between action and the reproduction of practices which constitute social systems. Thus, the firm can no longer be considered as a collective entity which simply conforms to rules.

Even if the definition of a rule differs among authors, there is a convergence concerning some of its characteristics (Reynaud, 1997). A rule constitutes a collective cognitive mechanism (Favereau, 1989) and a place where the collective knowledge is 'stocked'. Rules may guide collective action but they never govern it totally. They are incomplete and necessitate interpretation depending on the degree of their specification (Reynaud, 1998). Indeed, rules can be more or less precise, formalised and sanctioned. They emerge by negotiation and change through socialisation (Giddens, 1987).

The creation of rules is therefore a dynamic and recursive process: rules are produced by the system and at the same time they produce the system. Consequently, there are no stable rules but only regulation processes defined as creation and maintenance of rules. The regulation process of a firm is complex and combines different sources, levels and domains (Reynaud and Reynaud, 1994). Its dynamics can be understood through the analysis of its three constitutive dimensions: signification, power and legitimacy (Giddens, 1987).

Rules play a double role in the creation, accumulation and evolution of knowledge. Indeed, they serve as a basis for memorising existing knowledge. They equally constitute a coordination mechanism of knowledge dispersed throughout the firm. The regulation process can therefore be viewed as a determining element of learning processes and of dynamic capabilities.

The regulation process has both stabilising and evolutionary properties. In the first case, it allows the reproduction of social practices and relies heavily on existing rules and knowledge. In the second case, it allows the production of new social practices based on the creation of new knowledge leading to the emergence of new rules. Depending on its nature, the regulation process can privilege either organisational stability or organisational evolution. This underlines the problem of a trade-off between exploitation and exploration described by March (1991). A stable power and legitimacy structure favours the system's reproduction. In this case, the regulation process remains coherent if the signification evolves in a predictable and linear fashion. This is conceivable only in moderately dynamic environments. In contrast, in high-velocity markets which demand the rapid creation of situation-specific new knowledge, the firm is obliged to increase the dynamism of its regulation process in order to favour the emergence of new rules. Organic structures described by Burns and Stalker (1961) and Lawrence and Lorsch (1967) are typically associated with dynamic regulation processes.

In the post-rupture context of the economic transition, we suggest that competence renewal necessitates the emergence of a new regulation process based on deeply modified signification, domination and legitimisation structures.

METHODS

The principal questions asked in this research were: how did Polish industrial firms adapt to the new conditions of the emergent market economy? How did they overcome the difficulties of radical contextual changes? How did their organisational competencies develop and renew? The research perspective was longitudinal, narrative, and process-oriented. The empirical observation was non-participating and concerned the first ten years after the fall of a centrally planned system (1989–99). The unit of analysis was three Polish ex-socialist industrial firms with common characteristics: socialist past, lack of subsidies, profits in 1989 and localisation in the same urban environment.

Research Design

This empirical study was conducted as part of a doctoral research (Kaminska-Labbé, 2001). The exploratory case study method was based on constant iteration between theory and empirical reality. The choice of this particular empirical approach was motivated by the three criteria proposed by Yin (1989): research questions defined in terms of 'how', the novelty of the investigated field, and the exploratory nature of the research which makes control of actors' behaviour unnecessary.

Data collection took place between 1996 and 1999. As proposed by Yin (1989), the 'explanation building' involved the confrontation of the theoretical propositions with the empirical data. The initial propositions were confronted with the data collected in the first case. This allowed for the enrichment of the propositions which were once again confronted with the data collected in the first, the second and finally the third case. In practical terms, the first set of exploratory interviews led to the construction of an interview guide. The second stage consisted of interviewing a large number of employees occupying positions on different hierarchical levels. The objective of the final stage was to present the initial results to a small number of selected participants. A total of 45 employees were interviewed. Other sources of 'evidence' included direct observation and official documentation. Data analysis was conducted according to the methodology proposed by Huberman and Miles (1991). It involved data condensation, matrix construction and finally the formulation of conclusions.

Case Studies

Case one was created in 1951. Since 1958, it has been one of the biggest national producers of paints and varnishes for the construction and automobile industries as well as for consumer markets. In 1998, it employed over 1500 workers, held 22 per cent of the local market share and over 30 per cent of all Polish paint and varnish exports.

Until 1989, the company's production was destined mainly for the local market. It had a partial monopoly in its geographical zone of south-west Poland. Its director appointed in 1981 continually improved the company production systems. A recognised expert in his domain, and a charismatic leader, he managed to obtain sufficient funds from central authorities to invest in production equipment. In 1989, only four local firms were its direct competitors and the most important threat came from imports. Initially, international competitors occupied niches of highly specialised products such as automobile varnish, electric isolation paints, packaging and road marking, all of which were absent from the production range of Polish firms. However, the unexpected commercial success of these products on the Polish market motivated these competitors to extend their product range which put pressure on local firms.

During the first stage of adaptation (1989–90), privatisation became a priority. In 1990, the firm's status was changed allowing it to initiate the privatisation process. This generated internal conflicts between the top management who wanted to privatise the firm via the newly created financial market, and the unions who demanded an egalitarian distribution of the firm's capital among its employees. This resulted in several strikes and a period of instability during which the unions, protected by favourable legislation, retained the real power. During this time, the director spent most of his time convincing the employees of the opportunities of privatisation via financial markets and promised no layoffs without compensation. The employees slowly subscribed to his vision and trade unions' power kept diminishing. This strengthened the managers' legitimacy which was further reinforced by the acceptance of the stock-market proposal of privatisation. The latter was submitted to the Ministerial Committee in 1992, that is, less than a year after the creation of this institution. This innovative project proposed to issue two types of stock: stock A for the government, which distributed part of it among the employees; stock B for the stock market to finance the firm's investments. In 1992, the Workers' Council was dissolved and the Supervising Committee created in its place. In 1994, the firm was one of the first to be quoted on the Warsaw stock market.

The second period (1991–95) involved the evolution of the organisational structure, the production systems, and access to new markets. Starting from 1991, the firm redefined its product range (1991), improved quality, modernised equipment, adopted environmentally friendly attitudes (1993) and purchased new pigmentation technology (1995). It obtained numerous national prizes for excellence. The year 1991 was marked by the expansion to the former Soviet market, increased efforts in promotion and advertising on the national market (1992) and the development of distribution networks. New departments were created: sales and marketing (1991), development (1991), legal (1992) and export (1995). In 1995, the project of a merger with the major local competitor was presented. It was finalised in 1998.

The third stage of adaptation (1996–99) was marked by the continuation of reforms, quality improvement (ISO 9001 certification in 1996) and environmental protection (preparation for the certification ISO 14000 starting from 1998). Efforts were made to boost innovation with the strengthening of the research and development (R&D) team in 1997. Finally, a decision was taken in 1996 to develop European markets. In spite of the 1998 merger, the firm was unable to fulfil this strategic objective.

Case two was created in 1952. In 1959, its activity became the production of home appliances of which it remained the biggest national producer until the end of this research. In 1999, it had a workforce of approximately 5000 employees and held 35 per cent of the local market share. In 1970, an embryonic R&D department was created allowing the firm to diversify its production to washing machines and freezers. As from 1977, it modernised its production systems and expanded its product range. This enabled it to obtain numerous national and international prizes for excellence at various trade fairs. It was also able to reinforce its position on the national market and develop exports (10 per cent of production) to Western European countries. In 1989, the firm was in a good shape.

During the first stage of adaptation (1989–90), the privatisation project crystallised a conflict separating the workers from the director (who had been head of the firm for over 20 years) leading to his firing on the demand of the Workers' Council. This symbolic and political decision led to a long period of social unrest and a high turnover of successive directors (six in five years). The only change introduced during this tense period was the integration of an autonomous after-sales service unit.

The second stage (1991–95) coincided with the massive arrival of foreign competitors. In spite of the conflictual atmosphere, three decisions were taken by successive directors: elimination of a delocalised production site, selling after-sales centres and redefining distribution networks. They did not correspond to a clearly defined strategy.

As from 1992, the director of development began to modernise the production systems: he incorporated the R&D unit, and negotiated a loan with the biggest regional bank to modernise the refrigerator factory (1993). He became a CEO in 1995. When this case study ended in 1999, this person was still at the head of the firm. His nomination resulted in the ending of a five-year socially turbulent and destabilising period, and the initiation of a series of organisational and strategic transformations: launching of privatisation, finding new sources of financing, reorganising the firm and redefining its strategy. In order to gain the workers' support despite the announcement of the possible workforce reductions, he increased efforts in communication. The Supervisory Committee, whose role was to supervise the definition and implementation of strategy, was created in 1997.

The third period (1996–99) was characterised by changes in the structure, production systems and access to new markets (distribution, promotion and advertising). The strategy was to: become competitive on local markets, develop access to other Eastern European markets and forgo extending into Western markets. In 1998, the new models of refrigerators were out and the product range (dishwashers, dryers, microwave ovens, washer-dryer machines, air conditioning, vacuum cleaners) was extended significantly. The firm was quoted on the Warsaw Stock Exchange in 1998.

Case three, which in 1999 employed just over 500 people, was a leader in the local para-pharmaceutical market. Specialised since 1986 in the production and sales of adhesive plasters and bandages, it made significant profits over the term of this research. Thanks to the creation of a large R&D

unit, the firm had modernised its production systems in the 1960s. It had also innovated both in production methods and products. From the early 1970s, it was no longer subsidised by the government, began to generate profits and initiated its diversification (carpets, pneumatic chairs and construction materials). By the early 1980s, it was restructured to lessen the production of viscose, an important source of pollution. At the same time, it invested in new purification technology, clearly manifesting its concern for the environment.

In 1981, the Ministry of the Chemical Industry accepted the proposition of the CEO to diversify the production into bandages and adhesive plasters. The firm purchased the necessary technology from a West German firm and financed this project with a loan obtained from the Central Bank. Due to social and economic difficulties, this project was terminated in 1986.

For the company, the introduction of a market economy meant facing competition for both of its activities. On the viscose market, its most important competitors were Polish State-owned firms. On the para-pharmaceutical market, its competitors included major international groups. In spite of the loss of its monopoly, the firm continued to hold 73 per cent of the local market share at the end of the 1990s. In 1989, the top management decided to privatise the firm. Even though it was on the list of the first 15 Polish firms to obtain ministerial permission to launch the privatisation process, in reality the firm was not privatised until 1994. To preserve social stability, the compromise was established not to proceed with massive layoffs and to maintain most of the social benefits (financial help for needy families, holiday and meal subsidies, and so on).

During the second stage of adaptation (1991–95), the firm's mission was redefined and a new strategic vision was formulated. The decision was made to focus on the bandage activity and to eliminate viscose production by 1994.

As from 1991, a joint venture with a European partner 'X' for the production and commercialisation of diapers was created. This partnership had two main objectives: to utilise the unused production facilities made available by the elimination of viscose production and to transfer some of the former viscose production employees to this new production site. These employees were trained in the new technologies and activities of the firm. On the condition of 'no layoffs', the firm sold its equity in the joint venture to its partner in 1994 but continued to lease its unused space.

Then, product lines and ranges were expanded; new technologies were acquired and production processes modernised. Under important pressure from local and European environmental lobbying, the firm invested in environmentally friendly technologies and engaged in a very expensive anti-pollution programme. During this period, it improved its distribution channels in Poland and decided to develop the Eastern European markets. In 1994, it launched ISO 9001 and ISO 14000 certification programmes and reinforced its R&D by hiring new scientists.

The third period (1996–99) was marked by encouraging results and accelerated development. The firm was quoted on the Warsaw Stock Market in 1997 and obtained the ISO 9001 certificate, as well as four different prizes for the 'Best Polish Product' in the same year. The modernisation programme came to end in 1998. In 1998 and 1999, the firm innovated and conquered new local markets by creating new partnerships with hospitals and health care centres. Finally, after being on the list of the 80 most polluting Polish firms in 1990, it obtained the first national prize for respect of the environment in 1999.

DISCUSSION

The principal results concern the role of dynamic capabilities and the stages of competence building. The data concerning the competence accumulation process in three key domains for each firm studied show the role of path-dependency in competence building. However, the influence of path-dependency is limited: first, pre-adaptation is not significant and second, it is the dynamic capabilities which play a key role.

Path Dependency versus Dynamic Capabilities

In all three firms, the competence building process follows an order (see Table 4.1). Indeed, it started with building competencies relative to the production systems and it is precisely in this domain that capitalisation is the most significant. Then, the firms developed competencies in accessing the new markets. None of them possessed these competencies and were obliged to develop them by recombining their internal resources and/or by acquiring them externally. Even if competencies relative to the local markets are easier to develop, they do not seem useful when it comes to the development of other unknown markets. Firm one very quickly developed competencies relative to Eastern European markets. Indeed, if these markets are very difficult to develop for Eastern European firms, as witnessed by firm three, they are equally if not more difficult for Western firms. However, the development of Western markets seems very difficult for Polish firms and the absence of capital seems to be a principal barrier in building competencies of this sort (Boehlke, 1996). Finally, the three firms began to differentiate their products during the last period, suggesting that the development of these competencies is supported by those accumulated in the other two domains (production systems and access to markets). Firms one and three, which accumulated competencies more quickly in the two first domains, seem better at innovation:

specific products with a high added value (firm one), and new types of plasters (firm three).

According to the path-dependency perspective, all firms began building competencies by reinforcing their existing ones (production). At a first glance firm two seemed to be pre-adapted to the emerging market economy context. In 1989, it possessed quasi modern productive systems and commercial relations with Western European and North American partners. Paradoxically, it had more difficulty renewing and developing its competencies. Firm three appears to be the most handicapped at the moment of rupture. Its principal industrial activity was scarcely profitable and highly polluting. Interestingly, as from 1989 its competencies in the three key domains built up rapidly. One example of this may be the progress this firm made in environmental protection. Indeed, from being on the list of the 80 most polluting firms in 1990, it managed to obtain a national prize for becoming 'environment friendly' in 1999.

Two Stages of Competence Renewal

The first stage was a phase of stabilisation. Close to Lewin's (1951) 'unfreezing' step of organisational change model, it concerns the elaboration of a social compromise, making the radical change period more comprehensible and acceptable. It involves making the necessity of privatising the firm so obvious that all organisational members can accept it and participate in it. Very often the difficulty resides in the fact that this stage involves contradictory but simultaneous processes which require elaborating a compromise based on simple rules (Eisenhardt and Martin, 2000). In our cases these were: privatisation via financial markets and no massive lay-offs without compensation. These social and cognitive marks are indispensable for the organisational learning processes in a particularly turbulent environment (March, 1991). This stage concerned the establishment of a new 'system view' (Chiesa and Manzini, 1997), which is the ability of the firm to identify and understand the competitive context and the frame of reference of its actions. It used the managerial competencies and, more precisely, the ability to identify new opportunities congruent with the firm's existing resources (judgement and adaptation) or the ability to leverage these resources (imagination and ambition). It concerns the definition of major strategic options: markets, domains of activity, products and technologies. This period also involves making the employees understand and internalise that change is inevitable.

In the second phase, the objective was to start developing a portfolio of organisational competencies necessary for strategy implementation. This phase can be interpreted in terms of competence renewal, even if it is based on the competencies existing in the firm. As we have already pointed out, to

Table 4.1 Chronological matrix of competence accumulation

Competencies	Stage 1 1989–90	Stage 2 1991–95	Stage 3 1996–99
Production systems			
Firm 1	Leveraging industrial know-how	Improvement of the production system: quality, environmental protection, new technology	ISO 9001 certification Preparation for ISO 14000 certification Prizes
Firm 2	Leveraging industrial know-how	Modernisation of the production of refrigerators In 1995, launching of ISO 9001 certification process	Modernisation of the entire production site Certification ISO 9001 and preparation for ISO 14000 certification
Firm 3	Continuation of initiated reorganisation	Improvement of the production system: quality, environmental protection, new technology Progressive elimination of viscose production	Modernisation programme, terminated in 1998 ISO 9001 certification The national prize of 'leader in environmental protection'
Access to markets			
Firm 1		Development of promotion and advertising Development of distribution channels in Poland Development of ex-USSR markets	Reinforcement of the commercial position on Eastern European markets Difficulty in developing international markets other than Eastern European ones

Firm 2	Support from European partners to compensate for the fall in demand for national products	Development of distribution channels in Poland	Development of promotion and advertising Difficulty in developing Eastern European markets
Firm 3		Development of distribution channels in Poland	New distribution networks: hospitals and health centres Difficulty in developing Eastern European markets
Distinctive characteristics of product			
Firm 1			Development of innovation: products and processes Creation of interdisciplinary teams, reinforcement of R&D
Firm 2		Improvement of technical characteristics and design of refrigerators	Improvement of technical characteristics of washing machines New products, larger product range, design improvement
Firm 3		Cooperation with different research institutions Reinforcement of R&D team	Improvement of existing products (durability, water resistance, etc.) Production of a new type of plaster, VENAPLAST Development of specialised medicated products

65

achieve this goal the first change involved the production systems, then access to new markets, and finally the capacity to distinguish the products. This renewal was possible thanks to the ability to find new sources of financing, to combine new resources with the existing ones.

These results suggest that there are no pre-adapted firms and that the ones which survive are the ones capable of rapidly building new competencies. The question which then arises is: what are the specific mechanisms by which competence renewal can be enacted?

The Role of the Regulation Process in the Emergence and Development of Learning Capabilities

Privatisation played an important role in the emergence of a learning space. The privatisation processes in the three firms were very different. Even if privatisation followed the same stages, its development was very different: rapid in firm one, long and conflictual in firm two and long but non-conflictual in firm three. To explain these differences, it seems necessary to analyse the role played by different actors.

The directors of firms one and three had been at the head of their firms for a very long time and were recognised as experts in their respective domains (technical expertise in firm one; managerial expertise in firm three). These directors were also charismatic leaders. The director of firm two was engaged in open conflict with the Workers' Council. Moreover, during the first five post-rupture years, the workers of firm two resisted privatisation. It may have originated in the fact that firm two had always been supported by the banks and its international partners, who for the first few years after 1989 accepted absorbing a great part of its production. The employees who had no sense of danger and urgency then focused on the power struggle within the firm.

If the conflicts between the top management and the Workers' Council can partially explain the slow pace of the privatisation process in firm two, a different type of explanation is necessary to explain the same problem in firm three. The matrix shows a certain similarity in the three cases: each firm negotiated the privatisation via financial markets in exchange for guaranteeing no lay-offs without compensation. Firm three was in the process of abandoning the production of viscose. It was on the basis of this progressive reorientation that an acceptable privatisation project could be presented and implemented in 1994, the date which coincided with the elimination of viscose. However, this reorientation was very progressive in order to respect the essential 'no lay-off' compromise.

This stage consisted of making the radical change provoked by the fall of the communist system comprehensible and acceptable. The building of the 'system view' in the sense of Chiesa and Manzini (1997) was based on two rules: privatising the firm via the financial market and avoiding lay-offs without compensation. These two rules, accompanied by communication efforts, established the learning space of the firm by which a firm's competence changes and evolves. This stage focused on the first dimension of social regulation: the signification structure.

Dynamics of the Regulation Process as an Element of a Learning Process

The analysis of the three firms shows that the development of dynamic capabilities is embedded in social power bonds. We have seen that these power relations manifested themselves throughout the privatisation process. In firm two, the union objected to an evolution of the domination structure, which would be in favour of the managerial team. This attitude blocked the firm's evolution until 1995. On the contrary, the ability of the firm's managers (firm one) to change signification, domination and legitimacy structures, revealed itself to be a decisive factor in the firm's evolution.

The first stage, as we have previously seen, concerned all the signification dimensions in order to create a common understanding of the future dangers and opportunities. The second stage consisted of changing the power and legitimacy structures. The creation of new regulation sources (creation of services, nomination of new managers) on the one hand, and the modification of values on the other (efficiency, quality, market forces, ecology, and so on) led to the emergence of new practices and the renewal of competencies. During this stage, the role of quality and ecology programmes in the evolution of the legitimisation and signification structures needs to be emphasised. The importance of these programmes is partially linked to the way they are valued by the environment. In the past, State industries had a very bad reputation. Indeed they were known as great polluters and producers of low quality products. Therefore, as from 1991, the government invented a system of prizes in order to motivate firms to improve the quality of their products and invest in 'clean' technologies. These prizes were the first visible results obtained by the firms. The 'result' or a 'principle of reality' is a fundamental principle, especially for commercial organisations (Reynaud, 1999). These prizes therefore enabled managers to legitimise their actions. Moreover, great efforts were made to publicise these prizes in different local and national media. This enabled gradual change to take place regarding the signification structure throughout Polish society. Finally, it is noteworthy that these new representations, built up thanks to the concepts of quality and ecology, were in harmony with the philosophy of the transition towards a market economy and coherent with the former representations conveyed by the trade unions and the Catholic Church.

The third stage differed from one firm to another. It has not yet been initiated in firm two. Firm three was trying to stabilise this new social regulation process by formalising the changes both on the level of the power distribution (firm's structure), and on that of its value system (cost control, intensification of an environment protection programme). The objective of this period was to allow the memorising of new practices by stabilising new rules and routines. Firm one was trying to both stabilise and then dynamise the emerging regulation process by propagating the concept of 'total quality'. It was also trying to redefine the motivation system and improve cost control. At the same time, it tried to dynamise the regulation process by multiplying the regulation sources and their coordination modes (creation of the joint venture, of inter-disciplinary teams, reinforcement of cross-disciplinarity and work enrichment, and so on).

At this stage, there is a danger of not stabilising the emergent regulation enough and as a consequence, falling into the exploration trap (Levinthal and March, 1993). For example, in response to the pressure to increase exportation to the Western markets put on firms by the Polish government, firm one decided in 1996 to develop its exports. This decision highlighted the important lack of competencies to implement such a strategy. Apart from the merger with a local competitor in 1999, nothing had been done to build competencies to access Western markets. This incapacity to renew competencies results from the difficulty in identifying and understanding the Western competitive context, in other terms, the difficulty of establishing a new 'system view', essential for initiating a new learning cycle.

CONCLUSION

This chapter reported empirical findings about patterns of competence renewal in three Polish firms during the first ten years of the economic transition. We adopted a dynamic view focusing on the analysis of the competence building process. This perspective raised a number of key questions regarding the role of intentionality in fostering learning to develop dynamic capabilities with respect to the impact of history and path dependency and the influence of the social, political and economic environments.

The study showed that building new competencies is a complex process with multiple causalities. The influence of history and path dependency is visible, especially through the presence of the economy of scale in the competence accumulation process. However, we did not detect the existence of conditions prior to rupture which might be termed pre-adaptive in that they facilitated the firm's survival and development after 1989. The interactions with the social, political and economic environments are varied and often recursive. Managers, for example, often used environmental evolution to justify their actions and reinforce their position in the firm. Nevertheless, they often manifested innovative behaviour and brought this type of evolution. In general, our study highlighted the important role that managers played in their firms' development. The building of new competencies partially depends on the ability to develop the firm's learning mechanisms.

The main conclusion drawn then is that the regulation capacity is a key component of learning and a mediating variable of building new dynamic capabilities and competencies. The regulation process is studied through three of its dimensions: signification, power and legitimacy. The analysis of these dimensions can enrich our understanding of dynamic capabilities, especially in high-velocity markets which demand the rapid creation of situation-specific new knowledge. The case studies show that in the post-rupture deconstruction context, strategic renewal necessitates the emergence of a new regulation process based on deeply modified signification, domination and legitimisation structures. We suggest that this result can be extended to other post-rupture contexts marked by rapid environmental change.

IMPLICATIONS FOR INTERNATIONAL MANAGERS

Managers acquiring failing or ailing companies in transition economies sometimes fall prey to the temptation of simplicity. They see their principal strategic task as that of redeploying salvageable assets, and mostly transferring new competencies based on advanced technological and managerial practices. They ignore, at their own peril, the complex web of socio-technical interactions that tie the firm and its environment together and tend to underestimate the intricate manoeuvring required within evolving social and cultural contexts. And yet, without attention to these matters, new companies are likely to turn sterile.

In our research, all three firms confirmed the role of renewed social regulation as a mediating variable in building competencies, even if the way in which this renewal is conducted differed from one firm to another. There are some important lessons that international managers can learn from the experiences of Polish managers in terms of timing and style of introducing changes. The role of the managers was decisive in firm one. They acted very quickly and bypassed the unions. The latter still remains one of the most powerful actors in the Polish context. Many international investors in Poland experience major difficulties in restructuring the acquired companies because of the resistance from the local trade unions. Therefore, establishing a relationship based on compromise and mutual understanding seems essential prior to the introduction of any change programmes. However, there are innovative ways of modifying value systems even in the most unionised companies but they require different time frames. In firm one, a new regulation was developed and became legitimate thanks to the obtained results (privatisation, prizes, and so on). The managers of firm three preferred to establish a general consensus prior to any changes, which explains this firm's more gradual and slower rate of evolution.

REFERENCES

Barney, J. (1991), 'Firm Resources and Sustained Competitive Advantage', *Journal of Management*, **17**(1), 99–120.
Boehlke, J. (1996), 'Wspolpraca Przedsiebiorstwo z Kapitalem Zagranicznym a Bariery Rozwoju', in S. Sudol and W. Karaszewski (eds), *Proces Transformacji Rynkowej Przedsiebiorstw*, Torun: Wydawnictwo Uniwersytetu Mikolaja Kopernika, pp. 206–8.
Burns, T. and G.M. Stalker (1961), *The Management of Innovation*, London: Tavistock.
Chiesa V. and R. Manzini (1997), 'Competence Levels within Firms: A Static and Dynamic Analysis', in R. Sanchez and A. Heene (eds), *Competence-based Strategic Management*, New York: Wiley, pp. 195–214.
Cohen, W.M. and D.A. Levinthal (1990), 'Absorptive Capacity: A New Perspective on Learning and Innovation', *Administrative Science Quarterly*, **35**(1), 128–52.
Cyert, R. and J. March (1963), *A Behavioural Theory of the Firm*, Englewood Cliffs, NJ: Prentice-Hall.
Durand, T. (2000), 'L'alchimie de la Compétence', *Revue Française de Gestion*, **127**, 84–102.
Einsenhardt, K. and J. Martin (2000), 'Dynamic Capabilities: What Are They?', *Strategic Management Journal*, **21**, 1105–21.
Favereau, O. (1989), 'Marchés Interne, Marchés Externes', *Revue Economique*, **2**, 278–328.
Favereau, O. (1997), 'L'incomplétude n'est pas le Problème, C'est la Solution', in B. Reynaud, J.P. Dupuy and P. Livet (eds), *Les Limites de la Rationalité, Tome 2, les Figures du Collectif*, Paris: Edition la Découverte, pp. 219–34.
Giddens, A. (1987), *La Constitution de la Société*, Paris: PUF.
Hamel, G. (1994), 'The Concept of Core Competencies', in G. Hamel and A. Heene (eds), *Competence Based Competition*, New York: Wiley, pp. 11–33.
Hamel, G. and C. Prahalad (1994), *Competing for the Future*, Boston, MA: Harvard Business School Press.
Hatchuel, A. (1997), 'Fondements des Savoirs et Légitimité des Règles', in B. Reynaud, J.P. Dupuy and P. Livet (eds), *Les Limites de la Rationalité, Tome 2, les Figures du Collectif*, Paris: Edition la Découverte, pp. 183–210.
Huberman, M. and M. Miles (1991), *Analyse des Données Qualitatives*, Bruxelles: De Boeck-Wesmael.
Kaminska-Labbé, R. (2001), 'Cheminement Stratégique et Processus d'accumulation des Compétences: Le cas des Entreprises Polonaises Dans le Contexte de la Transition Economique', PhD thesis, University of Nice-Sophia Antipolis.
Lawrence, P. and J. Lorsch (1967), *Adapter les Structures de L'entreprise*, Paris: Les Editions d'Organisation.

Levinthal, D. and J. March (1993), 'The Myopia of Learning', *Strategic Management Journal*, **14**, 95–112.

Lewin, A. and H. Volberda (1999), 'Prolegomena on Co-evolution: A Framework for Research on Strategy and New Organisational Forms', *Organisation Science*, **10**(5), 519–34.

Lewin, K. (1951), *Field Theory in Social Science: Selected Theoretical Papers*, New York: Harper & Brothers.

Lewis, M. and M. Gregory (1996), 'Developing and Applying a Process Approach to Competence Analysis', in R. Sanchez, A. Heene and H. Thomas (eds), *Dynamics of Competence-based Competition: Theory and Practice in the New Strategic Management*, Oxford: Elsevier Science Publishing, pp. 141–64.

March, J. (1991), 'Exploration and Exploitation in Organisational Learning', *Organisation Science*, **2**, 71–87.

Nelson, R. and S. Winter (1982), *An Evolutionary Theory of Economic Change*, Cambridge, MA: Harvard University Press.

Penrose, E. (1959), *The Theory of the Growth of the Firm*, Oxford: Basil Blackwell & Mott Ltd.

Reynaud, B. (1997), 'L'indétermination de la Règle et la Coordination', in B. Reynaud, J.P. Dupuy and P. Livet (eds), *Les Limites de la Rationalité, Tome 2, les Figures du Collectif*, Paris: Edition la Découverte, pp. 235–54.

Reynaud, B. (1998), 'Les Propriétés des Routines: Outils Pragmatiques de Décision et Mode de Coordination Collective', *Sociologie du Travail*, **4**, 465-77.

Reynaud, E. and J.D. Reynaud (1994), 'La Régulation Conjointe et ses Dérèglements', *Le Travail Humain*, **57**(3), 227–38.

Reynaud, J.D. (1993), *Les Règles du Jeu: L'action Collective et la Régulation Sociale*, Paris: Armand Colin.

Reynaud, J.D. (1999), *Le Conflit, la Négociation et la Règle*, 2nd edn, Toulouse: Octares Edition.

Sachs, K. (1992), 'Spécificité de L'outil Industriel Polonais: Comment Investir?', *Analyse Financière*, 2e trimestre, 44–50.

Sanchez, R., A. Heene and H. Thomas (eds) (1996), *Dynamics of Competence-based Competition: Theory and Practice in the New Strategic Management*, Oxford: Elsevier Science Publishing.

Sudol, S. (1996), 'Wprowadzenie', in S. Sudol and W. Karaszewki (eds), *Proces Transformacji Rynkowej Przedsiebiorstw*, Torun: Wydawnictwo Uniwersytetu Mikolaja Kopernika, pp. 7–14.

Teece, D., G. Pisano and A. Shuen (1997), 'Dynamic Capabilities and Strategic Management', *Strategic Management Journal*, **18**(7), 509–33.

Van den Bosch, F., H. Volberda and M. Boer (1999), 'Coevolution of Firm Absorptive Capacity and Knowledge Environment: Organisational Forms and Combinative Capabilities', *Organisation Science*, **10**(5), 551–68.

Wernerfelt, B. (1984), 'A Resource-based View of the Firm', *Strategic Management Journal*, **5**(2), 171–80.

Yin, R. (1989), *Case Study Research: Design and Methods*, London: Sage.

5. Re-examining knowledge sharing in an intercultural context: findings from the transition economies of China and Russia[1]

Kate Hutchings and Snejina Michailova

INTRODUCTION

During the last two decades, there has been an unprecedented increase in the number of organisations that have internationalised their operations. In part they have been assisted and encouraged to do so by increased numbers of potential markets becoming available in developing nations, including former communist nations that are making the transition to capitalist market economies. Foreign direct investment (FDI) by multinational corporations (MNCs) has brought advanced technologies, marketing skills and easier access to export markets (Soubbotina and Sheram, 2000) but it has also presented challenges and opportunities for these organisations in establishing intra-organisational knowledge sharing.

Researchers and practitioners have suggested that knowledge transfer and knowledge sharing are vital in building organisational competitive advantage, and knowledge sharing takes on particular importance in MNCs as their ability to exploit knowledge is more efficient intra-corporate than through the market (Gupta and Govindarajan, 2000). While it has been argued that international businesses need to transfer distinctive knowledge to foreign subsidiaries to offset some of the disadvantages of operating in alien environments (Kogut and Sander, 2002; Von Krogh, 1998), such knowledge transfer does not always take place efficiently (Gupta and Govindarajan, 2000). Knowledge sharing, a learning process whereby there is an assimilation of ideas, involving direct contact and commitment on both sides of the exchange, is even more difficult to monitor for efficiency (Husted and Michailova, 2002) as it depends on the willingness of individuals to identify to the organisation the knowledge they possess and to share knowledge when required (Nonaka, 1994). Problems with knowledge transmission and knowledge reception are further heightened, though, where the gap between cultures is great. So, while knowledge sharing is of greater importance in the subsidiary operations of international businesses, it is also more problematic to achieve.

This chapter explores the challenges and opportunities in knowledge sharing in two transition economies, China and Russia, both of which have taken advantage of the rapid demand for entry by international corporations since the crumbling of communism in the late 1980s, and are of particular strategic importance to many international organisations that are relocating, and/or expanding their operations within the developing world. China is the world's largest recipient of international FDI and over the last decade, the Chinese economy's share of global output has doubled to 4 per cent (*Business Week*, 2004) and the gross domestic product (GDP) has grown at one of the highest rates in the world, with an average annual growth rate exceeding 10 per cent (World Bank, 2000) since the late 1970s. Further, its acceptance into the World Trade Organisation (WTO) in 2001 and Beijing's hosting of the 2008 Olympics has secured China's place as a major player on the international economic stage. While Russia's GDP growth rates are amongst the lowest in the world, its two periods of privatisation in the early 1990s did encourage foreign investors, who continue to be attracted by the large geographical area of the nation, its abundance of natural resources and a population of approximately 150 million. Given the sheer size of the Chinese and Russian markets, their cultural distance from Western nations, and their internal cultural and institutional diversity, understanding the drivers and inhibitors of knowledge sharing within these transition economies is of crucial importance to international businesses who seek to maximise competitive advantage in these countries and to researchers wishing to elucidate determinants of knowledge sharing in cross-cultural contexts.

Previous research has maintained that Chinese and Russians have a propensity not to share knowledge at all (Elenkov, 1998; Michailova and Husted, 2003). Our research suggests however that understanding knowledge sharing in China and Russia is more complicated than has been previously assumed. We argue that knowledge sharing may actually be greater in these locations than in Western nations if an in-group relationship exists between the respective parties. Via an examination of cultural and institutional influences on knowledge sharing in China and Russia, we examine the relationship between in-group dynamics and knowledge sharing. We do not undertake a comparison of China and Russia but rather examine this interplay in both nations by exploring in-group relationships as integral to knowledge sharing.

The chapter begins with an overview of the knowledge sharing literature that has specific reference to cross-cultural knowledge sharing in China and Russia and the role that in-groups play in determining the propensity of individuals to share knowledge within organisations in these two nations. This is followed by a review of the methodology employed in this research.

Subsequently specific cultural and institutional influences on knowledge sharing in China and Russia are explored with reference to interview data, where illustrative. The chapter concludes with some suggestions as to how international businesses may maximise intra-organisational knowledge sharing within their Chinese and Russian subsidiaries.

KNOWLEDGE MANAGEMENT AND KNOWLEDGE SHARING IN CHINA AND RUSSIA

Knowledge Sharing – a Naturally Occurring Phenomenon?

Within the knowledge management (KM) literature, there has been a general consensus that collective knowledge emerges from interaction and dialogue among the members of a community or organisation (Wenger and Synder, cited in Cabrera and Cabrera, 2002). Mueller and Dyerson (1999) argue that an organisation that invests in expertise may find that the returns from that investment may not be fully captured or easily appropriated and this certainly may occur in relation to knowledge sharing. Highlighting the interconnectedness of the individual and the collective, Glisby and Holden (2003, p. 30) point out that 'simply put, individuals must fundamentally be willing to share and exchange knowledge internally in the organisation as well as externally with suppliers, customers and other stakeholders'. While the value of sharing knowledge may be obvious to the organisation, from an individual standpoint, sharing knowledge can carry significant costs which can even offset the individual benefits, resulting in a situation in which individuals will be reluctant to share knowledge for the collective organisational benefit.

Knowledge sharing in particular is in reality not as natural as often presented in the KM literature. Sbarcea (2001) suggests that it is an ungrounded assumption that people will share the knowledge they possess with others or tap into the collective corporate knowledge base in order to find a solution to problems simply because such systems have been made available. Hutchings and Michailova (2004) argue that knowledge sharing can be beneficial to an organisation but it may equally prove detrimental to an organisation in that, once knowledge is codified and articulated, the organisation risks losing information to competitors. Similarly, individuals may also feel that in codifying and articulating information they may lose that information (and advantage) over their peers. Cabrera and Cabrera (2002) claim perhaps the most important cost associated with knowledge sharing is the vulnerability that may be assumed by revealing one's personal insights into certain organisational contexts. This individual cooperation dilemma may then translate into a public good situation in which a few individuals, seeing little reward for sharing knowledge, extrapolates into the group being trapped in a non-cooperating deficient equilibrium.

Knowledge Sharing in China and Russia

Glisby and Holden (2003) suggest that not only can knowledge sharing not be assumed but the conditions under which individuals are prepared to share knowledge vary between cultures. Indeed Holden (2002) argues that KM operates in a kind of a 'vacuum', in which diversity, including cultural and ethnic, is compressed into 'one giant independent variable', which does not allow for the influence of cultural factors as variables in understanding attitudes and approaches to knowledge sharing. Glisby and Holden (2003) further suggest that there is a need to understand how knowledge is constructed and constituted outside the confines of Japan and the Western world, and they decry the dearth of literature on KM in a cross-cultural context. Lam (2000) also maintains that the relative dominance of the different knowledge types, and the ability of an organisation to harness tacit knowledge as a source of learning, are powerfully influenced by broader societal and institutional factors.

While Nonaka (1994) maintains that efficient knowledge sharing depends on the willingness of individuals to identify to the organisation the knowledge they possess and to share knowledge when required, Husted and Michailova (2002) stress that such knowledge sharing cannot be assumed as the willingness to share knowledge is affected by knowledge being asymmetrically distributed in organisations. This asymmetrical distribution is of particular note in Russia where the potential value of knowledge sharing is often defeated by 'knowledge sharing hostility' (Michailova and Husted, 2003) which may result from: (1) the behaviour of knowledge transmitters; (2) the behaviour of knowledge receivers; or (3) the transmitter's and receiver's shared understanding of the content of the knowledge. Specific characteristics of Russians as knowledge transmitters are: lack of incentives for sharing knowledge; a departmental way of thinking and acting; and a fear of admitting mistakes. Further, Russian managers and employees are eager to accumulate knowledge but strongly resist sharing it and the strong focus on hierarchical status and physical distance is an impediment to knowledge sharing both top-down and bottom-up (Michailova and Husted, 2003). Moreover, according to these researchers, in knowledge sharing hostile environments, the 'not-invented-here syndrome' creates a general behavioural problem in which there is strong emotional group affiliation among individuals within an insider group with a high level of suspicion towards outsiders (especially foreigners) which works against intra-organisational knowledge sharing.

In China, it has been argued that the nature of the knowledge available for sharing, along with the knowledge owner's relationship to the potential recipient, may interact with the national culture in affecting people's openness in sharing knowledge (Chow et al., 2000). Indeed, if private knowledge has no potential to damage the sharer's self-interests, there is no significant difference between United States' nationals and People's Republic of China (PRC) nationals' willingness to share. However when examining knowledge that could potentially damage the sharer's self-interests while benefiting the company, Chinese respondents have a significantly higher propensity to share, thereby putting the interests of the collective ahead of their own. Chinese are also significantly less inclined to share information files with other employees who are not part of their 'in-group' (Chow et al., 2000).

In-groups and Knowledge Sharing in China and Russia

The distinction between in-groups and out-groups influences relationships to a high extent in the transition economies. Individuals feel a moral obligation towards their in-group and a lack of interest in those that are considered the out-group. The boundary between the individuals' in-group and other groups is very sharp and strong trust will be felt in in-group others but weaker or complete lack of trust in out-group others (Chen et al., 2002). The in-group becomes the mode of transaction for these societies (Boisot and Child, 1999).

In China, one's membership of in-groups affects all daily activities be they economic or social, and in-group value is inextricably linked to trust. Those who fall out of a personalised network are regarded as out-group members and they do not share benefits of networking with in-group members. Moreover, due to the interdependent relationships in an in-group, individuals are motivated to save face for in-group members (Sheer and Chen, 2003). Littrell (2002) suggests that, in China, the in-group is the source of identity, protection and loyalty and in exchange for such loyalty, knowledge can be expected to be shared within the group and withheld from those considered to be 'outsiders'. In Russia, strong collective instincts were born in the countryside in pre-revolutionary times with collective farming encouraged by the Tsars because of their fear of anarchy. Ethics of the obshina, the commune of villagers, was embedded in the peasant psychology and often carried from the farm to the factory when peasants migrated to cities (Smith, 1990). People who belonged to the obshina lived together, worked in the fields together and were accustomed to a common fate. Socialism has perpetuated this group thinking and behaving through ignoring the importance of individuals. Ashwin's (1996) research found that in Russia individuals outside one's own collective are defined negatively.

METHODS

The arguments developed in this chapter are drawn from relevant literature and knowledge acquired through the authors' fieldwork in Russia and China over an eight year period. The research involved both primary and secondary data with analysis of publicly-available annual company reports and internal company data as well as informal conversations and semi-structured interviews. In China, interviews were conducted with almost 100 expatriate Western managers and local Chinese managers in 1999, 2000, 2001 and 2003. In Russia, interviews were conducted with 48 expatriate Western managers and local Russian managers in 1996, 1997, 1999, 2000, 2001, 2002 and 2003. In China, interviews with Western and Chinese managers were undertaken in Shanghai and Beijing as these are the locations in which the majority of Western organisations' operations are concentrated. Informal conversations were also held with Western managers in the cities of Hangzhou, Nanjing, Suzhou and Wuxi. In Russia, interviews were conducted in Moscow and St Petersburg; also locations in which the majority of Western organisations' operations are concentrated. Qualitative interviews were conducted with the aim of hearing in detail and complexity how expatriate and local managers describe and contextualise their perceptions of and experiences with information and knowledge sharing in China and Russia, with particular respect to organisational structure, organisational culture, organisational change, human resource management, communication flows and business practices.

A pool of potentially suitable organisations with which to conduct research was initially developed from listings provided by the China Secretariat in Australia and various Western trade associations and chambers of commerce in China and Western consulates in Russia. From these initial databases, we extended our networks of potential interviewees as we undertook subsequent studies in China and Russia. The outsider status that can often be experienced as a researcher was partly offset by building rapport with the Western expatriate communities in these two countries while undertaking longitudinal research (for further discussion of insider/outsider status in conducting cross-cultural research, see Hutchings, 2004). The elimination of random sampling in favour of snowballing and convenience sampling through use of personal contacts (with business associations providing listings of organisations) does suggest the potential for bias on the part of the interviewer and the organisations providing contacts. However, it is a strategy that was also used by an international team of researchers currently reporting best practice in international human resource management (Von Glinow et al., 2002, p. 150). This approach was adopted given the difficulties associated with gaining an adequate sample when utilising random sampling in China (Nojonen, 2004).

The sample of organisations and managers was drawn from a multi-industry background of organisations and ranged in size from small, owner-operated businesses to large MNCs. The ethnic background of Western managers was primarily Anglo-Saxon-Celtic or European. By far the majority of interviewees were male. Despite the researchers' efforts to access female interviewees, the sample cohort reflects the predominance of male expatriate managers in Western organisations in China and Russia.

Interviewer and interviewee bias was minimised by the use of a neutral setting, by establishing trust and rapport by initial referral via business associations and subsequent follow-up research, and the use of funnelling and presentation of questions in unbiased form. A semi-structured interview was designed to be of one-hour duration. In practice, interviews were between 40 minutes and three hours in duration. In China, at the interviewees' request, interviews were not audio-recorded. The interview notes were transcribed and, where necessary, returned to the interviewees for clarification. If interviewees disagreed with how their comments were transcribed, they were requested to make the necessary corrections and return the interview notes to the researchers. None of the interviewees elected to make changes to notes of their personal interview. In Russia, interviews were audio-recorded and transcribed. In China, most interviews were conducted in English as the majority of interviewees had English as their first language. All Chinese interviewees were also fluent in English but the interviews with some of these people were conducted in a mix of English and Mandarin. In Russia, the Russian managers were interviewed in Russian while the Western managers were interviewed in English or Danish, according to each interviewee's preference. In Russia, expatriates from Germany and Brazil were interviewed in English. The difficulties of conducting interviews with Chinese and Russians in terms of accuracy of responses conveyed and willingness to 'open up' to outsiders is well documented (see Hutchings, 2004; Nojonen, 2004) and acknowledged but should not negate the value of the research findings. At all stages through-out the process, interviewees were assured that all information provided was given on a purely voluntary basis. Moreover they were reminded that their names, the names of their organisations and names of their employees who facilitated interview scheduling would be kept strictly confidential.

The transcribed interviews were analysed by qualitative inquiry by the researchers. Where interview data is presented in the remainder of the chapter, it is not intended to be comparative in nature in terms of representing specific numbers or percentages of organisational respondents concurring or disagreeing. Rather individuals' comments are included where informative and illustrative of the central arguments being advanced. Internal validity of this research was assisted by having the interviewees check interpretation of the data; the interviewees being involved throughout various stages of the research; and researcher/interviewer bias minimised. External validity was assisted by the use of multi-lingual, multi-disciplinary research teams in both countries; by having colleagues serve as external advisors throughout the research process; and the context from which the data was gathered being made clear.

DISCUSSION

Networks in China and Russia, being based largely on collectivist relationships, involve highly frequent exchanges and operate at both workplace and private levels (Bian and Ang, 1997; McCarthy and Puffer, 2003; Wright et al., 2002; Yergin and Gustafson, 1994). Moreover, just as relationship building must occur before business is transacted and before knowledge sharing will occur, relationship building takes a long-term orientation as it is integrally tied to the development of trust and shared context (Jandt, 2001). A Russian top manager in a Russian–Danish joint venture in the telecom industry commented,

> Westerners come and go. They usually stay for two, three years. Exactly after we have had some time to test them and made up our minds whether they are trustworthy or not, they leave. This is a pity. Two–three years are not a sufficient period to establish a good personal relationship. When the next Westerner comes, I simply decide that it is not worth investing the energy and the effort in a new friendship.

An important distinction between Western and Chinese/Russian practice is that for the Westerners, the ends can often justify the means but for the Chinese/Russians, the means are more important than the ends. Indeed the inclination not to share knowledge with outsiders means that the only way in which one is able to access information and knowledge from an outsider is to work towards the ascription of insider status or to work through intermediaries who already possess insider status. As an Australian manager in an importing company in China explained it,

> Get an intermediary – someone who sees, breathes, speaks China ... people with connections ... to be your advisors – they can mediate for you. They can tell you what to do. But be selective. These people can turn out to be charlatans. This can be a massive liability if these people get out of favour – you need to check their political background.

The cultural importance of in-groups in China and Russia has also been consolidated by the Communist political machinery and bureaucracy in these nations. In both China and Russia, various corporate departments within

State-owned enterprises (SOEs) have been linked to a large number of government constituencies, which implies that companies have depended heavily on higher authorities for their operations. As most of the SOEs performed poorly financially, they had to secure bank loans through government intervention. Moreover within organisations, there has been a high level of dependency on superiors, who are responsible for defining the tasks and assessing the performance of their subordinates. These factors have meant that organisational subunits in Chinese and Russian organisations have depended on relevant government agencies more than on their own organisation, and employees have directed their loyalty to their immediate superior rather than to the organisation as a whole. The departmental focus that arose (and continues to exist in most organisations in China and Russia) is in stark contrast to modern Western organisational practice.

Moreover, for the Chinese and Russians, knowing a lot about their in-groups but being reluctant to provide information to somebody they consider to belong to an out-group, are cultural traditions that were also reinforced by concern for security that was perpetuated during the communist regimes. In China and Russia, larger groups were imposed as merely structural configurations for executing work. It was within the immediate in-groups where people knew each other, could trust each other and, consequently, shared information and knowledge with each other. This sense of identification and belonging to the in-group, combined with hostility to out-group members, even from the same organisation, created a feeling of security that was, and still is, highly valued in China and Russia.

Cultural Influences on Knowledge Sharing in China and Russia

Intrinsically tied to the existence of in-groups and personal networks in China and Russia is the notion of trust. The decision to trust a person and share knowledge with him/her depends upon having knowledge of that individual. An Australian manager of a finance company in China characterised the situation thus,

> The Chinese talk about this trust thing and I think it is one of those things that I have found very hard. Basically when we start we have no trust and we have just met and let's do this deal first and then we can start talking about trust because then we will understand each other. Hence, the Chinese joint ventures having this opening paragraph about mutual understanding ... It is just really important to them.

The importance of emotional trust and implicit communication
In cultures such as China's and Russia's, implicit communication styles are used – meanings are either conveyed in physical context or internalised in

person and little information is provided in the coded, explicit, transmitted part of the message (Hall and Hall, 1990). As individuals already know much about each other by the time a relationship is formed and insider status ascribed, they do not need to disclose so much information in normal transactions – much knowledge is tacit. Indeed because tacit knowledge is part of the informal nature of the workplace, it is very difficult to move from outsider to insider status. Consequently it takes a long time to move into a situation of knowledge sharing because it depends upon tacit knowledge already existing. Though the richer the communication experience, the more effective the knowledge sharing, it will only occur where trust and in-group status is already established. One US hospitality manager in China noted that communication is the greatest difficulty of all. As he said,

> You need to take Chinese and turn it into Chinese English. The words that come out of my mouth – they hear it differently and the words that come out of their mouths I hear them differently ... They already have an understanding of what they are saying amongst themselves, and we (Westerners) are not really tuned into this.

A Russian employee in a Western-owned manufacturing company noted also that, 'The Westerners are too direct in the way they communicate. In this way they destroy a lot. One needs to be more careful'.

The role of face and status
Giving and saving face take on specific significance in China where it is absolutely critical to avoid words or actions that will cause embarrassment to others. To cause such embarrassment is a major *faux pas* in both social and business settings, but something of which many international managers are guilty. Moreover, face (*mianzi* in China) is something that should not be damaged (the concept of saving face) but it is also very important to give face – indeed, where face is saved, emotional feelings of attachment are developed. Such attachments (which reinforce in-group status) greatly facilitate a climate of trust in which people will have a greater inclination to share knowledge. Whereas Western cultures have a concern for privacy and autonomy and express self-face maintenance, Russian culture is concerned with interdependence and inclusion and Chinese culture with mutual-face or other-face maintenance. However it should be noted that giving and saving face are also very much linked to the importance of the group. When saving and giving face to an individual, face is automatically also given to that individual's in-group. Conversely when an individual is shamed, so too is the in-group shamed. Therefore it is very important for managers to be aware that they must be cognisant of the group when ensuring that they give and save face. A Chinese manager in a law company suggested that, 'Chinese play on face because it is a Western fear. If you offend in Australia or Canada or England, someone will

not do business with you. The idea is no different, but Westerners do not really appreciate this fact'.

In Russia, power and status are important. Inequality in status among participants is accepted and respected. At the same time this can be a strong inhibitor to sharing knowledge. Russian managers have difficulties accepting that they can learn from employees from lower levels of the organisation. The belief that people placed at hierarchically higher levels cannot learn from their subordinates is well expressed in the superiors' resistance and dissatisfaction when they have to work in a group with people from hierarchically lower levels, for example, in the context of management education and training programmes. The status- and power-based barrier to knowledge sharing is reinforced when the participants draw on distinct knowledge bases and ways of analysing and assessing information. A Western manager in Russia noted that,

> It is amazing how well-defined, strict and rigid the structures of the traditional Russian companies are. There are so many hierarchical layers. And there is so little transparency. At the same time when it comes to who is allowed to make a decision, suddenly the structure becomes entirely flat – there is only one person in the entire company who is authorised to make decisions, the top boss. Everybody is happy with this situation. Why? Because it is the best way in which the employees can avoid responsibility and the top boss is satisfied in his desire to exercise as much formal power as possible.

A similar view is shared by Russian managers and employees themselves. According to a Russian middle manager in a pharmaceutical company,

> The CEO is the top figure in each enterprise. This is how it is and nobody can question this fact. We all expect the CEO to have the precise answers to all important questions. He is paid for this and this is his prior responsibility. All the others have to make sure that the decisions are executed. It will be anarchy otherwise.

Institutional Influences on Knowledge Sharing in China and Russia

Historically the Chinese and Russian cultures value perseverance and hard work. Yet the communist era altered these traditional values in creating societies, in which stand-out performance was in general not valued and there were no rewards or incentives for achievement. A flow-on effect was that there was also no incentive for sharing knowledge. When Chinese and Russians work in market-oriented new organisations, they find it difficult to appreciate concepts of individual performance and incentives and rewards for individuals simply because in the SOEs, there was nothing to be gained by working harder or more efficiently. Moreover, the group focus and the need to not deviate from one's group mean that individuals have been conditioned not to take responsibility and to actually evade responsibility (Worm, 1997). Just as there was little incentive for performance as all employees were rewarded commensurate to each other, there was no incentive to be gained by sharing knowledge between departments and across the organisation. Indeed organisational cultures developed (and continue to exist) in which individuals view themselves as part of a department rather than an organisation. Their department became their work in-group and there has been indifference or even hostility towards the out-group (other departments). This division between groups and departments can also translate into problems in creating a sense of loyalty across an organisation. As an Australian manager in a trading company noted, 'Chinese are not loyal to the organisation. It is hard to get them to feel that sense of organisational commitment. They will leave you for 1 RMB (approximately US 10 cents)'.

Incentives and Rewards – a Group-based Approach

Where rewards and incentives have been introduced into the transition economies, there have been problems in their implementation. Chinese will be inclined to give greater reward allocation to, and be 'softer' in assessments of, in-group members than out-group members (Hui et al., 1991). In collectivist cultures, it is harder for in-group members to give and receive negative feedback from each other (Gomes et al., 2000); situations which work against sharing knowledge across groups. Feedback in Russian organisations is mainly given in negative terms, for example, when the boss notices a deviation from the defined standards and procedures, no matter how outdated and rigid these standards. In such a context, hiding mistakes is a well-justified and rational behaviour although it may cause chronic problems and financial losses from an organisational viewpoint. During the communist era, both Chinese and Russians were trained to not admit mistakes rather than view them as learning opportunities as is the norm in the Western context. Further Chinese and Russians have been employed in very hierarchical, authoritarian organisations in which mistakes were viewed as costly and to be avoided and hence not to be admitted. The corresponding absence of feedback and opportunity to reflect has contributed to an unwillingness to share learning experiences and knowledge of how to avoid repeating mistakes.

Chinese and Russian executives are generally reticent to believe that knowledge can be acquired bottom-up in organisations and have difficulties accepting that they can learn from employees from lower levels. Indeed, managers and employees perceive each other as belonging to out-groups, and international managers are perceived by local employees as belonging to a quite distinct group altogether. Subordinates often intentionally hoard their knowledge, anticipating that their superiors would not promote them if they demonstrate in public that they are more knowledgeable than their superiors. While the lack of rewards and incentives for sharing knowledge tends to work against employees initiating, the cultural traditions also reinforce the lack of institutional incentives for taking initiatives. That is, the strong hierarchical and authoritarian traditions within organisations mean that managers are threatened by participatory styles of management and employees do not want to involve themselves in decision making for fear of having their views rejected (Chen et al., 2002). Also in the case of China, for an employee to provide a suggestion to his/her senior manager would cause considerable loss of face for both parties. The manager looks inadequate and is disgraced for not having first thought of the idea and the employee is humiliated for shaming his/her superior. The institutional gap between managers and employees is further exacerbated when the people involved are foreign managers and Chinese employees as in these instances an even larger gap exists based upon an historical lack of networks and trust. Such distance enhances the in-group/out-group divisions which impact on knowledge sharing and organisational learning.

While Western reward systems are quickly being adopted in China and Russia as the number of strategic alliances with Western partners increase, traditions of formality, hierarchy and command are much slower to change. Moreover, it has been suggested that unethical behaviour continues to be tolerated in organisations in China because employees will not share knowledge of superiors' indiscretions (Jackson and Bak, 1998). Such systemic conditions suggest disincentives to share knowledge. Indeed, in withholding knowledge from members of the out-group, the in-group helps preserve its own stability. Maintaining stability and security is highly valued in the Chinese and Russian societal and organisational context (Ralston et al., 1997) and uncertainty can be a major de-motivator.

The legacy of a culture of fear
In addition to the cultural factors that may inhibit Chinese and Russians' propensity to share knowledge is the culture of fear that continues as a legacy of the communist era, in which Chinese and Russians were not only given no incentives to share knowledge but were actually encouraged to report to authorities the misdemeanours of others – a situation which reinforced the notion of in-groups and out-groups. A Western manager in Russia pointed out,

> We assume Russians will share information. However, until not long ago, they were punished for sharing information. Why should they suddenly change behaviour? It is deeply ingrained in them that it is much safer to be silent and only share very carefully and very selectively. I hate this in my managerial work, but I can also

understand the reasons for this type of behaviour. Or at least I believe I understand. Maybe I don't anyway ...

China's shift from communism to market economics, and its subsequent adoption of Western accounting practices, standards and legal regulations, has led many Chinese managers to argue for reliance on the rule of law (Wright et al., 2002). Yet in both China and Russia, even those who want to stay within the law may find it difficult to do so, since by observing one law they may be breaking another one. In Russia, the continued existence of loopholes in legislation encourages people and businesses to find other legal solutions. These legal ambiguities mean that interpersonal connections and in-groups are still the way through which many Chinese and Russians achieve their business ends, and many others are discouraged from sharing knowledge in case it should find them in trouble with authorities even though they may not be breaking an official law or regulation. The culture of fear has existed not only in relation to what has been loosely termed by successive Chinese and Russian governments as political 'secrets', but also within organisations in that employees who made mistakes were punished (Scarborough, 1998). There has been a suggestion that this culture of fear may begin to alter in China, with the changes flowing through since its accession to the WTO. However an Australian manager in a finance company in China claimed that,

> The WTO was never an overnight panacea ... just another signboard on the way to China getting from time zero to 21st century, whenever they got there. It is just another stepping stone ... another piece of administration to keep ... moving forward. But the culture of fear will also move slowly.

Systemic bribery and corruption

The widespread corruption and thriving black economies in China and Russia also have implications for knowledge sharing in that any knowledge can be acquired for a price so long as one has the necessary resources and insider contacts. Such a situation can cause difficulties for Western organisations trying to reconcile the pressure to engage in such practices whilst also attempting to stay within the confines of Western organisational ethics. In the case of China, it has been questioned whether corruption has become systemic (Hilton, 1996). The use of bribery is universally condemned, particularly now that there has been the introduction of laws specifically dealing with corruption and the government has made a point of executing thousands to make the point that it is serious about cracking down on corruption. Yet while giving cash is usually viewed as buying someone's services and hence is condemned, gift giving is universal (Yang, 2002) and the difference between what is an acceptable gift and what is an improper bribe depends on arbitrary, delicately poised cultural conventions that vary according to the situation

(Luo, 1997). Even so, while some practices are increasingly viewed as backdoor (Guthrie, 1998), many other historical conventions associated with in-groups remain *de rigueur*.

In Russia, gaining introduction to useful people remains extremely important. In cases when people have no resources to *blat*, people will resort to bribes (Ashwin, 1996). Bribery, corruption and the criminal 'second' society are all part of the criminal legacy of the 'economy of favours' in Russia (Ledeneva, 1998). This has important implications for knowledge sharing in general (and for the knowledge sharing between organisational sub-groups of Western managers and locals) in that it remains very difficult to develop and maintain good business relationships without engaging in some degree of favours, and knowledge sharing depends upon maintaining relationships through favours. Beyond that though, despite anti-bribery laws, paying bribes (to a member of one's in-group) is still a very effective way of ensuring access to knowledge as well as preventing knowledge from being shared.

IMPLICATIONS FOR INTERNATIONAL MANAGERS

Within the literature on learning organisations, suggestion has been made of the need for managers' mental models to be improved and shared amongst learners with the fundamental learning unit being not the individual but the team of managers who need one another to take new actions (Roth and Senge, 1996; Senge and Fulmer, 1993). Certainly in endeavouring to create intra-organisational knowledge sharing in subsidiary operations in China and Russia, there is a need for international managers to develop and engender new mental models or organisational learning and practice to create a collective wisdom that appreciates and works within Chinese and Russian cultural and institutional norms and frameworks of group membership.

Cabrera and Cabrera (2002) argue that to build organisational environments conducive to knowledge sharing, it is necessary for organisations to intervene to: reduce the costs of contributing; increase the benefits of contributing; increase the perceived value of collective gain; and send a clear message about the importance of knowledge sharing and creation for the organisation. To achieve these goals in China and Russia, however, requires that international managers create an orientation amongst organisational members towards the organisation rather than departments, and this will take both time and patience to achieve. Moreover, there are also key cultural and institutional influences associated with in-group membership that impact on the willingness or unwillingness of Chinese and Russians to share knowledge. These predispositions need to be recognised and accommodated by international businesses and expatriate managers.

First it is crucial that international managers recognise the long-term nature of China's and Russia's networking and development of trust (which is built on tacit knowledge being held), and that it is highly unusual for foreign managers to be incorporated immediately into these networks. It is important then for international managers to work through intermediaries within and outside their subsidiary operations while building relationships of their own with their employees and external business partners. In so doing, international managers need to be careful not to destroy existing networks (by immediately introducing cross-functional teams) and to utilise consultation with departmental managers to consolidate linkages with local employees.

Second, international managers also need to be cognisant of the fact that Chinese and Russian workers have been socialised not to deviate from the norm and to acquiesce to authority. Therefore international managers need to recognise that Chinese and Russians will be reticent to admit mistakes, do not want to be singled out from the in-group, and will be unlikely to question, or speak out against, superiors. To encourage knowledge sharing, international managers need to work towards creating a climate of trust but they also need to undertake their management and human resource management functions within the context of existing group relationships. Accordingly, training, performance assessments, motivation and rewards need to be done within the context of existing in-groups, while disciplinary action should be undertaken privately so as not to cause employees to be alienated from their group. International managers may also benefit from utilising personal recommendations from their existing employees when recruiting new employees. Moreover international managers need to be flexible and patient in attempting to create new networks for knowledge sharing and in redefining organisational perceptions of who is part of the in-group.

Finally, given the lawlessness that has been historically rife in Chinese and Russian society and still exists in some quarters today, it is important for international managers to realise that many Chinese and Russians will be too fearful to share knowledge because of the belief that they may be punished for doing so. In order to work within these confines, international managers need to build an organisational culture that values knowledge sharing by creating a subsidiary operation in which there is a high level of trust and in which people are incrementally trained to value intra-organisational knowledge sharing. It should be remembered also that Chinese and Russians who have been educated in or worked in the West will have a greater propensity to knowledge sharing across a whole organisation than those who have not had such exposure to Western organisational practices; and these people will often make very effective intermediaries.

Western managers need also to be aware that despite rapid developments in China and Russia, disparate educational levels, as well as vast regional differences and ethnic cultural differences remain. Despite China's commitments under the WTO accession agreement and the expectation to improve the predictability, transparency and competitiveness of the domestic business environment, and Russia's proximity to Western Europe, neither country is one economy. There are great disparities in living standards and business practices within the countries. In China, the Eastern seaboard exhibits elements of Westernised business practice while the inner provinces remain underdeveloped and largely agrarian. Russia spreads over eleven time zones, is a kaleidoscope of regions that differ enormously in terms of workforce, institutional environments and economic development. The multi-layered diversity within China and Russia does pose a major challenge for international businesses in their subsidiary operations but must be taken into account in order to create knowledge-sharing organisational cultures.

NOTE

1. Variations on this research have appeared in the edited book, *Cross-cultural Perspectives on Knowledge Management* and in the *Journal of Knowledge Management* and the *International Journal of Emerging Markets*.

REFERENCES

Ashwin, S. (1996), 'Forms of Collectivity in a Non-Monetary Society', *Sociology*, **30**(1), 21–39.
Bian, Y. and S. Ang (1997), 'Guanxi Networks and Job Mobility in China and Singapore', *Social Forces*, **75**(3), 981–1007.
Boisot, M. and J. Child (1999), 'Organisations as Adaptive Systems in Complex Environments: The Case of China', *Organisation Science*, **10**(3), 237–52.
Business Week (2004), 'China Economy', 3 May, p. 21.
Cabrera, A. and E.F. Cabrera (2002), 'Knowledge Sharing Dilemmas', *Organisation Studies*, **23**(5), 687–710.
Chen, C., M. Peng and P. Saparito (2002), 'Individualism, Collectivism, and Opportunism: A Cultural Perspective on Transaction Cost Economics', *Journal of Management*, **28**(4), 567–83.
Chow, C.W., F.J. Deng and J.L. Ho (2000), 'The Openness of Knowledge Sharing within Organisations: A Comparative Study of the United States and the People's Republic of China', *Journal of Management Accounting Research*, **12**, 65–95.
Elenkov, D.S. (1998), 'Can American Management Concepts Work in Russia? A Cross-cultural Comparative Study', California Management Review, **40**(4), 133–56.
Glisby, M. and N. Holden (2003), 'Contextual Constraints in Knowledge Management Theory: The Cultural Embeddedness of Nonaka's Knowledge-creating Company', *Knowledge and Process Management*, **10**(1), 29–36.
Gomes, C., B.L. Kirkman and D.L. Shapiro (2000), 'The Impact of Collectivism and In-group/Out-group Membership on the Evaluation Generosity of Team Members', *Academy of Management Journal*, **43**(6), 1097–106.

Gupta, A.K. and V. Govindarajan (2000), 'Knowledge Flows within Multinational Corporations', *Strategic Management Journal*, **21**, 473–96.

Guthrie, D. (1998), 'The Declining Significance of Guanxi in China's Economic Transition', *The China Quarterly*, **3**, 254–82.

Hall, E.T. and M.R. Hall (1990), *Understanding Cultural Differences*, Yarmouth, ME: Intercultural Press.

Hilton, R. (1996), 'Corruption in China: Has it Become Systemic?', *Asian Survey*, **36**(8), 741–57.

Holden, N.J. (2002), *Cross-cultural Management: A Knowledge Management Perspective*, Harlow: Financial Times/Prentice Hall.

Hui, C.H., H.C. Triandis and C. Yee (1991), 'Cultural Differences in Reward Allocation: Is Collectivism the Explanation?', *British Journal of Social Psychology*, **30**, 145–57.

Husted, K. and S. Michailova (2002), 'Knowledge Sharing in Russian Companies with Western Participation', *Management International*, **6**(2), 19–28.

Hutchings, K. (2004), 'Behind the Bamboo Curtain: Problems and Pitfalls in Researching Australian Expatriates in China', in E. Clark and S. Michailova (eds), *Fieldwork in Transforming Societies: Understanding Methodology from Experience*, London: Palgrave, pp. 136–56.

Hutchings, K. and S. Michailova (2004), 'Facilitating Knowledge Sharing in Russian and Chinese Subsidiaries: The Role of Personal Networks', *Journal of Knowledge Management*, **8**(2), 84–94.

Jackson, T. and M. Bak (1998), 'Foreign Companies and Chinese Workers: Employee Motivation in the PRC', *Journal of Organisational Change Management*, **11**(4), 282–95.

Jandt, F.E. (2001), *Intercultural Communication: An Introduction*, 3rd edn, Thousand Oaks, CA: Sage.

Kogut, B. and U. Sander (2002), 'Knowledge of the Firm, Combinative Capabilities and the Replication of Technology', *Organisation Science*, **3**(3), 383–97.

Lam, A. (2000), 'Tacit Knowledge, Organisational Learning and Societal Institutions: An Integrated Framework', *Organisation Studies*, **21**(3), 487–513.

Ledeneva, A.V. (1998), *Russia's Economy of Favors: Blat, Networking and Informal Exchange*, Cambridge: Cambridge University Press.

Littrell, R.F. (2002), 'Desirable Leadership Behaviours of Multi-cultural Managers in China', *Journal of Management Development*, **21**(1), 5–74.

Luo, Y. (1997), 'Guanxi and Performance of Foreign-invested Enterprises in China: An Empirical Enquiry', *Management International Review*, **37**(1), 51–70.

McCarthy, D.J. and S.M. Puffer (2003), 'Corporate Governance in Russia: A Framework for Analysis', *Journal of World Business*, **38**(4), 397–415.

Michailova, S. and K. Husted (2003), 'Knowledge-sharing Hostility in Russian Firms', *California Management Review*, **45**(3), 59–77.

Mueller, F. and R. Dyerson (1999), 'Expert Humans or Expert Organisations?', *Organisation Studies*, **20**(2), 225–56.

Nojonen, M. (2004), 'Fieldwork in a Low Trust (Post-) Communist Society', in E. Clark and S. Michailova (eds), *Fieldwork in Transforming Societies: Understanding Methodology from Experience*, London: Palgrave, pp. 157–76.

Nonaka, I. (1994), 'Dynamic Theory of Organisational Knowledge Creation', *Organisation Science*, **5**(1), 14–37.

Ralston, D.A., D.H. Holt, R.H. Terpstra and K.C. Yu (1997), 'The Impact of National Culture and Economic Ideology on Managerial Work Values: A Study of the United

States, Russia, Japan, and China', *Journal of International Business Studies*, **28**(1), 177–207.

Roth, G.L. and P.M. Senge (1996), 'From Theory to Practice: Research Territory, Processes and Structure at an Organisational Learning Centre', *Journal of Organisational Change*, **9**(1), 92–103.

Sbarcea, K. (2001), 'The Mystery of Knowledge Management', *New Zealand Management*, **48**(10), 33–6.

Scarborough, J. (1998), *The Origins of Cultural Differences and their Impact on Management*, Westport, CT: Quorum Books.

Senge, P.M. and R.M. Fulmer (1993), 'Simulations, Systems Thinking and Anticipatory Learning', *The Journal of Management Development*, **12**(6), 21–33.

Sheer, V.C. and L. Chen (2003), 'Successful Sino-Western Business Negotiation: Participants' Accounts of National and Professional Cultures', *The Journal for Business Communication*, **40**(1), 50–85.

Smith, H. (1990), *The New Russians*, New York: Random House.

Soubbotina, T.P. and K.A. Sheram (2000), *Beyond Economic Growth: Meeting the Challenges of Global Development*, Washington, DC: The World Bank.

Von Glinow, M.A., E.A. Drost and M.B. Teagarden (2002), 'Converging on IHRM Best Practices: Lessons Learned from a Globally Distributed Consortium on Theory and Practice', *Asia Pacific Journal of Human Resources*, **40**(1), 146–66.

Von Krogh, G. (1998), 'Care in Knowledge Creation', *California Management Review*, **40**(3), 133–53.

World Bank (2000), *Entering the 21st Century*, New York: Oxford University Press.

Worm, V. (1997), *Vikings and Mandarins*, Copenhagen: Kobenhavn Handelshøyskolens Forlag.

Wright, P.C., W.F. Szeto and L.T.W. Cheng (2002), 'Guanxi and Professional Conduct in China: A Management Development Perspective', *International Journal of Human Resource Management*, **13**(1), 156–82.

Yang, M.M. (2002), 'Rebuttal: The Resilience of Guanxi and its New Deployments: A Critique of Some New Guanxi Scholarship', *The China Quarterly*, **170**, 459–76.

Yergin, D. and T. Gustafson (1994), *Russia 2010 and What it Means for the World*, New York: Vintage.

PART THREE

Knowledge management in Asia

6. Knowledge management among Taiwanese high-tech industries and SMEs

Te Fu Chen

INTRODUCTION

In the past ten years, the USA has accumulated outstanding global talents to create and build uncounted knowledge, and successfully transfer it into commodity. The success of the USA has ushered the twenty-first century into an era of knowledge economy. This has had a great impact on Taiwanese high-tech industries as they have been cooperating with the US high-tech industries over a long period; thus Taiwanese firms see knowledge as a maintainable and sustainable competitive advantage. They have started to implement correct and effective development strategies, through knowledge management (KM) to bring continuous innovation and learning into organisational structures.

KM has been developed in high-tech industries in Taiwan for a long period. For example, the Acer group and Taiwan Semiconductor Manufacturing Company have moved KM into the stage of knowledge transfer and diffusion (Acer, 2006; Taiwan Semiconductor Manufacturing Company Limited, 2006). According to the survey conducted by the International Data Centre Taiwan (2006), Taiwanese firms highly value KM as 96 per cent of firms see KM as an important management tool. Most firms believe that 'knowledge' constitutes 50 per cent of the value chain, which consists of research and development (R&D), design, manufacturing, marketing and after-sales service. However, only 15 per cent of firms identified the value-production of knowledge to reach a decent level. This indicates that some firms, especially small and medium enterprises (SMEs), understand the importance of KM but do not fully grasp the concept of implementation. This situation is more applicable to Taiwanese SMEs as they are learning how to implement KM effectively from the high-tech industries.

Although the success of the high-tech industries has brought economic growth to Taiwan, it is unable to resolve the real economic problems as traditional industries are withering, the unemployment rate is rising and there is a large shifting of industries to China. This may be attributed to the Taiwanese government placing much emphasis on high-tech industries (that is information and communication technology) and ignoring traditional industries like the SMEs. This policy causes decreased competitiveness of SMEs as the situation of shifting out to China is serious. Hence the facilitation of SMEs' remaining foundation in Taiwan is imperative as it will determine the future of economic growth in Taiwan. Following the success of high-tech industries and the universalisation of technology and knowledge, it is believed that advances in technology of SMEs will enable them to upgrade and transform themselves into knowledge enterprises, thus enticing them to remain in Taiwan.

Currently, 98 per cent of Taiwanese industries consist of SMEs (Small and Medium Enterprises Administration, 2003). Though SMEs have the advantage of management flexibility, they have difficulties implementing KM as they face shortages in capital and management talents.

Particularly, past SMEs are traditional industries and their management model is totally different from the high-tech industries. Presently, more SMEs are following the trends of high-tech industries, hence this study aims to ascertain the future development directions for Taiwanese SMEs by learning how to integrate the management styles of SMEs and high-tech industries. This study also seeks to determine how SMEs utilise KM theory to implement value innovation.

KNOWLEDGE MANAGEMENT IN TAIWAN

The Development and Application of Knowledge Management in Taiwanese High-tech Industries and SMEs

To assist the Taiwanese high-tech industries and SMEs with the changing knowledge economy, the Taiwanese government will invest 364 billion to build 'Knowledge Taiwan'. In the meantime, KM has been popular in all industries, especially within the high-tech industries and SMEs. These industries have recently convened with the Taiwanese government to discuss the KM policy. During the past years, the high-tech companies which include Acer (2006), KHS (2006), Nissan (2006), Taiwan Semiconductor Manufacturing Company Limited (2006) and United Microelectronics Corporation (UMC) (2006) have been building up KM. SMEs have also directed e-business towards the knowledge management system (KMS), and some SMEs have adopted modified KMS of large enterprises like Lotus Note (IBM, 2006) and Microsoft KMS (Microsoft, 2006).

The 'Acer global information system' is an example of the application of KM in a high-tech industry. It is a platform operating on the Lotus Note software and can connect 51 branches globally to process real-time strategic distribution and feedback information. Acer also utilises on-line learning and distance teaching and training systems for their 'global training plan' to greatly reduce training costs (Acer, 2006).

Another example is Taiwan Semiconductor Manufacturing Company's 'real time of proposing system', where employees can propose suggestions through the internal groupware system's auto-working flow to related directors. This is highly beneficial as it draws on the collective thinking of employees and raises competitiveness within the company (Taiwan Semiconductor Manufacturing Company Limited, 2006). Through KMS, the employees at Nissan have also proposed over 90 000 ideas, with each employee averaging about 30 ideas. This has largely increased response and creative abilities for the firm (Nissan, 2006).

Most Taiwanese SMEs adopt KMS via external development, but most high-tech industries self-develop KMS. KMS is mainly used for document search and creation of knowledge communities, which share professional knowledge within firms. The learning website is also an important function of KMS as it facilitates learning.

IBM requests that employees share knowledge via a database between each project and produce a KM platform. This system of KM is called a 'process', as it involves seeking, editing, sharing and creating, and is mainly used in the USA and Europe. However, in Taiwan, industries are focused mainly on the 'results' of KM.

Knowledge Sharing and the Community of Practice in Taiwanese Firms

O'Donnell et al. (2003) argue that a community of practice (CoP) is about sharing experiences and knowledge in creative ways, and this can lead to new approaches in problem solving and innovation. Knowledge sharing is important to a CoP, and it can be defined as the circulation of knowledge throughout the organisation (Yang, 2004). Usually, sharing knowledge can be defined as the dissemination of information and knowledge through the whole department and/or organisation. Taiwanese firms encourage and reward their employees to transfer job-related knowledge, including experiences and routines, to others by developing and using a 'mentor system'. This leads to consistent customer services. In addition, this mentoring programme transfers individual learning, knowledge and experience to others.

In order to develop a sharing climate among employees, employees need to know that their sharing will be reciprocated. According to interviews from high-tech industries (Acer, 2006; Taiwan Semiconductor Manufacturing

Company Limited, 2006), people are educated with the concept that 'knowledge increases in value when it is shared'. Taiwanese firms share knowledge to refine their shared knowledge by the interactive dialogue process; knowledge forums, seminars and so on. Those who share knowledge can obtain knowledge from sharers. Consequently, the outcomes are multiplied beneficially among all parties.

Approaches to Sharing

The following approaches adopted by Taiwanese firms could be employed to facilitate the activities of sharing knowledge:

1. The development of motivation programmes, including intrinsic, extrinsic and social rewards.
2. Employees are required to share their information, skills and knowledge after they return from training sessions.
3. A company must open up its organisational communication channels and assist a person who is able to guide its employees, for inputting and participating in solving the company's problems, in order to match customer needs and interests.
4. Social interactions play a crucial role in accelerating knowledge sharing.

The Application of Knowledge Management in Taiwanese SMEs

To help Taiwan SMEs implement KM, the government devised a plan using 'technology' and 'experts' to establish 'knowledge business' (K-business) and make competitive core knowledge the best 'fighting power' SMEs possess to push forward in the global market (Small and Medium Enterprises Administration, 2003). The five year plan of 'KM application for SMEs' is impelled by the Small and Medium Sized Enterprises Administration (SMEA). The plan is a sub-plan of the 'Challenge 2008 National Development Plan', which expects to finish KM diagnosis and evaluation for 400 SMEs within the next five years. It also aims to guide and assist SMEs, introduce KM application for 80 SMEs, and cultivate 3600 talents for KM.

The plan for KM application for SMEs (2003–07) entails advertising and promoting KM activity; developing recognition of KM and its application for SMEs; assisting SMEs to apply information technology to introduce KMS; integrating core knowledge to create corporate value; increasing competitiveness; constructing knowledge paradigms and the basis of an application platform for providing knowledge sharing; and developing the related application technology of KM.

The Challenge 2008: National Development Plan in Taiwan

Taiwan is known throughout the world as an 'economic miracle'. Now at the outset of the twenty-first century, Taiwan has a new opportunity to pursue the next level of development. The 'Challenge 2008' National Development Plan draws on and integrates the many resources – including human resources, technology, capital, institutions and the cluster effect – built up during Taiwan's long-term economic development (Council for Economic Planning and Development, 2002). The plan's ten major investment projects are infused with themes of culture and quality. A feature of the plan is to transform culture, creativity and quality into economic industries. The plan serves as a blueprint for economic and social development, attaching equal importance to knowledge and innovation as well as the economy and the humanities.

Internationally, Taiwan faces technological challenges and a loss of investment and skilled managers to the Chinese mainland. Thus, the Executive Yuan has formulated four major investments in the national development plan. The four major investments include cultivating talent; research, development and innovation; international logistics; and a high-quality living environment.

Small Business Innovation Research

In November 1998, the Department of Industrial Technology (DOIT) of the Ministry of Economic Affairs (MOEA) launched Taiwan's small business innovation research (SBIR) promotion programme, mostly referred to as the SBIR US version (Army Research Office Washington, 2006). This was to encourage local start-up companies pursuing innovative research into industrial technologies and products (Department of Industrial Technology, 1998).

In accordance with the Knowledge Economics Development Act, passed by the Executive Yuan in August 2000, the SBIR promotion programme may enhance the private sector's R&D competitiveness through the promotion of technological innovation and IT.

An Overview of Knowledge Management in Taiwan

Taiwanese industries are in the transformation stage from original equipment manufacturers (OEMs) to original design manufacturers (ODMs), formally entering into the era of knowledge economy and profit making. Corporate management strategy has also transformed from a model of cost orientation to innovation orientation, which indicates a step towards KM. Though K-business is important, there is a lack of KM talent in Taiwan as firms do not recognise its importance to K-business.

According to the Institute for Information Industry (2006), the 2004 universal rate of e-business, supply chain management, customer relationship management, KM, e-learning and enterprise resource planning reached 67.3 per cent in large enterprises, 25.1 per cent in medium enterprises, and 5 per cent in small enterprises. This means SMEs still have opportunities to pursue larger businesses. It is evident that all of Taiwan's large enterprises utilise e-business and KM, which gradually impacts on SMEs. At present the application of KM in large enterprises has increased competitiveness but the main force of Taiwan's economy, which is the SMEs, is relatively insufficient in terms of resources and motivation, and they cannot acquire or accumulate the need for knowledge effectively and efficiently.

Therefore, the final objectives of the KM plan are to apply 'successful demonstrated cases' and a 'diagnosis and evaluation operation' to enable SMEs to understand the importance of KM. The next section analyses the successful demonstrated cases for Taiwanese high-tech industries.

CASE STUDIES ANALYSIS

One government case study for SMEs and two high-tech industries' case studies are examined in this part. Through content analysis and discussion, this section proposes integrated KM business models and strategies for Taiwanese SMEs and high-tech industries.

Case 1: How Can the SMEA Assist Taiwanese SMEs to Upgrade and Transform?

In the past 50 years, SMEs have contributed significantly to the rapid growth and development of Taiwan's economy and industries. Currently, there are over one million SMEs in Taiwan, which make up 98 per cent of all industries.

In recent years, economic liberalisation, industrial internationalisation and IT development have not only formed a borderless world, but also transformed the original production and marketing model. Subsequently, with Taiwan's entry into the World Trade Organisation comes the open pressure on domestic markets and the threat of low priced products from China. These factors have had a serious impact on the sustainable management of Taiwanese SMEs and their development direction.

Hence, the SMEA believes that the development policy of the government is vital to aid SMEs. The SMEA will adopt three ways to assist SMEs to face competition and challenge, and compete with global first-class firms and overcome difficulties as follows:

1. Raise international competitiveness of SMEs.
2. Cultivate innovation for SMEs.
3. Apply ten large assistance systems to help the development of SMEs.

The SMEA has also come up with a plan to assist SMEs in their transformation to knowledge enterprises. The four benefits of this plan are as follows:

1. Enhanced knowledge assets and corporate value of SMEs.
2. Increased problem-solving ability and improved response ability of SMEs.
3. Better quality products and services and increased competitiveness of SMEs.
4. A new knowledge base of professional service provided by the government for SMEs.

The outcomes of the KM guidance and assistance plan for SMEs in 2004 are as follows:

1. Recognise 120 KM consultants.
2. Cultivate 64 KM seed consultants.
3. Accomplish 300 KM reports of diagnosis and evaluation for SMEs.
4. Handle 30 KM programmes and the participation of 1152 people.
5. Guide and assist 25 SMEs to introduce the KM model.

The direction and key points of the KM guidance and assistance plan in 2005 are as follows:

1. Accelerate the impetus for guiding and assisting small and medium knowledge service industries.
2. Enhance the application ability of whole information.
3. Concentrate resources on beneficial areas such as multimedia, e-commerce and so on, and assist companies with raising capital and cultivating core talents.
4. Through the 'cultivation centre of entrepreneurship', and the university and research mechanisms, SMEs are fast catching up in the knowledge economy. Innovation not only impacts on technology, but on markets, marketing, management and business models too. Therefore, there are new opportunities everywhere. It can bring value and wealth for SMEs, but they must be willing to take risks. SMEs can reduce the risk of innovation by cooperating with the 'cultivation centre of entrepreneurship' and universities.

The four main results the SMEA hopes to achieve when assisting SMEs to implement KM and innovation are as follows:

1. Promote e-business and KM for SMEs.
2. Strengthen the capability of cultivating innovation for SMEs.
3. Impel 'the plan of upgrade and transformation for SMEs'.
4. Cultivate talents needed by SMEs.

Case 2: KM Application at Acer Inc.

Acer ranks among the world's top five branded personal computer (PC) vendors, designing and marketing easy, dependable IT solutions that empower people to reach their goals and enhance their lives. Established in 1976, Acer Inc. employs 5600 people in Taiwan supporting dealers and distributors in more than 100 countries. Revenues in 2004 reached US$7 billion.

A global winning formula

Acer has fortified its branding, technology and marketing know-how; as well as its effectiveness in managing global logistics, worldwide business channels and customer service. As its competitiveness grows, so do the rewards shared among its partners.

Two key factors ensure a lasting competitive advantage – an innovative business model and complete market intelligence. Optimum implementation of these factors makes Acer create a more effective, sustainable operation, and more value for their customers.

Acer employs over 20 000 employees worldwide. In addition to Taiwan, Acer also has production factories in Malaysia, China, Mexico and the United Kingdom and so on, and owns operations and sale centres in Holland, the USA and Japan. In a large enterprise like Acer, employees are situated around the globe and hence the collaboration of employees is necessary in raising the company's competitiveness. In the era of rapid product and knowledge updates, organisations should ensure that employees are equipped with the tools to learn new knowledge and update knowledge structures quickly. This will guarantee that they remain competitive.

Acer manages KM by cooperating with over 30 partners and suppliers via a virtual team platform. This platform permits affiliated counterparts to edit and share information, and video conference. In addition, the results of training can disseminate tacit knowledge across the organisation, allowing it to expand its supplier networks, customer networks and partnership alliance networks.

The corporate e-learning system

Acer provides over 100 training programmes annually to enhance the working abilities of employees and stay abreast of keen competition. It has established a corporate e-learning system to cope with the large number of training programmes. This system fully utilises existing Internet resources to carry out corporate-class on-line training plans, which can provide a large volume of training material for the whole company.

With the e-learning system, employees can adopt self-learning and collaborative learning with colleagues in a virtual classroom. They can also select programmes most relevant and valuable for their work and development. This reduces the travel time of the programme planner or instructor and enables them to concentrate solely on developing excellent training programmes. Through the e-learning system, programme administrators can also conveniently obtain the reports of various training programmes, and accurately evaluate students' learning progress.

Case 3: KM Application at Taiwan Semiconductor Manufacturing Company

Founded in 1987, Taiwan Semiconductor Manufacturing Company (TSMC) is the world's largest semiconductor company. Through continuous process improvement and innovation, TSMC has managed to accumulate precise and advanced OEM knowledge. The core advantage of TSMC is its excellent KM capability, which is not visible to other competitors. Through effective KM, TSMC has quickly expanded five factories in a span of 12 years – in locations like Tainan scientific park, Singapore and the USA. TSMC also established the first factory to produce 12-inch wafers of gallium phosphide in Taiwan. Thus, it is evident that TSMC employs an effective paradigm of KM and utilises a set of tight controls to update technology internally.

Employees at TSMC acknowledge that 'benchmarking' is the one of the key issues needed to stay competitive. They explore the best possible way of doing things from personal knowledge and handbooks, and distribute the information within the company. This form of knowledge sharing is known as 'data mining'. Cross-departmental communication is also very active, as TSMC aims to facilitate more communication. The outcome of all meetings is recorded and stored in the 'document centre', where files are saved into different categories, making them easily accessible to employees. The Singapore government was so impressed with TSMC's 'benchmarking learning' that they sent a team to Taiwan to study their KM operations. Over the past 12 years, TSMC has accumulated knowledge through the systematic creation of standardisation processes, which creates and stores files of knowledge. The success of TSMC is attributed to the collective intellect and effort of all its employees.

The most classic KM technique of TSMC is its 'technology committee', where employees attend committee meetings to exchange information. TSMC accumulates knowledge by recording the best machine equipment, material and process and transplanting this knowledge to every new factory. It uses a 'central team' to do a 'smart copy' of a factory and a 'copy executive' will ensure that all new factories are constructed and operated in the exact same way. There is also one person who integrates technology in every factory and he or she will share the knowledge with the 'technology committee'. A teaching handbook is also available to every new technician. In the human resource management (HRM) aspect, employees share their work experiences with each other. As such knowledge is stored and easily transferable, TSMC will not be at a loss even when employees with specialised skills leave the company.

The IT department plays an important role in the storing and sharing of knowledge, and supports TSMC in every aspect of KM. TSMC ensures that knowledge is well protected and stores data in computers located in two different buildings. The tangible intellectual capital of TSMC consists of patents, data, customers' files, manufacturing processes technology, company secrets, and so on.

At TSMC, every new worker has been led by a senior mentor. Its CEO, Mr. Chang-Chung-Mo actively builds the corporate culture of TSMC with 'vision, culture, strategy', as he believes that this world-class company needs a good honest culture. He also believes that in order for it to innovate continuously, it must first be a learning organisation. There is also a performance management and development system which ensures that employees strive to excel and learn in their jobs, or they will be eliminated. The reason why TSMC continues to accumulate and transfer organisational knowledge efficiently is attributed to the strong leadership of its CEO and his emphasis on 'learning'.

The learning development department continuously arranges various training programmes for employees. In 1998, 800 training programmes were scheduled for 35 000 employees, accumulating 230 000 hours in training. Employees' learning also extends outside the organisation as some undertake Masters Programmes at the university after work. At TSMC, learning is unavoidable and cultivates talent. TSMC believes that monetary allowance alone is insufficient to retain employees and focuses on providing employees with the chance of learning and development.

Success in the strategic execution of a business process or model may be accelerated with carefully chosen technologies. However, in the absence of good business processes and models, even the most sophisticated technologies cannot ensure corporate survival (Khosla and Pal, 2002). Therefore, the study explores the successful business model of real time enterprises (RTEs) in Taiwan through the case studies mentioned earlier.

The RTE is based upon the premise of getting the right information to the right people at the right time (Gartner Inc., 2006) in 'real time', that is without latency or delay. Enabling the RTE should lead to faster and better decisions, and enhanced agility and adaptability. RTE represents the future of knowledge enabled business processes, wherein digitised organisations interact with increasing and relentless speed and any specific 'event' results in a real-time 'response'. For instance, businesses such as Acer and TSMC are trying to minimise the delay between customer orders. The proponents of RTE technologies suggest that these technologies would help companies to learn to adapt, evolve and survive within increasingly uncertain business environments. RTEs are organisations that enable automation of processes spanning different systems, media and enterprise boundaries. RTEs also provide real time information to employees, customers, suppliers and partners and implement processes to ensure that all information is current and consistent across all systems, minimising batch and manual processes related to information. To achieve this, systems for a real time enterprise must be 'adaptable' to change and accept 'change as the process' (Khosla and Pal, 2002).

Applying Knowledge Community to Accelerate Corporate Innovation

When a community of practice (CoP) operation transforms into a knowledge community, firms are able to distribute knowledge like management strategy, through constant knowledge sharing. After implementing KM, firms will progress to the stage of organisational learning.

When firms realise how vital the speed of innovation and knowledge diffusion is to its competitive advantage, they use e-business to quickly develop knowledge communities and expedite the KM process. Firms use these knowledge communities to accelerate innovation as part of their corporate strategy.

Corporate knowledge communities are formed to achieve the operational goals of a firm. Regardless of whether a firm is virtual or physical, the main contribution of the knowledge community is not to make profits, but to create a learning organisational climate. This community aims to cultivate a culture which is willing to share and exchange experiences, and encourage innovation among employees.

Corporate Culture and KM

The reasons why KM is used only in slogans and not practised are because firms do not know what to do and how to do it. In order to implement KM, firms need to engage in organisational re-engineering which will incur additional costs, hence the easy way for most SMEs to introduce KM is to simply purchase group, e-document and engineering installation parameters

software. As a result, many KM investments are not in line with the firm's
vision and organisational operation, and become a consuming investment as it
is an inefficient use of resource allocation. Firms have a tendency to assume
that 'informationalisation' of knowledge is KM, however, they fail to realise
that KM is a combination of 'informationalisation' and corporate culture, and
not just 'informationalisation' alone. KM must also create corporate value.

Firms that do not combine strategic goals, corporate culture and culture of
KM but only choose to fulfil one or two components of KMS, will fail within
one or two years (Gartner Inc., 2006). The most vital component which
separates success from failure is the firm's corporate culture, as KM thrives on
a culture of 'trust and sharing' to succeed. If a firm's culture is bureaucratic, it
will be difficult to implement KM as information is tightly guarded. Hence,
the core solution will be to change the firm's culture and employees' behaviour
to a more open and sharing one.

Managers should not expect KMS software to solve knowledge integration
problems, as scholars and practitioners agree that a knowledge-sharing
supportive corporate culture must be present or nurtured for KM initiatives to
succeed. For example, TSMC have been successful in their KM initiatives as
their CEO encourages a supportive culture for knowledge-sharing.

The Most Profitable KM Business Model

As corporate resource is somewhat limited, companies should re-evaluate the
way they operate and consider adopting different management models and
implementing better leadership if they wish to cultivate optimum returns in
KM. Hence, it is evident that this management model is not only beneficial for
large firms' long-term development, but also for SMEs to establish the
foundation of KM competently.

The managers of both Taiwanese high-tech industries and SMEs have found
that focus on 'compound knowledge' will reap the most profits. However,
such a large volume of professional knowledge is often not shared with other
employees. This knowledge is often 'buried' and not applied, as it is acquired
behind closed doors and people with access to it are hard to contact. Therefore,
managers are striving to establish knowledge communities and learning
platforms to promote the rapid circulation of compound knowledge within the
organisation. This will help them provide better services to customers.

Necessary Strategic Actions for Taiwanese Industries
Under the Knowledge Economy

In the era of the knowledge economy, corporate strategy must focus on
expanding existing markets or creating new ones. Employing knowledge,
creativeness and the systematic use of economical commodities can produce

good returns, as with value innovation, technology innovation and value creation.

Different industries and companies possess different corporate values and KM accounts for those differences. For example, the corporate culture of the Acer group believes that their biggest asset is its people and focuses on retaining talent. On the other hand, TSMC adopts a Western thinking model of KM and focuses on retaining intellectual capital, that is manufacturing process technology or the standards for building new factories. This helps them speed up their processes. Through the analysis of the above case studies, there are three kinds of KM strategies as follows:

1. Systematisation strategy
   To reduce costs, firms should develop standardised KM processes, as it is a copyable and usable model which enables increasing numbers of users to reduce development costs and raise firms' profits. For example, Acer implemented KM systematisation and it became the global winning formula for the whole company.
2. Communitisation strategy
   To circulate company information and connect employees, firms should link technology and interpersonal networks to enable information to be accumulated and exchanged in a community. For example, TSMC's mentor system, IT and KMS.
3. Professionalisation strategy
   The strategy of TSMC is to provide the most sought after and valuable service in the market and cultivate professional talents in each field. Its KM strategy aims to establish standardisation, the foundation of common sharing, and to address professionalism and differentiation.

Knowledge comes in two forms – explicit and tacit knowledge. Firms can manage explicit knowledge through the information digitalisation model; however, managing tacit knowledge is a big problem. Firms can manage tacit knowledge on two levels – one is to guide employees through corporate culture and community and the other is through organisational norms.

In summary, there are three key elements of KM – content, community and technology. Firms must fuse the three elements together to create value-added knowledge. KM has paved the way for a new organisational style born under the e-management model – the 'knowledge community' that breaks through the old economic control system of a hierarchical organisation.

What Lies Ahead for Taiwanese SMEs?

In recent years, the increased protection of land, labour and environment in

Taiwan, and competition from low-cost products from developing countries, have caused SMEs to be disadvantaged internationally. The vitality of SMEs and their distribution systems with large enterprises have been the source of Taiwan's industrial flexibility and economic competitiveness. Therefore, if SMEs can upgrade and transform themselves efficiently, this will help increase the future competitive advantage of Taiwan. Possible approaches to upgrading and transformation are as follows:

1. Strengthen R&D in order to encourage innovation and industrial e-business, utilise the Internet to increase value-added products and services, and provide complete services.
2. Possible transformation strategies include transformation to a knowledge intensity manufacturing and service industry, and developing a link between creativity and the local characteristic industry.
3. Apply KM to construct a learning team and exchange platform. This will cultivate a collaborative learning culture and environment, and encourage team members to share knowledge, experience and learning abilities.

The aims of upgrading and transformation are as follows:

1. Cultivate individual, public and team knowledge.
2. Transform tacit knowledge to explicit knowledge.
3. Cultivate a team cooperation culture.
4. Cultivate an indispensable system.
5. Facilitate the exchange of successful experiences.

How Does Taiwan Prepare Itself for the Knowledge Economy?

In June 2000, the World Congress on Information Technology held in Taiwan attracted many global information leaders, with the USA leading the pack. The USA is economically advanced as it is backed up by sophisticated IT, and industrial and commercial management which encourages free competition, law and policy and a sound financial system. This spurs firms to venture out and strive for innovation to fulfil the 'American Dream'.

At the World Congress, Lester Thurow, a professor at the Massachusetts Institute of Technology, said:

> In the past five years, Taiwan has not been influenced by the Asian financial storm or faced with a long-term economic decline like Japan. However, the average income of its citizens is only a half of the USA and Japan. This is because although Taiwan has welcomed the knowledge economy, it failed to truly embrace it. The new knowledge economy, fuelled by IT, promises an alluring 'monetary vision', but firms need to create value by applying knowledge. In order for Taiwan to fully

embrace the knowledge economy, its government needs to cultivate a social organisation to inspire the growth of technology, education and creativity. It also needs to enhance educational resources to allow low income earners to have an equal opportunity in the knowledge economy. Firms must also apply digital technology to transform into a KM organisation. (World Congress on Information Technology, 2000a, 2000b)

The civil advancement of human history also applies to the advancement in KM, as both are developed through the interaction and accumulation of experiences and knowledge. The following section attributes the emphasis on KM to the external competitive and internal organisational environments.

Two Sides of Thinking for Knowledge Management

In order for firms to maintain external competitiveness, they have to create more value by shortening their knowledge cycle of customers and applying 'knowledge leveraging'. On the other hand, a competitive internal environment is nurtured through the 'knowledge sharing' of employees and fostering an open organisation where patented knowledge is shared throughout. KM stems from 'knowledge sharing' and regards organisational and social cultures as important. Members of firms must learn to trust each other and cultivate a willingness to develop and share knowledge, and create equality and responsibility among employees. This will create more value and profits for firms, and promote social knowledge sharing to eliminate privilege and achieve social equality and justice. The knowledge economy led by IT will bridge the digital gap and lessen unfair opportunities. Through knowledge sharing, it will discourage the monopoly of companies and bridge the gap between rich and poor.

CONCLUSIONS AND RECOMMENDATIONS

Conclusions

Organisational KM effectively records, sorts, stores, shares and updates experiences and knowledge throughout the organisation. Future firms must effectively manage various forms of knowledge in organisations and create a knowledge community and learning platform to facilitate sharing among employees, customers, suppliers and partners. It is impossible to merely focus on managing capital, equipment, products and employees any longer. Effective KM depends on KM strategies and business models, thus high-tech industries and SMEs have to create effective knowledge sharing strategies and a simple integrated KM business model for their employees.

Internet commercialisation opens a new era of digital and knowledge economies, and Taiwanese high-tech industries are transforming themselves into enterprises with strategic assets like knowledge innovation and value creation. However, traditional firms like SMEs face the pressure for transformation or risk being on the brink of destruction. This study was carried out to help industries maintain competitiveness and sustainable management in the knowledge economy. The proposed strategic actions for high-tech industry and SMEs in the knowledge economy are as follows:

1. Develop organisational innovation and knowledge sharing strategies.
2. Establish a knowledge community to facilitate knowledge flow and sharing.
3. Encourage employees to share knowledge and approach the sources of innovation information.
4. Accelerate organisational learning and diffusion of innovation knowledge.
5. Strengthen 'partnerships' for firms, suppliers and customers and establish an efficient interdependent model.
6. Establish an Internet foundational structure for 'complementary strategic alliance'.
7. Strengthen 'leadership mechanisms' through strategic outsourcing to reap the most management benefits.
8. Accelerate the circulation of value-added information to strengthen knowledge creation.

KM is an unavoidable trend as it is the future of management. Taiwanese SMEs face the future challenge and entry into the knowledge economy, and have to create a KM business model to nurture a suitable learning environment for sharing knowledge.

Recommendations

Suggestions for high-tech industries and SMEs
Different sizes of industries require different KM models and strategies. The study has proposed an integrated model that combines the 'knowledge community' and 'e-learning platform' to share knowledge, and RTEs to provide real-time information to employees, customers, suppliers and partners to ensure that all information is current and consistent across all systems.

A crucial aspect of KM is to share the available (and private) knowledge between employees, managers, departments and so on. The degree of knowledge sharing also depends on the organisational culture. One can share knowledge through projects, fact sheets, job rotations, internal secondments and lunchtime meetings. However, it is important that the correct knowledge gets to the right person at the right time.

Suggestions for government policies
To assist SMEs to upgrade and transform themselves in the knowledge economy, the government should provide sound infrastructure, and relinquish unnecessary control and red tape to allow firms to develop creativity and vitality. The government should also formulate rules for fair competition, to ensure that the big firms do not gain an unfair advantage and weaken the survival of SMEs. Additionally, the government can assist the SMEs with capital, technology, talent and information.

For example, the government can raise capital by creating an 'entrepreneur and investment fund' to assist innovative SMEs with developing potential, and help establish an R&D firm. It can assist with technology advancements through the SBIR plan, and provide a direction for industrial and technological development. And lastly, the government can ensure the availability of talent by establishing a professional database of university professors and give SMEs the option of seeking consultation on technology and KM. SMEs can also consult retired managers for advice on such issues.

IMPLICATIONS FOR INTERNATIONAL MANAGERS

In the wake of the knowledge economy, international managers need to recognise the value of knowledge; transform tacit knowledge to explicit knowledge; commit managers to fostering KM initiatives; create value-added knowledge and distribute it efficiently; and to absorb external knowledge to the firm's advantage.

Nine strategic approaches are proposed for the development and competition of high-tech industries and SMEs under the knowledge economy. They are as follows:

1. Focus on core expertise.
2. Emphasise management innovation.
3. Participate in international technology cooperation and the industrial network.
4. Build a learning organisation to cultivate a 'knowledge sharing' culture.
5. Implement business processes re-engineering.
6. Encourage intrapreneuring.
7. Enhance product and process innovation.
8. Plunge into R&D efficiently.
9. Fully embrace IT.

International managers face fierce global competition in the era of knowledge economies. It is imperative that they manage KM effectively through the facilitation of innovation and entrepreneurship, and increase the competitiveness of high-tech industries and SMEs.

REFERENCES

Acer Inc. (2006), 27 April, 2006, http://global.acer.com/
Army Research Office Washington (2006), 'SBIR Program', 28 April, 2006, http://www.aro.army.mil/arowash/rt/sbir/sbir.htm
Council for Economic Planning and Development (2002), *Challenge 2008: The Six-year National Development Plan in Taiwan*, Taiwan, ROC: Taiwanese Government Information Office.
Department of Industrial Technology (1998), *Small Business Innovation Research*, Taiwan: Taiwanese Department of Industrial Technology.
Gartner Inc. (2006), 'The Real Time Enterprise', 28 April, 2006, http://rte.gartner.com/
IBM (2006), 'Lotus Software', 2 May, 2006, http://www-306.ibm.com/software/lotus/
Institute for Information Industry (2006), 'Our Services', 28 April, 2006, http://www.iii.org.tw/english/
International Data Centre Taiwan (2006), 28 April, 2006, http://www.idc.com.tw/default_eng.htm
Khosla, V. and M. Pal (2002), 'Real Time Enterprises: A Continuous Migration Approach', 2 May, 2006, http://www.manyworlds.com/index2.aspx?from=/authorCOs.aspx&firstname=Vinod&lastname=Khosla
KHS (2006), 2 May, 2006, http://world.khsmusic.com/front/bin/home.phtml
Microsoft (2006), 'Knowledge Management', 30 April, 2006 http://www.microsoft.com/taiwan/business/km/
Nissan (2006), 30 April, 2006, http://www.nissan.com.tw/
O'Donnell, D., G. Porter, D. McGuire, T.N. Garavan, M. Heffernan and P. Cleary (2003), 'Creating Intellectual Capital: A Habermasian Community of Practice (CoP) Introduction', *Journal of European Industrial Training*, **27**(2–4), 80–87.
Small and Medium Enterprises Administration (2003), 'Foreword', 28 April, 2006, http://www.moeasmea.gov.tw/Eng/index.asp
Taiwan Semiconductor Manufacturing Company Limited (2006), 28 April, 2006, www.tsmc.com.tw.
UMC (2006), 2 May, 2006, www.umc.com.tw
World Congress on Information Technology (2000a), 'Lester Thurow', 30 April, 2006, http://www.polaris.com.tw/3good/news/topic/t890615_8.htm
World Congress on Information Technology (2000b), 2 May, 2006, http://www.worldcongress2000.org/
Yang, J.-T. (2004), 'Job-related Knowledge Sharing: Comparative Case Studies', *Journal of Knowledge Management*, **8**(3), 118–26.

7. Religion, caste, language and region: contributions to knowledge management in India

Simon Best and Rajni Kakkar

INTRODUCTION

Much has been written about the emergence of China as the place to do business. Recognised as having the fastest growing economy of any developing nation, it gets the attention it deserves (Kumar and Worm, 2004). However, China is not alone in having a fast growing economy amongst developing nations. India, too, is developing rapidly economically yet it does not match China in terms of attention. Although material on India is growing, there is still a significant gap between studies on China and studies on India (Pearson and Chatterjee, 2001).

The lack of attention on India does not do justice to those seeking to undertake a business venture in India. India has the second fastest growing economy and is overall the fifth largest economy in the world (Fusilier and Durlabhji, 2001; Nikam et al., 2004). Consequently, with the world's second largest population of over one billion, India is becoming a major nation in the global economy (Bever et al., 2005; Kumar, 2004). With GDP growth of 8 per cent and expected growth of 5 per cent per annum, it is anticipated that India will remain a growth nation for the foreseeable future (Economist.com, 2005). The World Bank has forecast India to be the fourth largest economy by 2020 (Budhwar, 2001). This makes India an extremely attractive country to invest in and participate in business activities now, for non-Indian firms and businesses. This alone indicates that business would benefit from significantly more studies on India, especially in the field of knowledge management (KM).

When doing business in India, apart from having to deal with the legal, political and bureaucratic systems, the cultural aspect also has to be considered. Anyone seeking to do business in India should understand the various aspects that construct the national identity as well as the individual identity of India and Indians (Fusilier and Durlabhji, 2001; Gopalan and

Rivera, 1997; Johnson, 2004). A lack of understanding about the culture mores of India can be a liability (Johanson and Johanson, 2004; Wilson, 2004).

This chapter seeks to diminish the gap in studies between India and China. In particular the chapter looks at the effect culture has at an individual level on sharing or managing knowledge and information. The methodology is presented first, followed by a discussion of the data collected. This data is then analysed and conclusions from the discussion and analysis are presented. The limitations of the study and the implications for international managers conclude this chapter.

LITERATURE REVIEW

As the first non-white country to gain its independence from colonial rule, India has developed slowly. Having been regularly invaded by foreigners over the centuries, it eventually obtained its independence from the British in 1947. This has given India a rich and varied cultural heritage (Budhwar, 2001; Nikam et al., 2004). However, this rich and varied culture has been the source of many of India's problems over its history (Hooker, 2003). India is an immense country with many variations in terms of religion, caste, language and region, amongst other things (Desai, 1999; Kumar, 2004; Singh, 1990). It has been considered as one of the most culturally diverse countries in the world (Gannon, 2004).

Several studies on culture have been undertaken that describe national cultures along various dimensions. These dimensions give an insight and a degree of predictability to a nation's behaviour and suggest a degree of homogenisation amongst the inhabitants. However, there are other aspects to culture as it consists of a series of beliefs about individual behaviour (Kumar and Worm, 2004). These beliefs are influenced by a number of different aspects relating to the social dimensions of the individual. In India, these dimensions can be collated into four broad categories: religion, caste, language and region. Although there have been many significant changes in India's culture since independence, these four categories still influence daily life and business (Johnson, 2004, p. 121). These four categories form the foundation of this study.

Religion

As a country that initiated three of the world's major religions, Hinduism, Buddhism and Sikhism, religious variation is a significant characteristic of life in India (Budhwar, 2001; Gannon, 2004). There are six recognised main religious groups. Hindus form the largest sect with some 80 per cent of the population, Muslims make up approximately 11 per cent of the population, Christians and Sikhs constitute 2 per cent with Jains and Buddhists making up the balance (Budhwar, 2001; Gannon, 2004). Communal animosity based on historical religious issues often affects interaction between individuals.

Caste

Although the caste system officially does not exist, it still permeates throughout India, predominantly in the Hindu community (Fusilier and Durlabhji, 2001). Linked to the Hindu religion essentially, the caste system is a hierarchy of positions which determines literally one's position within the community (Brown, 1985; Gannon, 2004; Overland, 2004). People who belong to a particular group will tend to act positively to members of the same group and discriminate against those who are not members (Gopalan and Rivera, 1997; Sinha and Kanungo, 1997). For example, some Hindus of a higher caste will still undertake a cleansing ritual after interacting with a person of a lower caste (Overland, 2004). This naturally has a restricting effect on relationships in that some people who still follow the caste system may seek to avoid interaction with people of a lower caste.

Language

Language can disunite people in a way that no other cultural aspect can (Gannon, 2004). Not being able to effectively communicate inevitably leads to misunderstandings. The constitution of India recognises 16 different languages, of which Hindi and English are the two most common (Budhwar, 2001). Apart from these recognised languages, there are several hundred other indigenous languages and dialects spread across the country (Fusilier and Durlabhji, 2001). This leads to some difficulties in determining the most appropriate language to use when communicating.

Region

Apart from language and religion, India can be divided into several regions based on geographical location (Brown, 1985; Hooker, 2003). The main regional divide runs across a North/South aspect (Gannon, 2004). One factor of this North/South aspect is that the South was less wrecked by war and invasion than the North. However, another divide lies across an East/West aspect, again based on substantial geographical differences (Budhwar, 2001).

These differences, as in most other countries, sometimes lead to a type of discrimination.

There have been many studies on the cultural differences that exist between various nations (for example, Hofstede, 2001) and, as a consequence, most studies on cultural issues tend to be external comparative studies between nations. Yet there exist within most countries cultural differences that can have a profound effect on the way KM occurs. For an expatriate doing business in India, it is as important to understand the similarities that hold the country together as it is to understand the differences that pull India apart (Fusilier and Durlabhji, 2001).

As a developing nation, there are no long established rules to treat knowledge as a resource (Banerjee and Bhardwaj, 2002). KM and sharing also face a cultural difficulty in India because information is often accumulated by individuals who are reticent to share the knowledge for different reasons (Banerjee and Bhardwaj, 2002). Knowledge is often collected for personal use rather than for sharing and integrating solutions (Kumar and Worm, 2004). However, there is limited research on KM and sharing in India primarily as it is a developing nation. In particular, there has been very little research in the way these four categories, religion, caste, language and region affect the sharing or management of knowledge and information. This study aims to consider some of the internal cultural differences and the impact they have on an expatriate manager in India in terms of managing or sharing knowledge and information.

METHODOLOGY

The data collected within this chapter has been sourced from a number of different approaches over a significant period of time. Both authors have been engaged in business activities in India as well as within Indian communities outside of India with a combined total of 20 years experience. As a result, the authors have had a number of experiences relating to cultural diversity and its impact on the sharing or management of knowledge and information. Using these experiences as a starting point for this study, they have been supplemented by a number of informal discussions with 28 business managers from a variety of industries. The data from these informal discussions has been presented in a series of anecdotal stories. The discussions focused on the issues of sharing or managing knowledge and information in a multi-cultural setting. The discussion was placed for the most part in a conversational context during and after business meetings. Where specific information was sought, specific questions were asked directly.

These informal discussions were then supplemented with a more formal approach to provide a degree of academic rigour to the study. Seventy-five business managers across a variety of industry sectors throughout India were chosen. The purpose of this was to gain as broad a response relating to the four categories as possible and eliminate any possible cultural biases that may have been found in a specific industry. They were asked about the cultural aspects of managing and sharing knowledge. The people chosen were approached based on their current or previous relationships with the authors. This use of insider relationships made it much easier to gain the trust and cooperation of the participants. This method of snowball sampling has some advantages and has been used in similar types of studies (Siu, 1996; Von Glinow et al., 2002). Of this sample, 59 interviews were usable, the others being either incomplete or the questions were not clearly answered. The participants were asked about their own religion, caste, language and region as well as their industry group. Not all the respondents provided the information. The answers are presented in Table 7.1.

Table 7.1   Participants' affiliations

Industry	%	Religion	%	Caste	%	Language	%	Region	%
Retail	1	Hindu	55	Brahmins	28	Hindi	48	North	39
Government	2	Muslim	10	Kshatriyas	30	English	21	West	21
Services	21	Sikh	15	Vaisyas	2	Kashmiri	1	East	19
Manufacturing	1	Christian	4	Sudras	0	Tamil	1	South	9
Media	1	Not stated	16	Not stated	40	Bengali	15	Not stated	12
IT	14					Telugu	1		
Medicine	2					Haryani	1		
Education	4					Not stated	12		
Not stated	54								

Each participant was asked if there were people from a particular religion that they were comfortable with when sharing or managing knowledge and information. The question was repeated for the other three categories: caste, language and region. If they answered 'yes', they were then asked what that religion, caste, language or region was and why they felt that way. A similar question also probed whether they had difficulty sharing or managing knowledge or information with people from a particular religion. As with the first four questions, this was repeated for caste, language or region. Again, they were also asked which religion, caste, language and region that was and why. The data from the informal interviews is discussed first, followed by the data collected in a more formal method.

FINDINGS

Informal Interviews

With a growing well-educated and well-travelled middle class, many of the traditional cultural aspects of India appear to be vanishing. However, based on some of the experiences of the authors, some aspects of India's culture continue to affect sharing or managing of knowledge and information. One telling experience from one of the authors was after thoroughly explaining a process for sharing and accessing information to a group of managers. During the presentation, all the members of the group appeared to be working and interacting with each other without any difficulties. Following the presentation, while relaxing, one of the authors was approached and told by one of the participants that they were certain that a particular person would engage in activities that would undermine his position by not cooperating. After some discussion the only rational explanation that emerged was that this other person was from a region noted for its shady and uncooperative characters. 'They are very ambitious from that region and do not like to help others succeed' was the reason given. In another incident, progress was slow on a particular project because of the perception of one person who believed that another was withholding or slowing information due to the different caste. Although there was no evidence of this, it still affected the progress of the project. Both authors have experienced similar situations where the sharing or managing of knowledge and information has derailed because of an unanticipated clash over religion, caste, language or regional differences.

During the informal discussions, several of the participants indicated that they had difficulty with different groups of people. Amongst one group of participants a common theme developed. This group, all from the Mumbai region, on hearing one of the authors had business dealings with people from Gujarat state were concerned because people from this state, while very good at business, were considered to be very unethical. When asked about sharing information, the participants expressed that they would have a reluctance to do so. One participant, a manager from a manufacturing business, stated that 'people from this state will tell you anything, they will make up information to gain an advantage'.

Other stories of fear of non-cooperation were common amongst the participants in terms of sharing knowledge and information. A manager in the hospitality industry described how he believed he had been thwarted in a promotion because of caste. He claimed that he was deliberately kept in the dark so that he would not apply for the position. In the discussions, there was a tendency by the participants to focus on negative aspects of their experiences of sharing or managing knowledge or information. All the participants felt they had been a victim at some stage of religious, caste, language or regional differences. Although the data was essentially anecdotal, it reflects on the ongoing experiences of the authors.

Formal Interviews

The data from the informal interviews has been collated into six tables that consider the responses across a number of measurements. Table 7.2 looks at the individual responses to each category and identifies the specific choices made in relation to who the respondents were comfortable with when sharing or managing knowledge and information.

Table 7.2   Overall individual responses – comfortable sharing or managing knowledge and information

Religion (20.70%)	%	Caste (17.20%)	%	Language (66.70%)	%	Region (32.20%)	%
Hindu	18.39	Brahmins	5.74	Hindi	34.48	North	16.09
Not disclosed	2.30	Kshatriyas	8.04	English	20.68	East	3.45
None	79.31	Vaisyas	3.44	Bengali	14.9	South	4.59
		Sudras	0	Telugu	2.30	West	1.20
		None	82.75	Punjabi	2.30		
				Tamil	1.20	Punjab	6.89
				None	33.33	Rajasthan	1.20
						Uttar Pradesh	1.20
						Tamil Nadu	1.20
						Bangladesh	1.20
						Pakistan	1.20
						None	67.89

Table 7.2 shows the breakdown of the responses to each of the first four questions as they were asked. The percentage total across the four categories exceeds 100 per cent because a number of respondents chose more than one category as being comfortable. The table also provides a breakdown of the respondents' specific answers relating to the four categories. It should also be noted that several people chose more than one language and more than one region when identifying the specific language or region.

The data suggests that the respondents are more comfortable sharing and managing knowledge and information with people from a particular language group, with Hindi emerging as the language most people are comfortable with. This reflects the fact that Hindi is the most common and widespread language (Budhwar, 2001; Fusilier and Durlabhji, 2001). Given that proportion, India has the largest English speaking population within the Asia Pacific region (Budhwar, 2001; Hooker, 2003), even though English is not the first language, it has the second highest ranking where a language was chosen. However, a substantial number of participants stated that there was not a language that they felt particularly comfortable with when sharing or managing knowledge and information. Given that two thirds felt more comfortable with a particular language is significant, in that it implies that sharing or managing knowledge or information would be better performed when the participants are using a language that they prefer. Therefore it could be argued that language does play an important part in the process of sharing or managing knowledge and information in India.

Almost a third of the respondents stated they are more comfortable with people from a particular region. This is to be expected as historically, there has been a degree of estrangement between various regions within India (Gannon, 2004). The regions chosen are presented based on the responses of the participants. By including Punjab, Rajasthan and Uttar Pradesh, the data indicates that an overwhelming majority are comfortable sharing or managing knowledge and information with people from the Northern regions. Two people chose countries, rather than regions within India. However the majority indicated that they did not necessarily feel comfortable with people from a particular region. This suggests that while region may affect the sharing or managing knowledge and information, it does not play as significant a role as language.

Although religion ranked third, 20 per cent or one fifth of the respondents felt that they are more comfortable sharing or managing knowledge and information with someone from a specific religion. Given the dominance of Hinduism (Budhwar, 2001; Gannon, 2004), it is to be expected that the respondents indicate that they are more comfortable with people from Hinduism. Despite this, such a high rate suggests that religion may influence the sharing or managing knowledge and information.

The last category, caste, implies with its low score that it does not necessarily influence sharing or managing knowledge and information to the same extent as the other three categories. With just over 17 per cent, it could be argued that caste is less of an issue when the sharing or managing knowledge and information than the other three. Of the castes chosen, the respondents were most comfortable with those from the Kshatriyas caste. None of the respondents indicated that they were comfortable with the lowest ranked caste, which is Sudras.

Table 7.3 looks at the individual responses to each category and identifies the specific choices made in relation to who the respondents had difficulties with when sharing or managing knowledge and information.

Table 7.3   Overall individual responses – difficulties sharing or managing knowledge and information

Religion (35.60%)	%	Caste (17.20%)	%	Language (54.00%)	%	Region (14.90%)	%
Muslims	22.98	Brahmins	3.45	Hindi	5.74	South	4.59
Christians	8.04	Kshatriyas	0	English	3.45	Bihar	4.59
Hindu	4.59	Vaisyas	0	South Indian	3.45	Gujarat	2.30
None	64.36	Sudras	13.79	Bengali	1.45	Kashmir	1.20
		None	82.75	Bihari	2.30	Orissa	1.20
				Urdu	1.20	West Bengal	1.20
				Any language except own	36.78	None	85.05
				None	45.97		

Table 7.3 shows the breakdown of the responses to each of the second set of four questions as they were asked. The percentage total across the four categories exceeds 100 per cent because a number of respondents chose more than one category as having difficulties. The table also provides a breakdown of the respondents' specific answers relating to the four categories. It should also be noted that several people chose more than one religion and more than one language when identifying the specific religion or language.

As with Table 7.2, language retains the highest ranking and caste the lowest. However, religion and region have reversed positions in Table 7.3 when compared to Table 7.2. Furthermore, religion has a significantly higher number of respondents in Table 7.3 as affecting the sharing or managing of knowledge and information than in Table 7.2.

As in Table 7.2, over half the respondents stated that they had difficulty sharing or managing knowledge and information with people of certain language groups. As stated earlier, the diversity of languages within India would inevitably lead to a degree of difficulty in terms of the sharing or managing of knowledge and information where there was no common language between the participants. This is supported by the result that when defining the languages specifically, the majority (36.78 per cent) of those indicating a difficulty stated that any language other than their own would create difficulties for them. Furthermore, most of the languages specifically mentioned tend to be minority languages (Budhwar, 2001). As indicated above, the data suggests that language would affect the sharing or managing of knowledge and information.

The second highest ranking category is religion. There is a significant number who felt they had difficulty sharing or managing knowledge and information with people of a particular religious background. With over a third indicating that they had difficulties with people from a particular religion, this suggests that another person's religious affiliations could be an impediment to sharing or managing knowledge and information. Of the religions identified, Muslims were singled out as the ones that difficulties arise from. Although India is a religiously plural society, there has been a level of animosity between some religions (Brown, 1985) and the responses probably reflect some people's attitudes.

Both caste and region had significantly low responses, neither above 18 per cent. Such a low response rate suggests that these two categories are significantly less likely to affect the sharing or managing of knowledge and information. However it is interesting to note the Sudras caste is singled out in Table 7.2. No one felt comfortable with people from this caste, and in Table 7.3 it was the caste that the respondents encountered the most difficulty with.

In summarising Tables 7.2 and 7.3, the data implies that one or more of the categories affect the sharing or managing of knowledge and information. From Table 7.2, people are more likely to feel comfortable with people of a specific language first, a specific region next and a specific religion thirdly. In Table 7.3, the respondents are more likely to have difficulty sharing or managing knowledge and information with people of a particular language first and a particular religion secondly. The next pair of tables looks at the combinations of responses across the categories.

Table 7.4 presents the participants' various combinations of responses about feeling comfortable according to their choices across all four categories. The table shows the number of people who chose only one category with which they were comfortable and the various combinations of each of the categories, through to those that chose all four categories and finally to those that did not chose a category.

There are four significant factors that emerge from this table. First, it is significant to note that the respondents who chose only one category chose language which ranked highly at 25 per cent, while the other three categories ranked very low as single choices by comparison. The second factor is that 24 per cent indicated that there were no specific categories that they felt comfortable with when sharing or managing knowledge and information. The third factor is that language and region categories combined also rated

Table 7.4   Combinations of answers – comfortable sharing or managing knowledge and information

Categories	%
Religion only	0
Caste only	1.15
Language only	25.29
Region only	4.6
Religion and caste	2.3
Religion and language	8.05
Religion and region	0
Religion, caste and language	3.45
Religion, caste and region	0
Religion, language and region	4.6
Religion, caste, language and region	1.15
Caste and language	3.45
Caste and region	1.15
Caste, language and region	4.6
Language and region	16.09
None	24.14

significantly as a factor. Although not as high as language alone, the combination of language and region was the second highest. This reflects the analysis of the data in Table 7.2, where the two highest categories were language and region. This suggests and supports earlier contentions that when feeling comfortable with people while sharing or managing knowledge and information, there is a tendency by the respondents to prefer people of a particular language and region over the other categories. Furthermore this choice is either as individual categories or as a combination of language and region categories.

The fourth significant factor is that the total number of people who chose two or more categories is 45 per cent. This is almost double the number of respondents who chose none. It is also greater than the number of people who chose only one category. The data suggests that the majority of people are influenced by at least one category and almost half are influenced by more than two categories when feeling comfortable sharing or managing knowledge and information.

Table 7.5 follows on from Table 7.4 as it provides the combination of answers across the categories based on the difficulties the respondents have. As with Table 7.4, there are a number of significant factors that emerge. First, there are two similarities between Table 7.4 and Table 7.5 in that both tables

Table 7.5   Combinations of answers – difficulties sharing or managing knowledge and information

Categories	%
Religion only	4.59
Caste only	0
Language only	20.68
Region only	0
Religion and caste	0
Religion and language	11.49
Religion and region	3.44
Religion, caste and language	5.74
Religion, caste and region	0
Religion, language and region	3.44
Religion, caste, language and region	6.89
Caste and language	4.59
Caste and region	0
Caste, language and region	0
Language and region	1.14
None	37.93

report the language only category and none as the two highest combinations of categories. However, the ranking in Table 7.5 of those who chose none is higher than in Table 7.4 and higher than language in both tables, while the language only choice is slightly lower than Table 7.3. The religion and language combination in Table 7.5 has replaced the language and region combination in Table 7.4 as the third most significant category, which also reflects the data presented in Table 7.4. The next significant factor is that in Table 7.5, people reporting no difficulties in sharing or managing knowledge and information constitutes the largest single grouping across both tables. This suggests that just over a third of the respondents are likely to not have any difficulties when sharing or managing knowledge and information, which is a significant number.

A significant number of respondents in Table 7.5 have chosen two or more categories as having difficulty sharing or managing knowledge or information. While not as high as Table 7.4, 37 per cent still represents a substantial proportion of the respondents. It is higher than those who indicated difficulty with only one category and almost equal to those who chose none. This suggests that at least one third would have more than one reason to find it difficult to share or manage knowledge and information.

By summarising these two tables, the data suggests that most people have

Table 7.6   Respondents' reasons – comfortable managing and sharing knowledge and information

Religion	'because we think alike and are more flexible' (6) 'I get on with them well' (5) 'we understand each other better' (2) 'very opened minded' 'they do not want to convert others'
Caste	'we are a very honest lot and there is an affinity between us' 'full of life and willing to take risks' 'knowledge level and better understanding of society and economy' 'as the roots are similar the mentality may match' 'they know the basics of business from childhood' 'they are honest and dedicated to their work' 'educated and cultured' 'there is a certain affinity'
Language	'easier to get work done' (4) 'there is no work with out communication' 'it is my language' (4) 'I can understand them better' 'they are the most acceptable languages in India' 'it is a universal language' (7) 'easier to understand' 'I can express myself better'
Region	'because they are very enterprising' 'because we have common traits' 'people are hardworking' (4) 'it is easier to get work done' 'there is a comfort level which can not be explained' 'I empathise with them' 'I identify with this region' 'we share the same environment' 'we understand each other' 'a very down to earth people' 'a lot of traits I can identify with' 'same attitude towards life' 'their attitude, mentality, ethics match mine' (3)

either two or more categories that they are either comfortable with or have difficulty with or both when sharing or managing knowledge and information. Table 7.5 indicates that the majority chose language only as their second choice as they are likely to have no preference in terms of feeling comfortable. The combination of language and region in Table 7.4 is the most popular combination. In Table 7.5, the majority chose none as the category and language was the second choice in terms of having difficulties when sharing or managing knowledge and information. Language and religion were the highest ranking combination. The last pair of tables look at the reasons why the respondents felt comfortable or had difficulties when sharing or managing knowledge and information.

In terms of religion, the responses in Table 7.6 centred on the concept of affinity, flexibility and understanding of each other. Caste also indicated a degree of affinity and understanding of each other as the reason for being comfortable with that caste. Language responses focused on the need to understand, with most people saying that the language they are most comfortable with is English because it is a universal language. Region had similar answers to religion and caste in that people felt comfortable with people they had an affinity with. It is also noted that many of the comments related to the ability to work hard. In general, the respondents tended to use emotive language to describe those they were comfortable with when sharing or managing knowledge and information in the three categories: religion, caste and region. However, much less emotive language is used when explaining why they are comfortable with certain language groups.

Table 7.7 shows the respondents' answers to why they had difficulties with people from particular religions, castes, languages or regions. The responses are diametrically opposite to the answers in Table 7.6. Essentially, the responses centre on a degree of rejection of those people in those particular categories. The same emotive language is used to describe their feelings about people from certain religious, caste and region categories and less emotive language with the language category.

In summarising Tables 7.6 and 7.7, the data implies that in terms of religion, caste and region, the respondents hold strong and emotive views as to why they may be either comfortable or have difficulties when sharing or managing knowledge and information. In Table 7.6, the respondents show a degree of connectivity. Alternatively, Table 7.7 indicates a desire to disconnect and avoid sharing. However, they tend to take a more pragmatic approach when describing their reasons for either feeling comfortable or having difficulties within the language category.

Overall, the data contained in these tables give a substantial indication that there are a number of cultural factors that affect the sharing or managing of knowledge and information in India. Comparing the overall data, there is

Table 7.7   Respondents' reasons – difficulties managing and sharing knowledge and information

Religion	'they are defensive and negative' 'not very many pursue higher education' 'not all that pushy' 'they are violent and aggressive' 'there is a religious gap' 'they are always trying to create trouble' 'some are very good but most of them mean trouble' 'they are fanatics and will not listen to anyone so easily' 'they are a stubborn lot' 'they are a lazy lot' 'they do not try to understand or analyse anything logically' 'a very rigid lot' (2) 'very destructive people' 'they are very close minded'
Caste	'because they do not want to educate themselves and compete on merit' 'always wanting an easy way out' (3) 'the government spoils them' 'in spite of getting privileges they are greedy for more' 'very narrow minded and tend to create trouble' 'exposure to the educated world is limited' 'they feel more superior to us and makes us feel uncomfortable' 'I was taught from childhood ... not to have any interaction with them'
Language	'difficult to work where language barriers exist' (3) 'practical difficulties arise' 'I cannot communicate in a language that I do not understand' 'it is difficult sharing knowledge when it is not your language' 'it is tough sharing information' 'I feel shaky when using that language' 'makes sharing information difficult' 'lost if I can not understand'
Region	'crooks thrive in that area' 'it is so corrupt' 'they lie through their teeth' 'it is a backward region' 'they are really backward people'

one final statistic to emerge. Of all the respondents that took part, only 16.05 per cent stated that there was no particular category they were more comfortable with, and there was no particular category that they had difficulty with when sharing or managing knowledge and information. This implies that the balance, 83.95 per cent, would either be comfortable with someone of particular characteristics or have difficulty if someone had particular characteristics or both. The implications prove that on an individual level, culture affects the concept of knowledge and how it is shared and managed (Pauleen and Murphy, 2005).

DISCUSSION

The emergence of the information and knowledge age has led to the need for generated information and knowledge to be transferred between people much more easily than in the past (Banerjee, 2003). The cultural backgrounds of people in developing countries often have the consequence of reducing the effectiveness of certain activities that are not similarly affected in developed countries (Chen et al., 2006). Furthermore, the success of a KM process is affected directly by cultural values (McDermott and O'Dell, 2001). The focus of this study has been to discover if cultural factors at an individual level impact on the sharing or managing of knowledge and information. The data suggests that this is the case.

As practitioners, the authors have learnt that the need to understand the subtleties of culture and its impact on the sharing or managing of knowledge and information at a functional level is critical. Relying on broad national definitions of culture at a functional level can be unhelpful. For example, although Indians may be presented as culturally collective (Hofstede, 2001; Sinha and Kanungo, 1997), this collectivistic behaviour by Indians may be limited to those who share similar traits and beliefs as Indians tend to demonstrate both collectivistic and individualistic behaviours (Kumar and Worm, 2004, p. 313; Sinha and Kanungo, 1997, p. 95). This study seems to indicate that, while we have not compared the responses of the participants to their own beliefs, they have particular biases that affect the sharing and managing of knowledge and information. A judgement has been made by the respondents on the basis of their framework of experience and fundamental personality (Mussweiler and Englich, 2005; Stumpf and Dunbar, 1991; Westaby, 2005). Furthermore, given the substantial variation of cultures within India, it is to be expected that a degree of social categorisation occurs in which people strongly identify groups to which they belong or do not belong to (Sawyer et al., 2006). This social categorisation creates restrictions which reduce communication (ibid.). The data across the four categories indicates that there is the chance of a significant reduction in the communication process across the various categories. This could have a limiting effect on how knowledge and information are shared or managed.

Indians tend to hold deeply entrenched views about one's status in the Indian community (Walsham, 2002). This is demonstrated in the reasons given for choosing a particular category. For example, although caste was not seen as influencing the sharing or managing of knowledge and information to the same level as the other categories, there was an element of status in the responses. Statements about the educational and cognitive abilities of people in certain castes indicated a degree of status. This is repeated to a lesser degree across the religion and region categories.

Cultural differences at all levels profoundly affect cognition (Pauleen and Murphy, 2005). This in turn can affect the sharing or managing of knowledge and information. The emotive language used when explaining why the respondents either felt comfortable or had difficulty with people of certain backgrounds gives a clear indication of the potential difficulties. One aspect of sharing or managing knowledge is the level of honesty and trust needed to ensure that the knowledge or information is viable and limits ambiguity (Banerjee and Bhardwaj, 2002; Kumar and Worm, 2004). Honesty and trust were notable comments by the respondents as to why they may be more comfortable or have difficulties with certain categories of people. If the levels of honesty/dishonesty and trust/distrust are as high as indicated in this study, then the sharing or managing of knowledge and information becomes complex and ambiguous.

Another influencing factor is the transition from traditional to modern that has occurred within Indian business processes. At times, this has created dualities that are difficult to follow and understand (Chatterjee and Pearson, 2000). This is reflected where some respondents indicated that while they are more comfortable with people from a particular region, they have no difficulties with people from a particular religion.

CONCLUSION

Despite years of experience of working in India and Indian communities, the authors are still occasionally caught out by their assumptions. Often when assuming that a particular person is able to work at sharing or managing knowledge and information with another person, small glitches begin to appear. While nothing is apparent at first, it is usually due to a difference based on religion, caste, language or region.

What this study has done is to advance the concept that while culture significantly affects KM, it is an understanding of the subtleties and variants of behaviour linked to cultural differences that profoundly affects the sharing or managing of knowledge and information on an individual level. When managing such a process, the author of such a process needs to have substantial concerns about the variants of cultural influences on the people implementing and utilising the process (Carliner, 2002). This understanding needs to occur at a functional level, not just at a national level or corporate level, particularly when considering countries that have substantial variations in cultural attributes. This study has also shown that these cultural differences can be extremely emotive at times in a way that profoundly affects sharing or managing knowledge and information.

LIMITATIONS OF RESEARCH

The essence of this study has been primarily from a practitioner's view. As business operators in India, the authors are well aware from an anecdotal position of some of the subtle difficulties that come along and unhinge progress within a business. This introduces a number of biases and limitations in terms of the application of the data presented, even though it matches the experiences of the authors.

There are two particular issues of bias that arise in this study: first, the relationship between the participants and the authors; and second, given the population size of India, the small sample size. There was link between the participants and the authors in that each of the people contacted to participate had a business relationship either directly or indirectly with the authors. To try to reduce the bias, the participants in the formal interview were contacted through a third party and the data sent back to the authors without any identifying marks. This allowed most of the data to be collected anonymously.

The bias relating to the sample size is harder to address. However, the data collected has been considered against the anecdotal experiences of the authors. In this case, there is a link between the anecdotal evidence and the data presented to suggest that the sample size is a good starting point for this study and suggests that further studies in this area using similar questions over a larger sample size would be appropriate. It would be beneficial to extend this study to include a much broader range of business people and to include both managers and employees.

One limitation is that none of the responses has been compared to the respondents' own positioning with the categories. It has not been discussed whether a speaker of Hindi is more likely to be comfortable than not using Hindi. There is no doubt that this comparison would add to the richness of this study, and is certainly an opportunity for further studies.

While this book looks at both cultural and institutional parameters of KM, this study has focused solely on the cultural aspects. There may be more widespread institutional issues that affect KM based on these institutional parameters that are worthy of investigating both independently and in conjunction with cultural issues.

IMPLICATIONS FOR INTERNATIONAL MANAGERS

The implications of this study are quite broad. KM is difficult even when there are limited cultural differences. In the case of India, the cultural differences are a significant factor. The diversity of culture in India makes even the use of local intermediaries difficult and not necessarily successful. Pulling together teams of people with substantial cultural similarities is also virtually impossible. With biases so widespread, sharing or managing knowledge and information in India is a balancing act.

Expecting complexity and responding in an unbiased way is often the only way to deal with these issues. In fact, this is one of the advantages of being a complete outsider when working amongst Indians. One is often viewed as being separate and not tainted by the various cultural structures that make up Indian life. This can make intervention easier. Consequently, for the non-Indian business person in India, understanding the nuances that occur adds to the complexity of working as an outsider in India. These nuances at times are often complex even for the Indians. International managers need a through understanding not just of the broad national cultural aspects but, in the case of India, the varied nuances that appear quite often unexpectedly. In particular, the following issues need to be considered by international managers:

1. While caste is officially non-existent in India, on an individual level it still plays a significant function in people's lives.
2. Although predominant in Hindu communities, caste is not restricted to Hindus. Muslims and Christians have sects that affect relationships.
3. Religious, caste and regional differences are very emotive issues for Indians.
4. Difficulties based on cultural differences are normal, consequently getting a balanced team is virtually impossible.
5. Indians are more likely to discuss these issues with an outsider (non-Indian).
6. Indians are just as likely to behave collectively as they are individualistically, depending on the situation.

REFERENCES

Banerjee, P. (2003), 'Narration, Discourse, and Dialogue: Issues in the Management of Inter-cultural Innovation', *AI and Society*, **17**(3–4), 207–24.
Banerjee, P. and K.K. Bhardwaj (2002), 'Constructivist Management of Knowledge, Communication and Enterprise Innovation: Lessons from Indian experience', *AI and Society*, **16**(1–2), 49–72.
Bever, E.J., E. Stephenson and D.W. Tanner (2005), 'How India's Executives See the World', *McKinsey Quarterly*, **3**, 34–41.
Brown, J. (1985), *Modern India: The Origins of an Asian Democracy*, Oxford: Oxford University Press.
Budhwar, P.S. (2001), 'Doing Business in India', *Thunderbird International Business Review*, **43**(4), 549–68.
Carliner, S. (2002), 'Designing Better Documents', *Information Management Journal*, **36**(5), 42–51.
Chatterjee, S.R. and C.A.L. Pearson (2000), 'Indian Managers in Transition', *Management International Review*, **40**(1), 81–95.
Chen, Y.N., H.M. Chen, W. Huang and R.K.H. Ching (2006), 'E-Government Strategies in Developed and Developing Countries: An Implementation Framework and Case Study', *Journal of Global Information Management*, **14**(1), 23–46.
Desai, R. (1999), *Indian Business Culture*, Oxford: Butterworth Heinemann.
Economist.com (2005), 'Survey: India and China', 3 March 2005, http://www.economist.com/surveys/displayStory.cfm?story_id=3689214
Fusilier, N. and S. Durlabhji (2001), 'Cultural Values of Indian Managers: An Exploration through Unstructured Interviews', *Journal of Value-Based Management*, **14**, 223–36.
Gannon, M.J. (2004), *Understanding Global Cultures: Metaphorical Journeys through 28 Nations, Clusters of Nations and Continents*, Thousand Oaks, CA: Sage Publications.
Gopalan, S. and J. Rivera (1997), 'Gaining a Perspective on Indian Value Orientations: Implications for Expatriate Managers', *The International Journal of Organisational Analysis*, **5**(2), 156–79.
Hofstede, G. (2001), *Culture's Consequences: Comparing Values, Behaviours, Institutions and Organisations across Nations*, Thousand Oaks, CA: Sage Publications.
Hooker, J. (2003), *Working Across Cultures*, Stanford, CA: Stanford Business Books.
Johanson, J. and M. Johanson (2004), 'Entering Emerging Markets: Ignorance and Discovery', in S.B. Prasad and P.N. Ghauri (eds), *Global Firms and Emerging Markets in an Age of Anxiety*, Westport, CT: Praeger Publishers, pp. 207–23.
Johnson, K. (2004), 'Globalisation and Culture in Contemporary India: Tradition vs. Modernity', in L.-H.N. Chiang, J. Lidstone and R.A. Stephenson (eds), *The Challenges of Globalisation: Cultures in Transition in the Pacific-Asia Region*, Oxford: University Press of America, pp. 119–30.
Kumar, R. (2004), 'Brahmanical Idealism, Anarchical Individualism, and the Dynamics of Indian Negotiating Behaviour', *International Journal of Cross Cultural Management*, **4**(1), 39–54.
Kumar, R. and V. Worm (2004), 'Institutional Dynamics and the Negotiation Process: Comparing India and China', *International Journal of Conflict Management*, **15**(3), 304–34.

McDermott, R. and C. O'Dell (2001), 'Over Coming Cultural Barriers to Sharing Knowledge', *Journal of Knowledge Management*, **5**(1), 76–86.

Mussweiler, T. and B. Englich (2005), 'Subliminal Anchoring: Judgmental Consequences and Underlying Mechanisms', *Organisational Behaviour and Human Decision Processes*, **98**(2), 133–43.

Nikam, K., A.C. Ganesh and M. Tamizhchelvan (2004), 'The Changing Face of India Part 1: Bridging the Digital Divide', *Library Review*, **53**(3/4), 213–19.

Overland, M.A. (2004), 'In India, Almost Everyone Wants to be Special', *The Chronicle of Higher Education*, **50**(23), 40.

Pauleen, D. and P. Murphy (2005), 'In Praise of Cultural Bias', *MIT Sloan Management Review*, **46**(2), 21–2.

Pearson, C.A.L. and S.R. Chatterjee (2001), 'Perceived Societal Values of Indian Managers: Some Empirical Evidence of Responses to Economic Reform', *International Journal of Social Economics*, **28**(4), 368–79.

Sawyer, J.E., M.A. Houlette and E.L. Yeagley (2006), 'Decision Performance and Diversity Structure: Comparing Faultlines in Convergent, Crosscut and Racially Homogenous Groups', *Organisational Behaviour and Human Decision Processes*, **99**(1), 1–15.

Singh, J. (1990), 'Managerial Culture and Work-related Values', *Organisation Studies*, **11**(1), 75–101.

Sinha, J.B.P. and R.N. Kanungo (1997), 'Context Sensitivity and Balancing in Indian Organisational Behaviour', *International Journal of Psychology*, **32**(2), 93–105.

Siu, Y.M.N. (1996), *Getting In, Getting On, Getting Out: The Role of Participant Observation Research in a Professional Organisation*, Working Paper 960202; Hong Kong: Hong Kong Baptist University.

Stumpf, S.A. and R.L. Dunbar (1991), 'The Effects of Personality Type on Choices Made in Strategic Decision Situations', *Decision Sciences*, **22**(5), 1047–72.

Von Glinow, M.A., E.A. Drost and M.B. Teagarden (2002), 'Converging on IHRM Best Practices: Lessons Learned from a Globally Distributed Consortium on Theory and Practice', *Asia Pacific Journal of Human Resources*, **40**(1), 146–66.

Walsham, G. (2002), 'Cross-cultural Software Production and Use: A Structural Analysis', *MIS Quarterly*, **26**(4), 359–80.

Westaby, J.D. (2005), 'Behavioural Reasoning Theory: Identifying New Linkages Underlying Intentions and Behaviour', *Organisational Behaviour and Human Decision Processes*, **98**(2), 97–120.

Wilson, E.M. (2004), 'An Outsider in India', in R. Marschan-Piekkari and C. Welch (eds), *Handbook of Qualitative Research Methods for International Business*, Cheltenham, UK and Northampton, MA, USA: Edward Elgar, pp. 421–38.

PART FOUR

Knowledge management in Africa,
the Middle East and Latin America

8. Mauritius: towards a knowledge hub and society

Mehraz Boolaky, Mridula Gungaphul and David Weir

INTRODUCTION

Knowledge is believed by many to be the driving force in today's economy (Bollinger and Smith, 2001). If this is accepted, then it is necessary for an economy to find ways of accessing existing knowledge and creating new knowledge if it desires to prosper and sustain prosperity. In this endeavour, Dosi and Malerba (1996) discuss the importance of an organisation's ability to learn, that is the willingness of members of the organisation to participate fully in the learning process to build and share knowledge. Countries need to recognise knowledge as a most valuable resource and develop mechanisms for tapping into the collective intelligence and skills of its human assets to draw maximum benefits from the unreserved participation of the whole population.

Commonly known as the Star and Key of the Indian Ocean, Mauritius is an island of about 1865 square kilometres with a multiracial population of about 1 230 000 inhabitants in 2005. Mauritius is widely cited as a model of economic and social development and in particular, an island of immigrants par excellence (History of Mauritius, 2001). This recent history is surprising and worthy of respect because of the parlous economic and social situation of the island state when it achieved independence in 1968. Its dependence on the monoculture of the basic commodity of sugar, its isolation from the major world markets and its rampant demographic explosion made it, in the eyes of many expert commentators, more likely to become an economic and social disaster than a success.

The rich plethora of ethnicities, the political stability, visionary leadership, wisdom, infrastructural development and the relatively high standard of living make the island one of the most favoured tourist destinations and business domains in the world. Much learning, experience and wisdom have been developed and acquired from the multi-faceted population and leadership; a relentless effort has been and is being made by the population to acquire knowledge, learn and pursue lifelong learning; and some countries have openly asked Mauritius to share its expertise and *savoir faire*. Propelled by these factors, Mauritius is now aspiring to and envisaging the opportunity of becoming a knowledge hub and society. We ask, can this happen?

THEORETICAL FOUNDATIONS

Earlier chapters introduced concepts related to learning, knowledge and knowledge management (KM). We illustrate applications of these concepts in this chapter and touch briefly on relevant literature. It is widely acknowledged that organisations require effective learning capability if they are to succeed in a complex, competitive and challenging world (Argyris, 1992; Senge, 1990). Competitive survival nowadays requires sustained learning and adaptation (Amin and Wilkinson, 1999). The organisational drive to knowledge needs to be mirrored in the institutions of the wider society and supported by the wider economy if it is to achieve success. When knowledge within the country is shared, it becomes cumulative. As Demarest (1997) puts it, knowledge becomes embedded within the country's processes, products and services. Grant (1997) also suggests that it is important to combine the various levels of expertise present to create new organisational knowledge, that in turn requires networking and communication channels that encourage sharing and collaboration.

Poynder (1998) views KM as more of a human resource issue with emphasis on organisational culture and teamwork, amongst others. For him, a strong, positive organisational culture is critical to promoting learning, development and the sharing of skills, resources and knowledge. Bollinger and Smith (2001) support the view that organisational knowledge develops and accumulates over time and enables organisations to attain better understanding and perception, which are characteristics of wisdom; wisdom is acquired as organisations gain new knowledge through the transformation of collective experiences and expertise. Wisdom contributes to success.

KM in an organisational setting relies on the building of a culture that is conducive to learning and the acquisition of knowledge. An organisation can develop a knowledge culture where KM is expressed through the application of various knowledge initiatives, tools and techniques (Moffett et al., 2003). Davenport and Prusak (1998) believe that a knowledge-orientated culture challenges people to share and contribute to knowledge organisation-wide. As explained in previous chapters, if people are to share, they have to trust and have faith in each other and hence transparency must be prevalent. We contend that not many countries and organisations operate in complete transparency where the population and employees are fully and equally knowledgeable and aware of what the vision is, what the country or organisation is trying to achieve, or where the country or organisation intends to focus.

As the wealth and prosperity of nations are increasingly based on the skills and knowledge of their workforces, it has been increasingly recognised that people's endowment of skills and capabilities, and investment in education and training, constitute the key to economic and social development. Skills and training increase productivity and incomes, and facilitate everybody's participation in economic and social life. Human resources development and training underpin the fundamental values of society – equity, justice, gender equality, non-discrimination, social responsibility and participation of all in economic and social life (International Labour Organisation, 2000). This point is echoed by Moffett et al. (2003) who suggest that organisations need to develop and implement activities such as education and training of employees, research and development, acquisition and transformation of knowledge, and innovation. Hence, countries and organisations have to trust their most valuable assets, that is, their human resources, in order to fully develop them and benefit from their total commitment and effort. This is of perhaps greater significance in developing economies, which are in the process of creating knowledge-oriented organisations and society.

To ensure sustainable total commitment, lifelong learning has become the new buzzword for education and training policies in the twenty-first century. According to the International Labour Organisation (2000), the lifelong learning framework emphasises that learning occurs during the entire course of an individual's life. Everybody must have access to learning and training so that everyone will be encouraged and enabled to continue learning throughout their life. In other words, businesses and citizens must have access to an inexpensive, excellent communications infrastructure and a wide range of services. Every citizen must be equipped with the skills needed to live and work in this new information society. The Lisbon European Council (2000) recommends that different means of access must prevent info-exclusion and the fight against illiteracy must be reinforced. It is sound judgement to recognise that individuals prefer to master their own lives and expect to contribute to the economy and society and be fully active citizens. According to the European Union Memorandum on Lifelong Learning (2003), the concept of active citizenship is the extent to which individuals and groups feel a sense of attachment to the societies and communities to which they theoretically belong to. This is closely related to the promotion of social inclusion and cohesion, as well as to matters of identity and values. Active citizenship also involves having information and knowledge upon which individuals can take action with some confidence, acquire experience in the process and have a fair say in the society in which they live. Individuals' independence, self-respect and well-being are essential to their overall quality of life and hence to knowledge sharing and management. Further, according to the International Labour Organisation (2001) and as echoed by others (Ernst and Young, 1999; Martin, 1998), the relevance of knowledge about facts is diminishing, while the need to learn how to access, analyse and exploit information and transform it into new knowledge is increasing. It is only by giving the individual the desire and tools, including financial means, to take charge of her/his own learning that he or she will be able to live and work in the knowledge and information society, both domestically and internationally.

METHODOLOGY

This chapter draws on empirical research conducted by the authors as well as personal experience and observations of the authors, and published documentation. The research questions posed within this chapter are:

- Is the aspiration to become a knowledge hub and society an over-ambitious vision for a minuscule island, a dot on the world map so to say, with highly limited resources?
- What do the indicators suggest?
- Can this vision become a reality?
- If so, what is the way forward?

We attempt to answer the above questions through an audit of the achievement of Mauritius in the areas related to KM. We argue that to acquire its privileged position and popularity in the Indian Ocean and the world, Mauritius has benefited fully from its most important assets, human resources and knowledge sharing and building. Moreover we argue that this experience is founded on a widespread sharing and understanding of social goals, both supported by and contributing to a social cohesion that is essential for the economic survival of a small, isolated island economy. The inflow of foreigners and the lessons learned from them, the shared civic vision, the entrepreneurial culture and the intra- and inter-community sharing and the strong value systems of the population in general are the ingredients for this economic and social success. In other words, we explore how Mauritius created, directly and indirectly, the right and most conducive environment for knowledge sharing and development that we term KM. We associate economic and social success directly to wisdom and KM. Our underlying hypothesis is that wisdom and KM have positively contributed to the well being and prosperity of Mauritius.

We thus provide some of the most prominent indicators to illustrate how Mauritius achieved through wisdom, its level of knowledge creation and building that resulted in wealth creation and societal transformation. Among these indicators, we illustrate how knowledge has accumulated from the entrepreneurial organisations and entrepreneurship. It is known that entrepreneurs strive to know more and more about their customers and build relationships and networks. In other words, entrepreneurial organisations produce people who are information seekers and disseminators, proactive, innovative and essentially relationship builders; these characteristics relate directly to KM as learning and skill development takes place and information is widely used and shared.

We briefly review the geography and history of Mauritius with particular emphasis on how history, leadership, initiatives taken, crises, responsible participation of stakeholders and a committed, cohesive population, help to consolidate the Mauritian culture and contribute to better sharing and mutual understanding towards nation building through KM.

MAURITIUS: IMPORTANCE OF GEOGRAPHICAL LOCATION AND HISTORY

Mauritius is located north of the Tropic of Capricorn, at a latitude 20 degrees south and longitude 57 degrees east of Greenwich. It is approximately 890 kilometres off the east coast of Madagascar and 200 kilometres from Reunion Island. Arab traders knew of Mauritius as early as the tenth century but never stopped to settle in. The Portuguese were probably the next to visit the island in 1498, and about 100 years later the Dutch landed on the island as immigrants and named it Maurice, in honour of Prince Maurice of Nassau. The Dutch barely exploited the island and only used it as a supply base. The Dutch left the island for good in 1710. In addition to presiding over the extinction of the dodo bird and leaving behind perhaps some runaway slaves, swarms of rats and ravaged ebony forests, the Dutch introduced a plant that was to be prominent in the island's future – sugar cane (Mauritius Country Studies, 2006).

The French were next to take control of the island during the eighteenth century. They named it Île de France (French Island). The settlement started in 1721. The development of the country started in 1735 with the arrival of the governor Mahé de Labourdonnais whose work is still visible today. During this period, a comprehensive civil infrastructure was commenced in particular the construction of Port Louis as military port and shipbuilding centre, the Château de Mon Plaisir in Pamplemousses, the Line Barracks in Port Louis and the Government House. The French East India Company took charge of the administration of the island until 1767. By 1726, the French erected the first sugar mill along with a road network and hospital. By 1750, the island's capital, Port Louis, became a free trading base and haven for corsairs who were mercenary marines paid by a country to loot the ships of its enemies. The long-term strategic ambition of the French was to create a base for the eventual attack on the English suzerainty of India. The English therefore took a strategic interest in the island particularly because of frequent attacks on their ships. In 1810, they battled with the French and were victorious in the Napoleonic war though it was the French who had gained the victory in the local hostilities. In 1814, the Treaty of Paris ceded Île de France, Rodrigues and the Seychelles to the British, but provided for the Franco-Mauritians to retain their language, religion, Napoleonic Code legal system and sugar plantations (History of Mauritius, 2005). The British renamed the island Mauritius (Maurice in French). This was a crucial decision for the long-term consolidation of a dual language culture in Mauritius, the effects of which can still be felt in the social and cultural experience of the island. In particular, it meant in effect a three-language solution to problems of communication with citizens of all strata of society having to learn to mediate between two distinct languages and ensured the emergence of a lingua franca of Mauritian Creole or Creole (Mauritius, 2006). At the time of independence over 40 per cent of Mauritians officially claimed Creole as a first language (Addison and Hazareesingh, 1999; Burton, 1965).

When slaves, the majority of whom had been imported from Africa, were liberated in 1835, workers were brought in from China and British India to supplement the labour force in the sugar plantations. Indentured labour from India continued to accrue. During the second half of the nineteenth century, there were also small flows of free immigrants from China and India (History of Mauritius, 2005). Those successive and sometimes overlapping waves of immigrants changed forever the demographic structure of Mauritius and its cultural mix. Indeed, we suggest that each wave of immigrants brought to the island new religions, cultures and languages, igniting with it the process of knowledge sharing and development through relationship building, under-standing and valuing each other's culture, mutual respect and team building.

Indians gradually made headway in the country's administration and management. In 1901, Mahatma Gandhi visited the island and in 1936, the Labour Party was founded to continue the struggle for labourers' rights. Following the Constitutional Conference of 1965 in London, general elections were held in 1967 and a majority of Mauritians voted in favour of independence. On 12 March 1968, Mauritius became independent. It remained a Sovereign State within the Commonwealth, with the Queen as its head, until July 1992, when the island became a republic. The British left behind the English language, a Westminster type of government, a civil service, a constitution, a British-based educational system and an embryonic welfare system (History of Mauritius, 2005).

We contend that it is fair to judge that the combination of British governmental procedures and French high culture in the arts and literature has melded with the largely Indian, but also Chinese and African influences in an especially supportive, dynamic and harmonious manner to produce a multi-racial blend that is uniquely multicultural and, perhaps most significantly in terms of KM, multilingual. This has had particular impact on language and communication capabilities. In terms of a population that is implicitly sensitised from a pre-school age to understand that communication is essentially an inter-cultural process, it is hard to imagine a better grounding than that provided in Mauritian society. Most adult Mauritians may be effectively at least quadri-lingual with English, French and Creole as a basis for their mother tongue, whether it be Hindi, Tamil, Urdu or Mandarin for example. Creole has been the language of general use since 1990. The population and language census showed that 71 per cent of the population used Creole as their mother tongue.

MAURITIUS: KNOWLEDGE-RELATED INITIATIVES

Emergence of the Entrepreneurial Culture

Studies support the view that culture has a great influence on the entre-preneurial capacity of a society, and that societies usually do not have homogeneous cultural settings. Loucks (1981) advocates that entrepreneurship is embedded in culture and therefore researchers on entrepreneurship should focus more on the cultural distinctions of the entrepreneurship phenomena, and how differences in values, beliefs, attitudes, shared norms and particu-larity of conditions influence what they do. Davidsson and Wiklund (1995) suggest that the variations in the levels of entrepreneurship are more apparent in cultural values and context.

Until 1970, Mauritius was a mono crop economy, depending mostly on sugar cane. Since independence in 1968 and the launching of the Export Processing Zone (EPZ) in 1970, the island learnt and realised that progress would only be possible if all the available human resources were fully utilised. The EPZ thus saw the emergence of an increasing number of women joining the workforce and that in turn resulted in an increasing number of working couples. Government and private institutions provided necessary training and support to make the couples better adapt to this new way of living. The belief once held that the woman's place is at home started to change, and changed drastically thereafter. The EPZ also brought with it an era of entrepreneurial activities that essentially helped to bridge the time lost for household activities while both members of the family were at work. Numerous people with entrepreneurial flair were quick to exploit the windows of opportunities that accompanied the simultaneous absence of both husband and wife from their homes. Many entrepreneurs invested in vehicles to take care of the transportation of small children at a very reasonable rate. They would pick up the children in their respective neighbourhood early in the morning, take them to their classrooms and drop them back home after school. Others invested in the sales of fruits, vegetables and other household products close to the factory premises. There was not much time for the parents, in particular the housewife, to fetch these from the market. Others opened takeaway and eat in restaurants, beauty parlours and hairdressing saloons, garment manufacturing, and so on. In brief, the EPZ brought alive a community that felt the desire and need to improve, learn, acquire new skills, and share experience in the spirit of helping each other and giving better meaning to life (Boolaky and Gungaphul, 2003).

These social changes provided a real wake-up from lethargy. Just prior to independence, the island was suffering from perhaps its worst social and economic problems and no magic solution presented itself at that time. The drastic changes that Mauritius suddenly witnessed during that period gave new life and hope to the population. In fact, the economic activities became so dynamic during that period that people started to assume more and more responsibility and started having stronger faith that their life could improve further if they worked harder. The negative influences of social problems decreased gradually to their minimum level. More girls started going to school and parents believed that educating their children was a top priority.

Since those days, the entrepreneurial culture in Mauritius has been well established and gathering momentum at an increasing rate. The Mauritian government has spared no effort in encouraging entrepreneurial activities in Mauritius by providing a supportive environment that includes an array of incentives and institutional support. There is a fully-fledged ministry to take the responsibility for small and medium enterprises. However, apart from a supportive environment and government programmes and policies, the development of entrepreneurship also requires subjective mindsets of individuals. These subjective mindsets are usually shaped by a broad cultural framework, and according to Pfeifer (2003) cultural factors that inhibit change are found both at the individual level and the societal level. Education and training in the field of entrepreneurship are being recognised as a must to support entrepreneurs. In Mauritius, short courses and training are dispensed to entrepreneurs by a variety of institutions from both the public and the private sector. Formal entrepreneurship education is also delivered at the university level. These initiatives enable entrepreneurs and would-be entrepreneurs to become more knowledgeable about running their businesses and at the same time improving their competence in conducting a business. Training helps entrepreneurs to find orientation and growth strategies that will provide success and prosperity for the individual and the community.

Visionary Leadership and Initiatives in the Education Sector

One of the most decisive initiatives in the Mauritian economy and history that contributed almost directly to knowledge sharing and development was that taken by the Mauritian government, under the Prime Ministership of Sir Seewoosagur Ramgoolam (also known as the founding father of the Mauritian nation), to provide free education to the population at all levels. That decision ignited the cause of education in Mauritius and significantly increased enrolment in both primary and secondary schools. With the emancipation of women and their growing numbers in the workplace, and the increase in the number of nuclear families, more and more people are sending their children to nurseries and then to pre-primary schools and on to full primary, secondary and tertiary study (Mauritius, 1982–83). The Tertiary Education Commission (TEC) was set up in 1988 to foster post-secondary education, coordinate activities within the sector and offer guidance to tertiary education institutions on planning matters. Five government-funded institutions fall under TEC, namely the University of Mauritius, the University of Technology Mauritius, the Mahatma Gandhi Institute, the Mauritius College of the Air and the Mauritius Institute of Education. In 2003, around 15 000 students were enrolled in these institutions and it is estimated that some 13 000 other students are enrolled in other institutions in Mauritius and are studying abroad (Tertiary Education Commission, 2006). The University of Mauritius is a flagship institution, aspiring to meet the highest international standards. The Industrial and Vocational Training Board (IVTB) also aims to do this in the vocational sector. Education has become a motif, infusing every aspect of social policy, and as of today it is still free in Mauritius, even at the tertiary level. Government after government created new ministries to support education, manpower planning and development, information technology, entrepreneurship, and so on. Government education budgets continue to increase relatively in spite of a minimal population growth rate; clearly indicative of a commitment to creating a knowledge state. To give an idea of the figures involved in the education budget, we quote the Central Statistical Office Report on Economic and Social Indicators (2005).

> Total government expenditure estimates for the financial year 2005/2006 is Rs 51,750 million, out of which Rs 7,379 million (14 per cent) has been allocated to education. Government capital expenditure on education, estimated at Rs 1,179 million, represents 14 per cent of total government capital expenditure (Rs 8,600

million), and recurrent expenditure on education estimated at Rs 6,200 million, that is 14 per cent of the government total recurrent expenditure (Rs 43,150 million). Out of the recurrent budget of the Ministry of Education for the year 2005/2006, 43 per cent is allocated to secondary education, 30 per cent to primary education, 13 per cent to post secondary education, 2 per cent to technical and vocational education, 2 per cent to pre-primary education and the remaining to other expenses of the Ministry. (Central Statistical Office, 2005)

Vocational Education

The Mauritius Research Council was set up in 1992 as the leading body to promote and coordinate national investment in research and advise the government on all matters pertaining to science and technology (Mauritius Research Council, 2006). The government envisions transforming Mauritius into a knowledge hub and a centre of higher learning. It is formulating a strategy to provide the necessary framework for internationally reputed universities to set up subsidiaries in Mauritius. The system of education at all levels is being reviewed to incorporate new trends in education and training.

Mauritius is increasingly taking the lead in Indian Ocean and African regional initiatives in education and is regarded as a vanguard country in those regions. Mauritius participated in the Special UNESCO–UNEVOC Workshop 'Focus Southern Africa' held during the Tenth European Congress and Specialist Trade Fair for Education and Information Technology (UNEVOC, 2002) in Karlsruhe, Germany to discuss topics such as 'How can educational technologies help improve the quality of technical and vocational education and training (TVET)? Can they reduce its delivery cost? Do they increase access? What can be done to facilitate the sharing of knowledge and expertise in TVET in Southern Africa? Is the digital divide an obstacle to e-learning, or can it even be used as a tool for the unreached to catch up with global developments?' The workshop was held as part of the initiative 'Learning for Life, Work and the Future: Stimulating Reform in Southern Africa through Subregional Co-operation' that had been launched jointly by the Department of Vocational Education and Training of the Ministry of Education of Botswana and by the UNESCO–UNEVOC International Centre in late 2000. Key personnel in the areas of TVET and information and communication technology (ICT) came from Botswana, Lesotho, Malawi, Mauritius, Mozambique, Namibia, South Africa, Swaziland, Zambia, Zimbabwe, United Republic of Tanzania and the Human Resource Development Sector of the Secretariat of the Southern African Development Community. Mauritius has had especially longstanding links with the region exemplified by these countries, and its off-shore location and lack of political embroilment have given it a privileged status as a role model and mentor.

Workforce and Training Initiatives

Parallel to the TEC, the Technical School Management Trust Fund (TSMTF) was set up in 1990 by an Act of Parliament to manage technical education and training. The TSMTF manages three technical training institutions, namely Lycée Polytechnique Sir Guy Forget, Swami Dayanand Institute of Management, and Institut Superieur de Technologie. It also advises the Ministry of Education on short- and long-term plans for technical education and on the need for appropriate research in the field of technical education. The Training and Skills Development Programme (TSDP) was set up to bridge the gap between education and work for unemployed graduates, diploma holders and higher school certificate school leavers. The TSDP provides on-the-job training to develop employable skills in relevant fields, through one-year training attachment in a public or private organisation with a stipend. The programme also aims at giving greater opportunities to unemployed graduates and diploma holders to acquire employable skills and widen their employment prospects (Tertiary Education Commission, 2006).

The IVTB was created in 1988 to act mainly as a regulator, facilitator and provider of training. The IVTB has evolved over time and is now fully involved in training of the workforce, providing training to school leavers who could not pursue further education for various reasons, and re-skilling and multi-skilling currently employed, unemployed and retrenched workers from different sectors. The IVTB operates 11 training centres among which are the Hotel School of Mauritius, the School of Design, the School of ICT and the Sir Ramparsad Neerunjun-East Wing. IVTB also intends to develop itself as a knowledge organisation to better promote KM and be more responsive to demand for training in Mauritius and in the region (Industrial and Vocational Training Board, 2006).

The Human Resource Development Council has been recently set up to promote an integrated and coordinated approach to human resource development in line with national economic and social objectives. The Council also aims at stimulating a culture of training and lifelong learning at individual, organisational and national levels for enhancing employability and increasing productivity, so as to inculcate the necessary skill base and human resource thrust to transform Mauritius into a knowledge economy (Portal of the Republic of Mauritius, 2006).

In response to the initiatives taken in the training and education field, Mauritius has a workforce that is productive, disciplined, adaptable, highly literate and multilingual (English, French, Creole, coupled with an Asian language such as Hindi, Bhojpuri, Mandarin and Urdu, and so on). The high level of education as well as vocational training of the workforce ensures good communication, courteous service, and harmonious industrial relations. In addition, there is a national consensus among government, employees, trades unions and political parties on the need to increase productivity and to maintain a peaceful labour climate in order to achieve rapid development across all sectors of the economy. To achieve this, the National Productivity and Competitiveness Council (NPCC) was set up in 1999 through an Act of Parliament and became operational in May 2000. It is a tripartite body with a national mandate. The NPCC act allows it to have a council composed of members representing respectively the interests of the government, the private sector and the trades unions. The council acts as the decision-making body (National Productivity and Competitiveness Council, 2006).

These initiatives have been translated into workable systems and practices at the organisational level. One of the authors reviewed a total quality programme introduced into a textile company that manufactures shirts for the European market. The management talked the talk, but a more revealing sign that the principles of self-inspection and conformability to quality norms had been internalised came with the sight of a banner over a table where sleeves were being selected for re-work. It read, in Creole '*Si Pa Korrek, Mo Met Korrek*' (If it's not right, I'll make it right). It translated a generic prescription into an understandable and do-able action.

Information Technology Initiatives

The following extract from the President of the Republic of Mauritius' address at the opening of the First Session of the Third National Assembly of the Republic of Mauritius (Address by the President, 2000) gives a good indication of initiatives in the information technology (IT) sector: 'The Government is fully conscious of the importance of the "new economy" of information and communication technology and the opportunities which it brings to countries like ours. The Government will develop the IT and Communications industry to increase national wealth, create new opportunities and jobs'.

Thus to transform Mauritius into a 'cyber island', the government took bold initiatives to ensure training and development of its workforce in the area. Human resource development in the area thus became a priority, and rightly so. Massive investment in IT education as well as the training of IT professionals resulted in ten government-funded and 30 private institutions, in collaboration with reputed foreign universities and international training centres, to provide tertiary education as well as specialised professional training courses in IT. Public servants are sponsored to attend academic training programmes at a tertiary level.

The National Computer Board (NCB) was established in 1988 and is a parastatal body which operates under the aegis of the Ministry of Information

Technology and Telecommunications. The role of the NCB is to e-power people, businesses and the public sector by developing and promoting ICT and ICT-related services in line with national goals and policies. The NCB is a key enabler in transforming Mauritius into a cyber island and, amongst others, advises the government on the elaboration of national policies for the development of the ICT sector in Mauritius. With the objective of e-powering people, the NCB undertakes various activities to bridge the digital divide and create an information-based society in Mauritius (National Computer Board, 2006).

To better understand the use of IT in Mauritius, the NCB carried out a study on the household usage of IT in 2000 and a similar one in 2002, using a structured questionnaire as a research instrument and a sample of 2000 households in Mauritius. According to the results of the survey, both home computer ownership and home internet connection of households having telephone connectivity have increased to 29.4 per cent and 23.8 per cent respectively. As far as on-line shopping is concerned, a gradual progress has been observed since the last survey in 2000. In the rural areas, computer ownership increased from 18 per cent in 2000 to 27 per cent in 2002. The proportion of urban and rural computer household ownership was 31 per cent and 27 per cent respectively. There has been a marked increase in internet penetration with 23.8 per cent of households having telephone connectivity reporting having access to the internet in June 2002, compared to 12 per cent in September 2000. Internet penetration among households having telephone connectivity and owning computers increased from 58 per cent in year 2000 to 81.1 per cent in 2002. Internet access and usage have increased in the lower income group (Rs 20 001–30 000) from 28 per cent in 2000 to 39 per cent in 2002. On-line purchases have increased from 1 per cent in year 2000 to 2.2 per cent in 2002 (National Computer Board, 2003).

To help residents of the most isolated places in Mauritius gain access to IT facilities, the NCB launched the Cyber Caravan project in November 2000. The NCB presently operates two cyber caravans, which are equipped with nine and ten personal computers respectively, and internet connection. Registered IT instructors provide training on board according to the needs of people, regardless of age, education background or profession. As at 31 March 2006, more than 43 000 people have attended the ICT Literacy and ICT Awareness Courses (National Computer Board, 2006).

To promote and stimulate the development of the ICT industry, the government has recently introduced the Scheme to Attract Professionals for Emerging Sectors to encourage and attract foreign IT talents to work and live in Mauritius. This scheme provides a three-year work and residence permit to professionals in the IT and financial services, with the option to apply for permanent resident status thereafter. Such professionals can also buy residential property on the island and their spouses may take up employment.

An attractive tailor-made incentive scheme is offered for those willing to operate in the ICT sector. For example:

- Tax exemptions up to 2008 and a 15 per cent corporate tax thereafter.
- For call centres or back office operations, the company can opt for a uniform corporate tax of 5 per cent.
- Duty-free import of equipment.
- Accelerated depreciation allowances for ICT equipment in the form of investment.
- Allowance of 50 per cent plus annual allowance of the total investment over three years.
- Fifty per cent relief on personal income tax for a specified number of foreign IT specialists per company.
- Duty-free import of personal belongings of expatriates excluding vehicles.
- Fast track processing of visa, work and residence permits for expatriates (Invest Mauritius, 2006; Permanent Residence in Mauritius, 2006).

To show its commitment to develop a strong information-based economy, the government of Mauritius recently introduced the following incentives to foster industrial development: the liberalisation of access to the international gateway via satellite dishes through call centres; preferential corporate tax rates to network service providers, internet service providers, IT training schools and other service providers such as multimedia development and hosting of web sites; and the deduction of funding contributions from taxable income by companies providing initial funding to start-up companies in information technology, multimedia and telecommunications.

The latest development in the island is the Ebène Cybercity, which is a new generation knowledge park. It is located only 15 minutes from the capital city Port Louis and 40 minutes from the SSR airport. The Ebène Cybercity (Business Parks of Mauritius, 2006) is an integrated mega project of 64 hectares comprising a cyber tower, a business zone, a knowledge centre, a commercial centre, a world class hotel, an administrative block to house government offices, and a residential and recreational complex. The cyber tower provides 40 000 square metres of ultra modern office space equipped with high bandwidth connectivity at competitive rates. The Business Parks of Mauritius runs and operates the Ebène Cybercity (Business Parks of Mauritius, 2006).

The Informatics Park and the Freeport Trade and Marketing Centre are other intelligent buildings dedicated to IT activities. Across the islands there are cyber cafes, including those run by Mauritius Telecoms that offer space suitable for ICT activities at reasonable rates. The government recently launched a project of equipping post offices with internet facilities to enable the population to have free internet access for various purposes. The cyber mobile caravans are another avenue to promote the use of IT and the internet.

Mauritius is also fast becoming the destination for IT projects via the business process outsourcing (BPO) procedures. It offers an ideal investment climate for international BPO companies that aim at diversifying into the French market as well as exploiting the African continent for IT ventures. The outcome of the initiatives taken is that an increasing number of IT companies from the United States, India and Europe are setting up businesses in Mauritius in the following areas: software development, high value-added data processing, CD-ROM and internet publishing, development of multimedia applications, translation services and e-commerce (Invest Mauritius, 2006).

This IT revolution in Mauritius is creating an explosion of work in computer-based operations such as data processing, computer-aided design, software design, electronic publishing and telephone services (call centres). Mauritius now houses the regional headquarters of IT MNCs such as Microsoft, IBM, Infosys Technologies and Infinity BPO (Cybercity Mauritius, 2004). Appropriate legislations and enforcement ensure protection of intellectual property rights. To further promote and encourage e-business and e-commerce, the government has recently introduced an Electronic Transaction Act. These characteristics of Mauritian society can be and are marketed as positive advantages to the globalising off-shore industries. Thus, a current web-site advertising off-shore accounting services announces that the plus points of Mauritius are: a democratic republic based on the Westminster model, market-friendly policies, a skilled professional and educated work force, proficient English language skills, an emerging ICT sector, good industrial relations, a diverse culture, wonderful living conditions and very competitive costs. Other globally active organisations, like the international banks, are continuing to find in Mauritius well-qualified recruits for their international operations.

THE WAY FORWARD

In pursuing its journey towards the knowledge hub and society, Mauritius will be well advised to address the following issues.

Keeping Control of the Knowledge Gap

Mauritius should take continual steps to minimise the widening of the knowledge gap between those with low level, outdated or no employable skills and those who developed their skills through educational and training opportunities. A knowledge society should create equal opportunities for all to learn, as disadvantaged groups will not participate fully in the social, political and cultural life of the society. Apart from the costs that such exclusion carries, the environment will not be conducive for knowledge creation, sharing and building. KM requires full participation from all spheres. Thus, the Mauritian government should pursue the bold initiatives taken to promote access to education, training and skills development in different ways for women, young workers long-term unemployed, older displaced workers and workers with disabilities. This will help the country to maintain its political, social and economic stability.

Recognise Individual Differences

It is the responsibility of the individual to learn and share information. As the amount of information exposed to an individual is increasing very rapidly, it is the individual's job to select, use and transform the information for knowledge creation. He or she is expected to organise his or her own learning. Thus, a paradigm shift is required if an economy wishes to become a knowledge society. The person must actively, and interactively, participate in the learning process with teachers and trainers who support the learner's acquisition and sharing of knowledge. This is already on the agenda in Mauritius. Curricula are being revised, teachers and trainers sent back to school and education is taking various shapes and styles that do not resemble the conventional ones, for instance, the initiatives taken by the University of Mauritius to introduce the Transferable Outreach Skills Programme (TOSP), which is a small module meant to enhance students' knowledge, skills and attitude for greater employability. The TOSP aims at producing broadly educated, self-motivated graduates, with a thirst for life-long learning, being aware of their heritage, conscious of their civic obligation, and ethically responsible for their professional career (University of Mauritius, 2005). Examples of such modules are Active Citizenship, Honest Living, Project Management, and Team Building; secondary school teachers receive training free of charge in the area of computers, all syllabuses are being revised, lifelong learning is a reality, and the whole system of education at all levels is undergoing reforms. ICT and e-learning are making their way into schools, colleges, community and other centres, training institutions and universities. Such initiatives and efforts must be sustained to enable all individuals to find their place in the Mauritian society.

Look Ahead for Knowledge Entrepreneurship

To create a growing proportion of wealth within an increasingly knowledge-based economy, entrepreneurs need to understand how to access, work with and share information, and create conditions which lead to the development and application of knowledge. The skills and competencies required to do this are distinct from those needed to manage money and machines, as different forms of relationships have to be established and sustained (Coulson-Thomas, 2000). There is a need to step up from information management to knowledge entrepreneurship. As pointed out by Cabrera et al. (2006), the transformation from information management to knowledge entrepreneurship opens up opportunities for knowledge entrepreneurs who know how to acquire, develop, package, share, manage and exploit information, knowledge and understanding, and introduce related job support tools. Further, as opportunities for increased participation are created for individuals, families, small enterprises, large corporations and societies, it can be safely assumed that people will have to struggle to keep up with the flow. Much of the information might be outdated and not relevant to contemporary priorities and concerns. The challenge is to maintain the balance. In other words, there will be ample opportunities for those who can help cope with the information overload. Information needs to be sifted, screened and sorted, presented in ways that make it easier to absorb and understand (Coulson-Thomas, 2000). The new challenge for KM is how to manage information overflow.

CONCLUSIONS AND LESSONS LEARNT

The main conclusion of this study is that Mauritius can certainly aspire to become a knowledge hub and society. The level of development and achievement in the knowledge area in Mauritius is remarkable for an island of its size. However, the achievement needs to be sustained. One of the most important things to bear in mind is that KM invites analyses, initiatives and willingness to address situations in order to minimise the negative influence of degradations. KM and wisdom have been the drivers for success. Efforts in this direction must be maintained.

Mauritians are known for their entrepreneurial flair and spirit. We conclude that this entrepreneurial spirit has not happened haphazardly but it has developed from learning in all its forms – double loop, symbolic or vicarious; more so because entrepreneurship absorbs people of varying education levels, gender and age groups. In other words, entrepreneurship helps a country to obtain synergy from the population, where all members participate and are given an opportunity to participate. Entrepreneurs are essentially knowledge workers. They innovate, they are proactive, they build relationships and networks, they are quick to learn and adapt – all these require information and information processing and management, or, expressed differently, they require KM. There is enough evidence to illustrate these facets of entrepreneurship in Mauritius and our empirical research confirms this. We observe in our everyday life the extent to which women are joining the entrepreneurial sector, how the person with absolutely no school education is managing his or her business successfully, and how the entrepreneurs keep on innovating and building relationships around them.

Of the question: 'Is the environment in Mauritius conducive to encourage learning and KM?', we conclude that the answer is definitely affirmative. As discussed and illustrated earlier, the right environment implies commitment by the government and administrators to the cause of education, training and development, which requires setting up the right institutions and other frameworks, and provision of resources and continuous support to all members of the population without discrimination. Mauritius has been addressing and continues to address this important aspect of its economy and thus it provides ample evidence that knowledge building does take place in an environment of sharing, equity and trust. Mauritians have trained and continue to train themselves to fit and respect a knowledge-sharing environment. International managers can rely on the team spirit and mutual respect that are so crucial for organisational competitiveness in these days of turbulence. The specific Mauritian context of a well-informed civil society and honest and capable administration has provided the basis for a relevantly positioned economic development that has avoided some of the extremes of many of its African and Asian counterparts.

We further conclude that in spite of its size and limited natural resources, Mauritius offers great business opportunities thanks to a close-knit and committed population that has devoted full belief and faith in education, training, learning and development – the essence of KM. The learned population ensures that the visitors are in safe hands and are well taken care of.

The important lessons to draw from this study are that human resources can develop capabilities and become capable. For this, it is necessary to understand situations and to react to cues even if they are minor ones that might have serious consequences. Relationship building, discipline, mutual respect and in particular creating the right learning environment are essential ingredients of capability and capacity development. These capabilities are embodied in the civic culture of Mauritius.

Another important lesson from this study is if the population is not ready to understand, evaluate and support education and training initiatives, these investments might prove futile. The buzzwords in Mauritius today are lifelong learning, knowledge hub, and knowledge society. It is not just by coincidence that the keynote address of the President of India, Dr A.P.J. Abdul Kalam, during his recent visit in Mauritius to the University of Mauritius students was entitled 'Dimensions of Knowledge Society'. The President identified the components of a knowledge society as being driven by societal transformation and wealth generations. We can assert that these are visible cues in Mauritius. We have identified the willingness of Mauritians to pursue lifelong learning and economic indicators do suggest that the national cake is becoming bigger and bigger. Of course, sustainable efforts are required to maintain the momentum.

Mauritius is one of the rare countries of the world that does not belong to one ethnic group, be it the majority or minority. Everyone in Mauritius is aware of this and embraces the multiculturalism. It is perhaps this understanding that helps keep the different communities well knitted together and, most importantly, this belief has never been put to question even for a fraction of a second. Mauritians find themselves at ease learning from each other and collaborating with each other. Mauritians strive to build the Mauritian nation. KM will enable this.

REFERENCES

Addison, J. and K. Hazareesingh (1999), *A New History of Mauritius*, Mauritius: Editions de l'Ocean Indien.

Address by the President (2000), At the Opening of the First Session of the Third National Assembly of the Republic of Mauritius, 26 May, 2006, http://labour.intnet.mu/mlp/pr20001003.htm

Amin, A. and F. Wilkinson (1999), 'Learning, Proximity and Industrial Performance: An Introduction', *Cambridge Journal of Economics*, **23**(2), 121–5.

Argyris, C. (1992), *On Organisational Learning*, Oxford: Blackwell.

Bollinger, A.S. and R.D. Smith (2001), 'Managing Organisational Knowledge as a Strategic Asset', *Journal of Knowledge Management*, **5**(1), 8–18.

Boolaky, M. and M. Gungaphul (2003), 'Innovation and Creativity in Entrepreneurship: The Mauritian Experience', in *Proceedings of the Global Conference on Business and Economics*, July 2003, London.

Burton, B. (1965), *Mauritius: The Problems of a Plural Society*, London: Pall Mall Press.

Business Parks of Mauritius (2006), 26 May, 2006, http://www.e-cybercity.mu/

Cabrera, A., W.C. Collins and J.F. Salgado (2006), 'Determinants of Individual Engagement in Knowledge Sharing', *International Journal of Human Resource Management*, **17**(2), 245–64.

Central Statistical Office (2005), 26 May, 2006, http://www.gov.mu/portal/sites/ncb/cso/indicate.htm

Coulson-Thomas, C. (2000), 'Developing and Supporting Information Entrepreneurs', *Industrial and Commercial Training*, **32**(6), 196–200.

Cybercity Mauritius (2004), 26 May, 2006, Cyber Operators http://www.e-cybercity.mu/operators.asp

Davenport, T. and L. Prusak (1998), *Working Knowledge: How Organisations Manage What They Know*, Boston, MA: Harvard Business School Press.

Davidsson, P. and J. Wiklund (1995), *Cultural Values and Regional Variations in New Firm Formation: Frontiers in Entrepreneurship Research*, Wellesley, MA: Babson College.

Demarest, M. (1997), 'Understanding Knowledge Management', *Long Range Planning*, **30**(3), 374–84.

Dosi, G. and F. Malerba (1996), *Organisation and Strategies in the Evolution of the Enterprise*, London: Macmillan.

Ernst and Young (1999), *Country Profiles: Africa Analysis*.

European Union (2003), 'Learning for Active Citizenship: A Significant Challenge in Building a Europe of Knowledge', 26 May, 2006, http://europa.eu.int/comm/education/archive/citizen/citiz_en.html

Grant, R.M. (1997), 'The Knowledge-based View of the Firm: Implications for Management Practice', *Long Range Planning*, **30**(3), 450–54.

History of Mauritius (2001), 26 April, 2006, http://www.intnet.mu/iels/hist_mau.htm

History of Mauritius (2005), 26 April, 2006, http://uk.geocities.com/maurivilla_com/history.html

Industrial and Vocational Training Board (2006), 26 May, 2006, http://www.gov.mu/portal/sites/ncb/ivtb/index.htm

International Labour Organisation (2000), *Joint Meeting on Lifelong Learning in the Twenty-First Century: The Changing Role of Educational Personnel*, April 2000, Geneva: International Labour Office.

International Labour Organisation (2001), 'Life at Work in the Information Economy', *World Employment Report 2001*, Geneva: International Labour Office.

Invest Mauritius (2006), 'ICT Scheme', 26 May, 2006, http://www.boimauritius.com/en/schemes/ict.html

Lisbon European Council (2000), 'Presidency Conclusions', 26 May, 2006, http://ue.eu.int/ueDocs/cms_Data/docs/pressData/en/ec/00100-r1.en0.htm

Loucks, K.E. (1981), 'A Survey of Research on Small Business Management and Entrepreneurship in Canada', in K. Vesper (ed.), *Frontiers of Entrepreneurship Research*, Wellesley, MA: Babson College, pp. 111–29.

Martin, B. (1998), 'Tied Knowledge: Power in Higher Education', 26 May, 2006, http://www.uow.edu.au/arts/sts/bmartin/pubs/98tk/, 1998

Mauritius (1982–83), *Report of the Commission of Enquiry on Education: 'We have all been Children'*, Port Louis, Mauritius: Government Printing Office.

Mauritius (2006), 'Encyclopædia Britannica', 28 April, 2006, http://www.britannica.com/eb/article-4719

Mauritius Country Studies (2006), 26 May, 2006 http://www.country-studies.com/mauritius/early-settlement.html

Mauritius Research Council (2006), 26 May, 2006, http://www.mrc.org.mu/

Moffett, S., R. McAdam and S. Parkinson (2003), 'An Empirical Analysis of Knowledge Management Applications', *Journal of Knowledge Management*, **7**(3), 6–26.

National Computer Board (2003), 'ICT Penetration within the Mauritian Society', 26 May, 2006, http://www.gov.mu/portal/goc/ncb/file/ICT%20Outlook2002.pdf

National Computer Board (2006), 26 May, 2006, http://www.gov.mu/portal/site/ncb

National Productivity and Competitiveness Council (2006), 26 May, 2006, http://www.npccmauritius.com/history/

Permanent Residence in Mauritius (2006), 'Procedures to Obtain Permanent Status', 26 May, 2006, http://www.maurinet.com/residency.html#sapes

Pfeifer, S. (2003), 'Modification of Entrepreneurial Behaviour by Cultural Factors in Emerging Economy', in *Proceedings of the International Council for Small Business 48th World Conference*, June 2003, Northern Ireland.

Portal of the Republic of Mauritius (2006), 26 May, 2006 http://www.gov.mu/

portal/site/?content_id=627f5a10a66e7010VgnVCM100000ca6a12acRCRD

Poynder, R. (1998). 'Getting to the Nuts and Bolts of Knowledge Management', *Information World Review*, **135**(20), 135–55.

Senge, P.M. (1990), *The Fifth Discipline: The Art and Practice of the Learning Organisation*, New York: Currency Doubleday.

Tertiary Education Commission (2006), *Report of Tertiary Education Commission of Mauritius*, Port Louis, Mauritius: Government Printing Office.

UNEVOC (2002), 'Special UNESCO–UNEVOC Workshop: Focus Southern Africa', 31 May, 2006, http://www.unevoc.unesco.org/southernafrica/learntec2002/index.htm#2.LEARNTEC

University of Mauritius (2005), 'Prospectus Chapter 3', 26 May, 2006, http://www.uom.ac.mu/admissions/prospectus/chap3.htm

9. Managing knowledge in the Middle East and North Africa

David Weir

INTRODUCTION

The first section of this chapter discusses the background and context in which knowledge management (KM) operates within the MENA (Middle East and North Africa) region. A subsequent section reviews some recent developments that show promising signs of improving the situation for KM in the MENA region. Some aspects of the internal organisation of companies are considered with special reference to their modes of decision making. In conclusion, there is an overview of future prospects and some general conclusions.

The MENA region enjoys a vast territorial domain, extending from Morocco to Iran. MENA's territorial area of six million square metres is almost equal to that of the European Union, and one and a half times larger than that of the United States and of China. The inhabitants of the MENA region comprise 6 per cent of the total world population, and one third of the population of China. The population of this region is almost equivalent to the population of the European Union and one and a quarter times larger than the population of the United States. Within the next decade, MENA's population is projected to exceed that of the European Union (EU) by 20 per cent (growing at a rate of 3 per cent versus 0.8 per cent in the EU). MENA's vast consumer market is projected to double in size in approximately 18 years, while the EU market is expected to double in approximately 87 years. The consumer market growth of MENA is further reinforced by the skewed structure of its population breakdown. More than 45 per cent of MENA's population is below the age of 15, compared to the EU's 18 per cent. MENA is a leading player in international trade. World trade (imports and exports) of the MENA region in 1994 reached over US$320 billion, while the gross domestic product (GDP) of MENA for the same year reached US$500 billion. The contribution of MENA's international trade to its GDP stood at around 65 per cent (World Bank, 1998).

The MENA region is an important player on the world's economic stage, but its diversity and breadth of experience mean that it is even more difficult to formulate general conclusions about it than compared to what may be said about the USA, Europe or China, especially in the field of KM.

THE PARADOXICAL REGIONAL BACKGROUND

As we have seen, it is the Maghreb countries of the Eastern Mediterranean and the Arab and Moslem-dominated societies of the Middle East that together comprise the MENA region. The MENA region demonstrates in some ways both the best and the worst aspects of KM in the contemporary world. Moreover the region comprises such a range of performance in relation to KM that it is scarcely possible to generalise in an informed way.

Population is growing and living standards are on average not rising. There are more educated people than ever before but poverty and unemployment are on the increase. Eighty million people in the region, or 30 per cent of the population, live below a United Nations (UN) poverty line of less than two dollars a day. Unemployment affects 15–20 per cent of people in some countries in the region and this figure includes a disproportionate number of young graduates. Women's labour force participation rates are so low that in some statistics they are not entered into the calculation of unemployment rates. The authoritative United Nations Development Programme (UNDP) report on social indicators concluded that on a wide range of social measures the MENA region showed signs of concern (UNDP, 2002).

Lack of education per se does not appear to be the main concern in this region. These depressing figures are due to on average a higher percentage of GDP spent on education compared to developing countries in other regions. An improving pattern of literacy and enrolment rates over the last two decades added to it. Overall more than 90 per cent of males in these countries and almost 75 per cent of females are enrolled in primary school. In secondary level education, the enrolment rates were 60 per cent for males and 50 per cent for females. At the tertiary level, male and female enrolment in Arab countries is higher than in all developing regions except for Latin America (Page, 2002).

More specifically in terms of the spread of KM, the authoritative World Bank study has concluded that the MENA region is substantially deficient in employment opportunities for a growing population (Aubert and Reiffers, 2003, p. 63).

MODERNISATION: ONE MODEL OR MANY?

Much of the scholarly discussion about the lack of relevant modernisation in the Arab world has been framed by a group of sociological and institutional theorists who have been concerned that this world has not followed the paths of the West in developing a truly 'modern' economy.

Education as the basis for knowledge has traditionally been a central value in the Moslem world. The relative lack of impact of modernism cannot be simply attributed to ignorance. In fact, young people in this region typically know much more of the West than do their Western counterparts of the MENA region. Thousands of young Arab men and women travel to the West to study and obtain qualifications. But rather few young Europeans or Americans make the converse journey.

Are the deficiencies revealed in the World Bank study to be attributed then to a weakness in political and social organisation? Is there a wide-ranging 'democratic deficit' that impairs the spread of knowledge and its organisational influences? Our characteristic Western narratives of modernity seem to imply that with economic globalisation and the force of political liberation exercised through Western military might, democratic ideals and practice would become universalised.

But some Arab scholars question these certainties, albeit with some apparent regret, for Sharabi's (1998) concept of neopatriarchy describes a condition of patriarchy in Arab society that has arisen from a 'distorted development'. The MENA world tends in many ways to be dominated by familial models of social, political and business organisation but these are not necessarily to be construed as oppressive rather than facilitative of the career aspirations of women (El-Kharouf and Weir, 2005). A priori there is much to recommend the inference that Arab business people are well-attuned and have been for several generations to the requirements of a global economy linked by bonds of trade and family connection.

CURRENT REALITIES IN THE MENA REGION

The current situation in relation to the knowledge economy as evidenced by most objective statistical and comparative reports is not good. Aubert and Reiffers (2003, p. 2) conclude that

> the MENA region's readiness for the knowledge economy is low, although a number of governments have begun to adapt their economies to meet the new challenges. Compared to other parts of the developing world, the region trails East Asia, Eastern Europe, Central Asia, and Latin America. It is somewhat ahead of South Asia and Sub-Saharan Africa. In general terms, the MENA countries' knowledge economy is somewhat lower than their overall level of economic development as measured by GDP.

Jean-Louis Sarbib, Vice-President of the World Bank has commented that despite the reverence and high budget allocation given to education in the

MENA region, there is little evidence that education has contributed to economic growth. This is contradictory at a time when literate, educated human capital has become critical to gaining competitivity in a global economy, driven by advances in knowledge and technology, and when developing countries with an educated labour force such as Korea and Brazil are raising their economies' share of high value-added productive activities. In contrast, Arab countries' share of international outsourcing – which has fuelled the transfer of technology and employment to developing countries in Asia and Latin America – has been negligible (Sarbib, 2002).

But if we are to eschew simplistic cultural explanations for these paradoxes, it is clear that we can find little solace in simplistic economic and financial stories either. This region includes some of the poorest but also some of the richest nation-states in the world, and within the Gulf Cooperation Council (GCC) sub-region alone such exemplars as United Arab Emirates, Bahrain and Kuwait, in terms of per capita income and urbanisation (Djeflat, 2002).

In terms of the more specialised indicators of KM such as the average spend on research and development, the publication of scientific papers per million inhabitants and the share of investment in GDP, the MENA region has admittedly started from a low baseline. More specifically, the region is low, perhaps the lowest in the world, in terms of websites originated and in Internet usage generally, and as Sarbib points out, these measures indicate the level of integration into the global knowledge economy (Sarbib, 2002).

Yet these are not incompatible with a high level of interest in new technology in the consumer population at large, and some startlingly visible evidence of official support for such high-tech showcase projects as Dubai's 'Knowledge Village' and 'Internet City' and the 'Silicon Hills' of Jordan. Moreover the region can boast some state-of-the-art organisations like Emirates Airlines that can legitimately claim to be among the 'best in class' on a world scale.

Sarbib (2002) identifies four pillars on which a knowledge economy should be founded:

- An economic incentive and institutional regime that encourages entrepreneurship, the development of new activities and more generally the modernisation process throughout the economy.
- A skilled and flexible labour force, in which people have opportunities for quality education and lifelong learning.
- A dynamic information and telecommunications infrastructure that provides efficient services and tools available to all sectors of society.
- A system in which regional firms, science and research centres, universities and other organisations can interact to promote innovation and create new products and services.

It has been argued elsewhere that in the near-universal practices of Guanxi and Wasta, the MENA countries and China share a similar basis for business networking. In contrast to Western nations, and like China, the basic rule of business in the Arab World is to establish a relationship first, build connections, and only actually come to the heart of the intended business at a later meeting. As in the case of China, this process is very time-consuming, yet once a relationship has been established, verbal contracts are absolute and an individual's word is his/her bond. Failure to meet verbally agreed obligations leads to termination of a business relationship. Wasta involves the social networks of interpersonal connections rooted in family and kinship ties and implicating the exercise of power, influence and information-sharing through social and politico-business networks. It is intrinsic to the operation of many valuable social processes, and central to the transmission of knowledge and the creation of opportunity (for further discussion of Wasta and Guanxi, see Hutchings and Weir, 2006).

Although these practices enable business and contribute to a framework of discourse and status that both enables effective trading and dealing and empowers business people (who do not suffer the generally low esteem perceived for business in some Western countries), they are a mixed blessing in the Information Age. Where society itself is de-personalised and fragmented, contacts made through electronic means are as good as any other; in their novelty and immediacy, they may indeed be better. But where the whole basis of business lies in the personalisation of relationships, they are bound to appear as an inferior substitute. It is not easy to become a trusted intermediary, worthy of respect, via electronic means alone.

But while Wasta itself becomes more complex, the social networks that give rise to it and enable it to function do provide a substrate of socialisation that is significant. In the Arab and Chinese worlds, network relations can exist despite a lack of spatial contiguity. Family and, in the Arab case, religious affiliation provide bases for social bonding. Potential social relations can cohere with actual ones as individuals are positioned by membership of social unities that do not depend on knowing exactly who the other partners in a social transaction are. This can become an enabling force for KM.

Another striking feature of the MENA region is its lingua franca of Arabic. It is the language of worship, trade and society. But it is a mixed blessing to the knowledge economy. Aubert and Reiffers (2003, p. 33) claim that

> the region includes a very large linguistic block within which trade and commercial exchanges, so far surprisingly very limited, can be intensified; similarly, cooperation in science, education and culture needs to be developed, using new technological opportunities and approaches such as open and virtual universities. The sense of a broad nation felt by the Arabo-Islamic world would find a direct

application in such initiatives. International organisations, including the World Bank, have also a crucial role to play for accompanying the movement.

There is much apparent logic in this argument but one has to wonder why, if these benefits were going to accrue to the linguistic universalism of Arabic, they have not occurred hitherto. In practice, the deficiencies in basic literacy, governmental restrictions on freedom of information and the lack of inclusion in the business communities of significant groups such as women, coupled with the variations in spoken Arabic between one region and another, effectively vitiate these bases for optimism. In some ways, the Arabic of the mosque is an impediment to the use of Arabic as a medium of commerce, particularly e-commerce, and it is English that is more widely used in the KM communities, especially for more advanced applications, and English that is the preferred language for strategic business discussions.

There are continuing economic problems in the region that hinder the growth of KM. Underlying problems include low productivity, slow annual growth rates, high unemployment, often masked by social measures, pluralism of jobs and ineffective use of human resources. Capital markets function imperfectly under variable and unsupportive regimes dominated by centralist thinking, even when it wishes to be generally beneficent, and they are hindered as governmental sectors are generally by bureaucratic distortions sometimes of stupefying complexity. The inefficient application of capital to new and more potentially productive sectors is compounded by skill shortages as well as by a lack of foreign direct investment (FDI) that can, of course, find more attractive opportunities, most recently in China and India (Keller and Nabli, 2002).

Historically, the capital-rich nations in this region have tended to be net exporters of financial capital, but this situation has been showing signs of change since 9/11 and its consequential events. In lieu of substantial opportunities in manufacturing, it is possible that investment in knowledge-creation opportunities will appear more attractive to capitalists in the region. But infrastructure of a more conventional type, and in particular urban residential developments, may nonetheless exert a stronger pull. In the recent past, even quite large-scale projects in infrastructure have often tended to bypass the possibility of raising capital from local sources and Wilson (2001) shows that the development of the gas sector in Saudi Arabia for example has followed this international route.

The economic picture is not the same throughout the whole region. Aubert and Reiffers (2003) show that the range of dispersion is in fact greatest of all the regions surveyed by the World Bank, with three distinct groupings of countries. Jordan and Kuwait are above the MENA average in the World Bank benchmarking exercise; Tunisia, Morocco, Egypt, Saudi Arabia, Iran and Algeria are in the middle; while Syria and Yemen fall below. All countries in the region except Jordan show a pattern in which their GDP per head ranks relatively better than their performance in knowledge economy-related activities.

A striking feature of all the studies undertaken on economic aspects of movement towards the knowledge economy, is that oil-rich states do not necessarily make the most strides. It is Jordan, a resource-poor state with significant problems over the last two decades in relation to its involvement in the geo-political scene and Dubai, and the only one of the United Arab Emirates without a strong natural resource base in oil and gas, which has moved forward.

Within the knowledge-based sectors of secondary and especially higher education, the systems again work imperfectly. These processes effectively hinder the development of the 'learning economy' (Lundvall, 1999). Higher learning is perceived and managed in terms of ascription rather than achievement. It is impossible to obtain a position in a university or college without possession of a doctoral diploma, but there are no pressures to publish and promotion is likely to be based in large part on seniority rather than output. Professors on the whole do not publish like their European and North American counterparts. Empirical research is undertaken for doctoral qualification and then often not returned to after the first two or three papers. This is counter to the basic precepts of KM thinking, where the actual stock of knowledge matters less than its renewal, and the generation of systems for knowledge-sharing.

In order for a knowledge economy to function effectively, the knowledge and its holders have to operate in a climate of transparency and on the basis of shared presumptions. However, in the case of the MENA region, different rules apply. Knowledge is seen as located in certain positions and roles, as conferring special status and exclusive rights, and the more significant it is in value, the less it is codified. Lifelong learning that is central to the new knowledge economies is perceived as threatening by existing power and status position-holders. Innovation can be resisted because it calls into question existing arrangements. Organisational decision making may be highly consultative but is nonetheless highly centralised. Interfaces between organisational components may be highly opaque and mobility restricted. Organisational structures may be highly resistant to change. None of these factors enhances the possibility of widespread support for KM as it is understood.

So in fact the first two 'pillars' of a knowledge economy as recommended by Sarbib (2002) are quite hard to find in the MENA region, despite many protestations and fine words. The basic prerequisite conditions for these two pillars are not yet in place.

The third pillar identified by Sarbib (2002) is 'a dynamic information and telecommunications infrastructure that provides efficient services and tools available to all sectors of society'. Here, there are more promising signs in particular locations. Overall, many countries in the region have made significant investments in information and communications technology (ICT) infrastructure. In the Gulf States, especially in Dubai but markedly also in Bahrain and Kuwait, this has been accompanied by a boom in retail and services. Tourism has become a dynamic focus for investment in these locations with several prominent developments that have ratcheted up the requirements for information technology (IT) support.

Mobile phone technology has been prominent but the shortage of landlines has inhibited the region's standing in terms of Internet use. But a more profound limitation is imposed by the relative underpreparation and formation of qualified scientific and engineering skills within the indigenous communities. These GCC countries in particular still rely on expatriate labour to provide the most needed skills. Practically every state in this region has promulgated legislation to favour indigenous candidates for key jobs and practically every one has failed to achieve these goals, leaving the long-term prospects for obtaining an appropriate skill-balance rather weak.

There are two exceptions to the general pattern, Jordan and Dubai. They have several features in common. Both have benefited from consistent and strong political leadership, both have sought to blend public and private policy-making in an integrated vision of the future and both have explicitly targeted knowledge per se as a development priority. Moreover both nations have developed a philosophy that has sought a customised solution to what each has identified as national economic needs, in terms of a vision of what each can offer on a wider stage, regionally and internationally.

Jordan has long fostered education and particularly higher education as a national strategic priority. It has developed both public and private universities of good standing. More recently, His Majesty King Abdullah has led a comprehensive programme involving international support especially from the USA and Britain and combining the resources of the public and private sectors. Initiatives include the Jordan IT Community Centres scheme to develop the use of IT and promote sustainable development especially in rural areas that has now established 20 centres. The Economic Opportunities for Jordanian Youth is seeking to increase the provision of relevant training in IT to increase skills at the point of entry into the labour market. REACH is an initiative directed to create an export-oriented IT services sector to facilitate the emergence of Jordan as a regional leader in IT products and services.

Dubai has become the richest growth pole in the region by explicitly planning a development strategy based on a diminished reliance on natural resources, an increase in trade and services and, especially in recent years, those related to the knowledge economy. Over the decade of 1995–2005, the dependence on oil-based revenues has been cut by half and a 30 per cent increase in GDP has depended on a massive growth in services, of which a quarter has been in the knowledge sector.

Specific initiatives have been directed towards establishing Dubai as the regional leader in these sectors and as an inescapable hub in the global knowledge economy. These initiatives have formed a part of a wider strategy in which tourism, air transportation for both passengers and cargo, and financial services have been attracted to Dubai as a hub interfacing between Europe, the USA and Asia. The strategy is backed up by supportive developments in education and other soft infrastructures.

Dubai University College (DUC) is a recently created higher education institution formed under the aegis of the Dubai Chamber of Commerce and Industry. Its programmes give strategic emphasis to IT and business in close cooperation with the local business communities. The strategic priority for the faculty is to concentrate on building up a high-quality research base in the United Arab Emirates (UAE), with priority being given to research with especial relevance for business and industry in the region. To this end, they are emphasising research methodology teaching in the curriculum and utilising student projects undertaken on jointly supervised internships leading to dissertations, to improve the quality of knowledge about business and industry in the UAE. The Business Faculty has built a reward system to encourage regular publication based on systematic empirical research. Its Centre for Management and Professional Programmes is currently offering courses for executives in IT, Logistics and Supply Chain Management, Total Quality Management, Quality, Negotiation, and Corporate Governance. The College of IT (CIT) is next door on an integrated campus and offers a BSc programme in Internet Computing and Computing Information Systems. Like the Business School, the CIT is also in the process of accreditation of their BSc programme from the Accrediting Board for Engineering and Technology. There are over 400 students in CIT and over 900 students in the College of Business.

In the next two years, the DUC will move to a new site that will enable it to play a bigger role in developing the knowledge economy. The new developments costing AED 150 000 000 (USD 41 million) will see the DUC occupying a new site some 10 kilometres from the centre, in the new Academic City, close to the Knowledge City. The site will also include a Business Research and Development Centre, a Centre for Leadership Training and Research, a Business College, an IT College and a College of Law and Arbitration (Dean of the DUC Business School, April 2006).

The Dubai Internet City is a prime focus of the drive to establish the knowledge economy in the region, by fostering a dynamic international community of ICT companies including global giants like Microsoft, Cisco Systems, IBM, HP, Dell, Siemens, Sun Microsystems, Computer Associates,

PeopleSoft and Sony Ericsson. Many small and medium businesses and promising entrepreneurial ventures are also part of the community. The cluster comprises companies from a variety of sectors – Software Development, Business Services, Web Based and e-Commerce, Consultancy, Sales and Marketing and Back Office (see Dubai Internet City, 2006).

The Knowledge Village was launched in 2003 and is the core of this most ambitious and well-integrated strategy. Dubai Knowledge Village, launched in October 2003, places Dubai on the map as a destination for learning excellence. Its one kilometre long picturesque campus provides a supportive environment for a variety of knowledge-based entities, including prominent international universities, training centres and learning support entities (see Royal College of Surgeons in Ireland and Dubai, 2006).

These developments may be successful in their short-term aims of establishing Dubai as a regional and global hub, but achieving the long-term objectives of changing the approach to knowledge economies in the MENA region will be a greater test. Over the next decades, these initiatives can affect the whole of the MENA region. But it is far from clear that this will happen easily. Dubai's claim to regional economic leadership will continue to depend on an acceptance by other states that they can go down the same route or that they will succumb to Dubai's claims of hegemony. But the chief danger is that while these developments may work well and become embedded in the urban and corporate spaces of Dubai, they will not be generalised to the wider communities of UAE enterprises and public organisations but will remain dimensions of the expatriate economy. Thus, skills will not become embedded locally but will remain as transient as the careers of the mobile population of transnational managers (Harry and Banshi, 2004).

PATTERNS OF MANAGEMENT AND LEADERSHIP IN ORGANISATIONS IN THE MENA REGION

It is well understood that management resonates to different formal practices in the MENA region from those in the West. The dual pull of tradition and modernity is evident in the characteristic responses of Arab managers to the problems of managing authority and relationships in organisations. I have previously identified these practices as together constituting a 'fourth paradigm' of management values, styles and behaviours (Weir, 1998, 2000).

Al-Rasheed's (1994) study illustrates that in the Arab context, the personalised concept of power leads to feelings of uncertainty and loss of autonomy among lower-level organisational participants. Problems tend to be ascribed to personal failure rather than to organisational or administrative shortcomings. Leadership is a fundamental aspect of life in the Arab world, but its connotations are not necessarily the same as those in the West. The 'leader' is one who has to be acceptable to peers or colleagues to guide activities, ensure progress towards some agreed goals and to coordinate disparate efforts. But leaders, once agreed upon, can expect to be followed, unless they transgress severely. In Islamic tradition, much weight is placed on the concept of the 'just ruler' and this emphasis on how the ruler exerts authority takes precedence over considerations of how the power and position were obtained and whether this can be defended as legitimate according to general rules of decision. Thus the discourse of 'democracy' is not as significant as the discourse of 'justice'.

A common model is control through close supervision. Thus plant managers go to considerable lengths to demonstrate that they are highly active in supervising the behaviour of employees who cannot be trusted to act responsibly of their own accord. Concepts of stewardship of resources exercised over relatively long time-spans may be more significant in accounting for the perceived legitimacy of managerial authority than the maximisation of returns on assets. The typical form of decision making in Arab organisations is consultative, with delegation the least widely used technique. Loyalty is prized above all other organisational values, even efficiency. Loyalty can be guaranteed by surrounding the executive with subordinates whom he can trust. Arab managers have a more flexible interpretation of time than Western management, and often run several meetings simultaneously. The basic rule of business with Arab managers is to establish the relationship first and only come to the heart of the intended business at a later meeting, once trust has been achieved. This process may take considerable time. Verbal contracts are absolute and an individual's word is his bond. Failure to meet verbally agreed obligations may be visited with dire penalties and will certainly lead to a termination of a business relationship. Nonetheless, the Arab world is essentially a trading world, governed by an implicit and extensive understanding of the requirements of commercial activity (see Weir, 2000).

A concise overview of the impact of Arab culture on Arab management practice is Al-Faleh's (1987) article on cultural influences on Arab manage-ment development in Jordan. He identifies the importance of status, position and seniority as more important than ability and performance. The central control of organisations corresponds to a low level of delegation. Decision making is located in the upper reaches of the hierarchy, and authoritarian management styles predominate. Subordinates are deferential and obedient, especially in public in the presence of their hierarchical superiors. Consultation is one-to-one, rather than on a group basis. Decisions do not emerge from the formal process of decision making. Prior affiliation and existing obligation are more influential than explicit performance objectives.

Ali and Ali-Shakhis (1985) have undertaken several studies of the relationship between managerial decision styles and work satisfaction. They reinforce the general finding that Arab managers prefer consultative styles and are unhappy with delegation. They point, however, to the experience of political instability and to the growing fragmentation of traditional kinship structures as the origins of an ongoing conflict between authoritarian and consultative styles and the need for Arab managers to resolve this conflict by developing a pseudo-consultative style in order to create a supportive and cohesive environment among themselves. They contrast Saudi-Arabian with North American managerial styles in that the Saudi managers use decision styles which are consultative rather than participative. Their value systems are described as 'outer-directed', tribalistic, conformist and socio-centric, compared to the 'inner-directed', egocentric, manipulative and existentialist perspectives of the North Americans.

Whereas American organisations are tall, relatively decentralised and characterised by clear relationships, Saudi organisations are flat, authority relationships are vague, but decision making is centralised. In the West, typically the norm is that staffing and recruitment proceed on principles which are perceived or can be defended as objective, based on comparability of standards, qualifications and experience. On the other hand, in Saudi organisations, selection may be perceived as highly subjective, depending on personal contacts, nepotism, regionalism and family name. Performance evaluation in Saudi may be informal, with few systematic controls and established criteria and the planning function is typically undeveloped and not highly regarded (Ali and Ali-Shakhis, 1985).

But it is unwise to over-generalise the younger generation of managers, who are often Western-trained and may hold different expectations. Al Hashemi and Najjar (1989), for instance, document the emergence of a managerial class in Bahrain in a series of publications which draw a picture of a well-educated and sophisticated cadre of professional managers, who may not be able to find the fulfilment that their Western counterparts would seek in their work, because of the tight constraints of organisational and administrative structures.

Central to an understanding of what is basically distinctive about the styles of organisational decision making in the MENA region is the Diwan. A Diwan can thus signify a couch, a room, the holder of an office of state, a place, an organisation and a style of decision making. It can also be a historical account or a mode of literary production. Its multiplicities and connotations are understood by practically everybody in the Arab and Islamic worlds and by practically no one outside of these milieux. To understand Diwan is to penetrate to the heart of why decision making is a fundamentally different social process from the Western organisations, why strategy and implementation are different, and why the rhythms and pace of management are distinct.

In the Diwan, decisions are the outcome of processes of information exchange, practised listening, questioning and the interpretation and confirmation of informal as well as formal meanings. Decisions of the Diwan are enacted by the senior people, but they are owned by all. This ensures commitment based on respect for both position and process. Seniority and effectiveness are significant, but to be powerful, the concurrent consent of those involved has to be sought, and symbolised in the process of the Diwan. Hierarchy is a feature of the Diwan and it can be clearly noted in the layout of the Diwan and in understanding who moves through what aspects of the space. But the hierarchy is modified by fluid movement, what Baumann (2005) calls 'liquidity'. This is a highly-ordered interactional event. In the Diwan, people observe a characteristic pattern of social networking reinforcing existing strong bonds of family and kinship.

These patterns of social networking are not of course restricted to the Arab Middle East and they appear in differing forms in the Arab and Chinese business worlds (Hutchings and Weir, 2006; Weir and Hutchings, 2005). But in a specific cultural milieu we can also see the operation in a precise and well-understood framework, of an activity that creates the spatial manifestation of a method of managing and generating social knowledge, which can lead to business and political opportunity. The Diwan is a matrix for KM that embodies openness to the possibility of new knowledge that can emerge as the Diwan progresses. Within the Diwan, ideas can be reviewed and positions checked without the formalities of official reporting or precise financial announcement. The Diwan is a KM device that permits both openness and closure. The bounds of interaction are self-limiting and an interactional homeostasis is the outcome of events that are in precise terms unplanned. Agendas are not issued, nor minutes taken. But what has happened is transparent.

The Diwan is however a place of tacit knowledge and unspoken implications. Managing this knowledge requires a strong appreciation of context as well as content. It is not clear how the more formalistic approaches to KM typical of Western KM theory can apply to these dimensions of knowledge.

CONCLUSION AND IMPLICATIONS FOR INTERNATIONAL BUSINESS OF KNOWLEDGE MANAGEMENT IN MENA

Earlier I quoted Sarbib's (2002) framework of the four pillars that should support a knowledge economy. What are the prospects for each of these pillars? I argued above that in principle, the MENA region seems to be not deficient in generic attitudes to education so any presumed preference for a 'traditionalism' that encompasses a preference for ignorance over knowledge can be swiftly rejected. Even within the frameworks of a culturist explanation, this preference would be unlikely. Historically, this region and these cultures are largely though not exclusively dominated by the tenets of Islam, and have prized education even more coherently than the nations of Western Christendom.

Some critics of the MENA region have indeed presumed that globalisation as an all-encompassing process will merely increase the discrepancies between the dominant paradigms of the West and East and that the MENA countries will sink into a trough of despond in between. But this negativism is far from inevitable. The global world is indeed upon us, but whose world will it in fact turn out to be? 'Globalisation' is often taken to imply the inevitability of current market realities, only written on a larger canvas. But tomorrow's tastes can rarely be predicted from today's fashions.

While analysis of the increasingly 'global' economy and changing patterns of information-use and data transmission are based on the assumptions that current trends will continue and the industrial and commercial hegemony of the West will persist (not merely unimpaired but strengthened by the new technologies of virtuality), I propose that a longer-range perspective on the ways in which knowledge emerges is created and used in practice to produce some interesting possibilities, and that the MENA region will not continue to be at the bottom of the pile forever.

In principle, I have argued in earlier publications that the ways in which the world order is moving may not all be especially helpful for the West's continuing hegemony, nor are they especially negative about the prospects for other regions and in particular for the MENA countries (see Weir, 1998, 2000, 2003). So for the purposes of the present discussion, I wish to consider the extent to which the bases of knowledge-based business in the Arab Middle East are likely to be strengthened or attenuated by the forces that are changing the world. In practice, our sciences of management are dominated by Western cultural paradigms and the bulk of writings on business are written implicitly or explicitly from a Western perspective and assume Western preconceptions and understandings. Possibly we should consider what we mean by 'knowledge' and whether a broader definition may yield some insights into the special circumstances of this region.

Although I earlier eschewed simplistic culturalist explanations for the lack of progress, there is in fact little evidence from the global scene as a whole of wholesale cultural convergence in business matters, especially as these are impacting on the role of cultural factors or social networks on business processes. So it is unwise to assume that as technology advances it will bring adherence to Western norms of business behaviour. Indeed there is some evidence of an increasing divergence and diverse cultural framework for business. Singularity may not be as evident as centrifugality. Within this more complex framework, network models may be more promising than structural models.

In the past few years, there has been unambiguous support for Western hegemony in economic matters. However, it is now apparent that in some respects, the present Western model is suffering a series of setbacks. It is not yet in full-scale retreat, but some warning notes are being sounded. It is not as clear as it was that a state-based model of economic development cannot bring rapid prosperity to China, or that Western ideas of democratic political government are the necessary basis for continuing Arab business wealth. In Latin America and in the emerging Africa, much attention is currently being paid to alternatives to the Western capitalist paradigms.

There may be inherent advantages in the modes of doing business characteristic of this region compared to the Western models, where the new virtual environments are concerned. The reasons for this relate to the strong cultural bases, the universalising cultural paradigms and the potential for network structures implicit in the bonds of family, kinship and social bonds in these societies.

Nonetheless and notwithstanding all these arguments that could encourage an optimistic view, the knowledge era clearly has not dawned in the MENA region. There are some bright spots but overall the outlook is not encouraging. The reasons relate not so much to endemic cultural reasons but to some more specific geo-political and economic realities.

Over the past decade, there has been a worsening of the political ambience between this region and the West. Thirty years ago, Iraq emerged as one of the better prospects for an education, qualifications and knowledge-based route to economic growth, however, it has now been reduced to a state of civil war. Third world social indicators have been depressing, the more so because they were largely avoidable. Enforced pauperisation of whole communities, whether in Gaza or in Fallujah, do not facilitate the growth of trade or enhance the credentials of those whose civilising mission comes firstly through the pilotless drone or the Humvee. Business cannot be enforced by military means. There is a generalised anxiety felt about the future throughout the entire MENA region.

The discourses of 'confrontation' and 'clash of civilisations', however inept from a scholarly perspective, have served their turn in marginalising and isolating relevant modernism within the Moslem world. Being a moderniser in business technology may entail risks for some professionals in this climate of anxiety about the West and its true intentions.

While the prospects for the more backward players in the MENA region have worsened significantly in some cases, at the other end of the scale, the oil-rich nations have profited from a war boom and a general inflation of oil prices. This has meant too much easy money and even less incentive to modernise.

The introduction of new geo-political forces in terms of China, India and some countries of South East Asia, especially Malaysia, has brought with it the prospect of new economic models and success paradigms. When the MENA region finally moves, there is possibly even less reason to expect that it will move towards the Western models.

Finally, I argue that styles of organisational governance and operational management in this region, especially as represented in Diwan styles of decision making, need to be more thoroughly understood before they can be readily incorporated in the largely Western-rooted theories of KM that currently constrain our discourse.

REFERENCES

Al-Faleh, M. (1987), 'Cultural Influences on Arab Managerial Development', *Journal of Management Development*, **6**(3), 19–33.
Al-Hashemi, I. and G. Najjar (1989), 'Strategic Choices in Management Education: The Bahraini Experience', in J. Davies (ed.), *The Challenge to Western Management Development*, London: Routledge, pp. 29–39.
Al-Rasheed, A.M. (1994), 'Traditional Arab Management: Evidence from Empirical Comparative Research', in *Proceedings of the Second Arab Management Conference*, University of Bradford Management Centre.
Ali, A. and M. Ali-Shakhis (1985), 'Managerial Value Systems for Working in Saudi Arabia', *Journal of Social Psychology*, **127**, 183–9.
Aubert, J.-E. and J.-E. Reiffers (2003), *Knowledge Economies in the Middle East and North Africa: Towards New Development Strategies*, Washington, DC: World Bank.
Baumann, Z. (2005), *Liquid Life*, London: Polity Press.
Djeflat, A. (2002), *Challenges for MENA Countries from the Knowledge Revolution*, Washington, DC: World Bank.
Dubai Internet City (2006), 'Dubai Internet City Official Website', 20 April, 2006, http://www.dubaiinternetcity.com/
El-Kharouf, A. and D. Weir (2005), 'Women Managers in Jordan', in *Proceedings of the Fifth European Academy of Management*, May 2005, Munich, Germany.
Harry, W. and M. Banshi (2004), 'Transnational Managers in the Middle East', in *Proceedings of the Irish Academy of Management*, April 2004, Dublin, Ireland.
Hutchings, K. and D.T.H. Weir (2006), 'Guanxi and Wasta: A Comparative Examination of the Impact of Internationalisation and Modernisation on Traditional Ways of Networking in China and the Arab World', *Thunderbird International Business Review*, **48**(1), 141–56.
Keller, J. and M. Nabli (2002), *The Macroeconomics of Labour Market Outcomes in MENA countries in the 1990s: How Growth has Failed to Keep Pace with a Burgeoning Labour Market*, Working Paper 71, Washington, DC: The World Bank.
Lundvall, B.A. (1999), 'The Learning Economy: Challenges to Economic Theory and Policy', in K. Nielsen and B. Johnson (eds), *Institutions and Economic Change: New*

Perspectives on Markets, Firms and Technology, Cheltenham, UK and Northampton, MA, USA: Edward Elgar, pp. 33–54.

Page, J. (2002), 'Structural Reforms in the Middle East and North Africa', in P. Cornelius and K. Schwab (eds), *Arab World Competitiveness Report 2002–2003*, Oxford: Oxford University Press, pp. 62–79.

Royal College of Surgeons in Ireland and Dubai (2006), 'Dubai Knowledge Village', 20 April, 2006, http://www.rcsidubai.com/kv/index.html

Sarbib, J.-L. (2002), *Building Knowledge Societies in the Middle East and North Africa*, Washington, DC: World Bank.

Sharabi, H. (1988), *Neo-patriarchy: A Theory of Distorted Change in Arab Society*, Oxford: Oxford University Press.

UNDP (2002), *United Nations Development Programme: Arab Human Development Report 2002*, New York and Oxford: Oxford University Press.

Weir, D.T.H. (1998), 'The Fourth Paradigm', in A.A. Shamali and J. Denton (eds), *Management in the Middle East*, Kuwait: Gulf Management Centre, pp. 60–76.

Weir, D.T.H. (2000), 'Management in the Arab World', in M. Warner (ed.), *Management in Emerging Countries: Regional Encyclopaedia of Business and Management*, London: Business Press/Thomson Learning, pp. 291–300.

Weir, D.T.H. (2003), 'Human Resource Development in the Arab World', in M. Lee (ed.), *Human Resource Development in a Complex World*, London: Taylor and Francis, pp. 69–82.

Weir, D. and K. Hutchings (2005), 'Cultural Embeddedness of Knowledge Sharing in China and the Arab World', *Knowledge and Process Management*, **12**(2), 89–98.

Wilson, R. (2001), 'New Regionalism and GCC Trade: New Directions', in K. Lawler and L. Sedighi (eds), *International Economics, Theories and Debates*, New York: Prentice Hall, pp. 148–71.

World Bank (1998), *World Development Report 1998–1999: Knowledge for Development*, Washington, DC: World Bank.

10. Latin American cultural values and their impact on knowledge management

Luis Felipe Calderón-Moncloa

INTRODUCTION

Management theories coming from industrialised countries flow between borders and continents very easily. What is not easy to understand is the undesirable direct and side effects that the application of those theories can have, when naive academicians and managers try to implant them without taking into account all the cultural complexities involved. When implanted in a power-oriented culture, like our Latin American organisational culture, concepts like participative management and flatter organisations acquire different connotations from those originally intended. If managers try to practise participative management, they might create confusion among employees who feel that it is inappropriate for the boss to share responsibilities with the subordinates, and thus the managers may lose some authority in the process. In a similar manner, managers can use re-engineering, downsizing, outsourcing and flatter organisations as excuses to fire employees for the sake of budget savings, resulting in fewer employees and longer hours without extra compensation. This situation is highly common in Latin America now.

My intention in this chapter is to introduce the Latin American environment and culture and try to explain the general blockages that Latin American managers experience when trying to implant knowledge management (KM) recommendations into the organisations. A note of caution before proceeding to the analysis – an implicit paradigm that permeates some of the academic analysis is a Western-centric biased vision, implying that theories coming from Western academia are the correct ones and that third world organisations are wrong if they fail to adopt them. What this paradigm ignores is the existing distance between academic theory and real organisational practice in the Western countries.

Trying to establish a generic pattern for how knowledge is shared and disseminated in Latin America is, optimistically speaking, a highly difficult task. To understand how huge this difficulty is, it is necessary to explain, as briefly as possible, the complexity of Latin American societies, based on their history, social evolution and present socio-economic situation.

The very concept of 'Latin America' is highly controversial. In its more simplistic definition, the name Latin America alludes to a part of this continent that was invaded by European countries whose languages originated in Latin, mainly Spain (most of South and Central America and extended parts of North America) and Portugal (Brazil) and secondarily France (that is Quebec, Louisiana, French Guiana, Haiti and many minor Caribbean islands). But inside some parts of this same territory, it is also possible to recognise zones that were invaded by Britain (Belize, Guyana and many Caribbean islands) and the Netherlands (Surinam, Aruba, Curacao and many other Caribbean islands), which are still under their control and/or influence.

California, Arizona, New Mexico, Colorado, Texas and Florida were originally invaded by Spain (and, in some minor share, by France) but they were later integrated into the United States. But the dynamics of immigration in the last century have transformed some parts of those territories, mainly the Spanish speaking regions, making it difficult to establish if they are a part of Latin America. The same problem occurs with the Canadian province of Quebec that it is a French speaking region but is not considered part of Latin America despite conforming to the basic definition. But, as intricate as all this seems, this is only the simpler part inside a more complex history.

Latin American History: Implications for Management

After the 'discovery' of America in the late fifteenth century, the invasion of European countries in the early sixteenth century, three and four centuries of political and military domination, which included the extermination of tens of millions of the native population, and more than one century of political and economic influence of the USA, the fracture inside the Latin American countries continues to be immense. There are sometimes extreme differences within each of these countries, as there is a mosaic of independent, overlapping, contradictory and submissive social groups and cultures. There are even overlapping cultural worlds with Westernised and conservative native minded people in the same country, city and even company, who pretend that they understand each other perfectly and that they are not that different. Hence, it is nearly impossible to generalise the 'Latin American' culture, management style or KM practices.

In the 1970s and 1980s, many Latin American countries, sometimes by means of military coups d'état or democratic elections, turned to 'nationalist' governments. The most well known examples of this are Salvador Allende in Chile, Omar Torrijos in Panama and General Juan Velasco in Peru, who started a wave of nationalisations and expropriations, which created immense state-owned companies and protection of the national companies. These governments demanded and tried to impose a different relationship between their countries and the dominant capitalist countries and their transnational companies and, as a consequence, many transnational companies were forced to or decided to leave the region. However, some of them learnt how to play the new game and stayed in the region, profiting from the advantageous conditions created by protectionism.

But in the 1980s and 1990s, after years of 'nationalism' and anti-liberal policies, most Latin American countries again turned to liberal policies. This attracted big transnational companies back to Latin America and it was expected that they would transfer advanced management and technical knowledge into the economies.

This wave of liberalism supposedly had brought free markets, development and prosperity, but the experience seems to be somehow disappointing considering that one South American electorate after the other is turning their vote to non- or less liberalistic options (Hugo Chavez in Venezuela, Inacio Lula da Silva in Brazil, Tabaré Vásquez in Uruguay, Néstor Kirschner in Argentina, Evo Morales in Bolivia and Ollanta Humala in Peru). (Because these are ongoing events, it is too soon to have literature reviewing these cases. This information can only be found in journals and newspapers.)

These less liberal governments are relatively new so it is too soon to evaluate how far this wave will take these countries, and how this will affect the local and the transnational companies and their KM practices. What seems crystal clear is the tendency of these countries to change politically from one extreme to the other, without building a consistent long-range national policy. One exception to this is the case of Chile. Despite having a moderate socialist government, it continues to have highly liberal policies implanted by General Pinochet from 1973 and is the fastest growing economy in the region.

Although there are big differences among the Latin American countries, some general damaging regularities prevail. The two best known are the complexity of the regulatory systems (De Soto et al., 1986) that pushes the economies towards informality, and the intense and pervading corruption that affects citizens' everyday and organisational lives. There are no exact statistics addressing the size of the informal economy but some reasonable numbers estimate its rough size to be 50 per cent.

At the individual level, a highly important characteristic that marked the last decade is an increasing unemployment rate (especially executive unemployment) in most countries (International Labour Organisation, 2004).

There are many reasons for this. The first and most important is the economic crisis that started in Asia in 1998, which had long lasting recessive consequences in Latin America. Other contributing factors are the wave of mergers and acquisitions, the 1980s and 1990s privatisations, and the tendency for radical cost reduction and outsourcing.

At the same time, the number of B-School and MBA graduates is skyrocketing, making the executive market increasingly competitive. Hence, holding an MBA is no longer a guarantee for obtaining or maintaining a good job. This makes jobs harder to obtain and easier to lose, thus executives feel insecure and lose their negotiating power with their bosses, resulting in increasingly submissive behaviour. Despite popular ideas about participative, flatter and democratic management styles in managers' discourse, real world management practices are not necessarily changing, except in some particular cases (Casado-González, 2003). In fact, these discourses encourage an epidemic of hypocrisy, as they point to some socially accepted direction but are not practised correctly.

A MOSAIC OF CULTURES, A WORLD OF PROBLEMS

Contrary to the apparent homogeneity that occurs with Chinese, Japanese and Western European countries, Latin American countries are far more heterogeneous.

Despite the differences between countries, it is possible to affirm that within each country there are multiple independent cultures that co-exist, dominate, submit and sometimes pretend that the other cultures do not even exist, or that the others are not different. But, at the same time, all those cultures are in an intense *mestizaje* in blood, language, customs and values. *Mestizo* (Portuguese, *mestiço*; French, *métis*: from Late Latin mixticius, from Latin mixtus, past participle of miscere, 'to mix') is a term of Spanish origin used to designate the people of mixed European and indigenous non-European ancestry. The term has traditionally been applied mostly to those of mixed European and indigenous Amerindian ancestry who inhabit the region spanning the Americas; from the Canadian prairies in the north to Argentina and Chile's Patagonia in the south (Wikipedia, 2006d).

In almost every big Latin American city, it is easy to find whites, native Indians, Negros, Asians and *mestizo* populations. However, depending on the race or social class, it may also be possible to find people with different degrees of *mestizaje* living a Westernised and/or a traditional lifestyle.

Adding to this complexity is the intense process of internal immigration from the rural and extremely impoverished zones to the cities, creating huge shanty towns (also known as misery belts, favelas, barriadas, callampas, bidon villes). These towns surround every big and small Latin American city, creating social and economic problems and increasing the informal sector – the street vendors and the informal micro companies.

Latin America is a complex mosaic, made up of at least three socio-cultural groups from each city. First, there are the modern, Westernised, affluent upper and middle class groups. Second, the poor, mostly Westernised, group, and third, some new forms of *mestizaje* produced in recent decades that have created new subcultures and marginal groups composed of immigrant peasants living in a completely different culture (De Soto et al., 1986). In some countries, this culture is called the Chicha culture. The number of people making up the Chicha culture is so big that their own mixed culture is becoming stronger and relatively autonomous from the city's culture, making up nearly 60 per cent in some cities. It is so strong that it has started a process of *inverse acculturisation* (Arellano and Burgos, 2003), whereby instead of this 'marginal' group being acculturated by the city group, the city group culture is strongly affected by the marginal culture.

This complexity is, of course, reproduced inside the organisations because different organisational layers usually come from different social groups and origins. Shareholders and management usually come from the first group, white collar workers normally come from the second and blue collar workers usually come from the third group.

Ignoring the Cultural Complexity Inside Organisations

Because Latin American managers are usually unaware of these cultural differences and/or they despise those cultural groups, their management of workers coming from those social groups is mostly based on authority and the capacity to manage a reward/punishment system.

Another problem that increases managers' inability to manage the cultural differences is the role of Westernised management education in universities and business schools that tries to emulate their developed counterparts and ignore their own cultural peculiarities. In fact, almost all management education in Latin American universities and business schools is based on translated American books, and hiring professors with US-awarded PhD degrees is highly prioritised.

However, the organisations in the informal sector are mainly constituted by people coming from the third group and their values and practices are not always the same as in the formal, Westernised sector.

As a result of the historic, social and economic dynamics, what characterises Latin American cultures (and consequently, their organisational cultures) is a widely present and socially accepted high 'power distance' (Hofstede and Hofstede, 2005). This is derived from huge socio-economic, racial and educational asymmetries, where social and organisational relationships are based on 'domination' because of race and/or socio-economic position and/or educational level. As stated by Hosfstede (ITIM International, 2003), power distance focuses on the degree of equality, or inequality, between people in the country's society. A high power distance ranking indicates that inequalities of power and wealth have been allowed to grow within the society. These societies are more likely to follow a caste system that does not allow significant upward mobility of its citizens. A low power distance ranking indicates that the society de-emphasises the differences between citizens' power and wealth. In these societies, equality and opportunity for everyone is stressed.

In today's Latin America, there are two phenomena similar to the Europeans' 'Kapo syndrome' (Frankl, 1997) and the 'Stockholm syndrome'. Kapo was a term used for certain prisoners who worked inside the Nazi concentration camps during World War II. The name stood for *Kameradenpolizei* (comrade police), and referred to prisoners who had been recruited by their captors to police their fellow prisoners. They received more privileges than normal prisoners, towards whom they were often brutal. Their tasks included transporting victims of gassing to the ovens, cleaning the gas chambers of human excrement and blood, removal of gold from the teeth of the victims and shaving the heads of those going to the gas chambers. Kapos were given special privileges within the concentration camps, but were seen as betraying their fellow prisoners for personal gain (Wikipedia, 2006a).

On the other hand, the Stockholm syndrome is a psychological response sometimes seen in a hostage, in which the hostage exhibits seeming loyalty to the hostage-taker, in spite of the danger (or at least risk) the hostage has been put in. The Stockholm syndrome is also sometimes discussed in reference to other situations with similar tensions, such as battered woman syndrome, child abuse cases, and bride kidnapping (Wikipedia, 2006b).

In the Latin American culture, there are two phenomena similar to the above mentioned. They are known as *malinchism* and the *yuppie criollo* (the Creole or *mestizo* yuppie). Both were derived from the hate/love paradox of identification with the predator that some victims feel.

'Malinchism' is a word derived from Malinche (the name of the Hernan Cortez native lover) who has been wrongly considered as a betrayer of her people (Lanyon, 2000; Messinger-Cypess, 1991; Romero and Nolacea-Harris, 2005). Malinchism causes what in psychiatry is known as a Dissociative Identity Disorder, which is derived from repetitive micro-traumas or ritual abuse usually inflicted in childhood. Dissociative identity disorder is described as the existence in an individual of two or more distinct identities or personalities, each with its own pattern of perceiving and interacting with the environment. At least two of these personalities are considered to routinely take control of the individual's behaviour, and there is also some associated memory loss, which is beyond normal forgetfulness (Carreón, 2000; Wikipedia, 2006c).

Malinchism is the situation where Latin American locals, from native, negro and/or *mestizo* ancestors, adopt the values and play the role of the dominant side, identifying with them and interjecting their values and behaviours, and treating their native subordinates worse than the powerful foreigners and local whites do.

Yuppie criollo is the name given to a Latin American executive, usually a *mestizo*, who over-adapts his/her thinking and his/her external behaviour to that of an American yuppie executive (in his/her language, clothing, life and management style, and so on). This *yuppie criollo* normally holds an American, European or Latin American MBA degree and superficially seems to have the same profile as an American or a West European executive. But this similarity is only partial and mostly apparent because in his/her ideology, it is possible to identify both ways of thinking – the *mestizo* and the Western ideology.

It is hypothesised (Domínguez, 2004; Passuth, 2004; Tenorio, 2006) that an important number of Latin American managers and political leaders are malinchists and/or *yuppie criollos* and that their managerial behaviour is marked by one or both of these profiles. This could explain why their real world practices are distant from Western expressions even though their management discourses are formally Westernised. They could inflict abuse, mistreatment and oppression on their subordinates without expressing remorse because of the Dissociative Identity Disorder. They are not capable of ethically reviewing their own abusive behaviour and, when asked to think about it, they assume it is legitimate. The implications of these phenomena in the real world practice of KM are huge. For example, knowledge sharing is recognised as a key condition for KM, however knowledge is only shared with some subordinates (the in-groups), which depends on the social distance they feel with each cultural group inside their organisation. In this way, invisible but strong barriers are created against knowledge dissemination across out-groups.

In Latin America, punitive ideologies are widely accepted, hence both bosses and subordinates tend to accept that bosses have the legitimate right to inflict punishment. These relationships of subordination are accepted as natural and legitimate as evidenced by Hofstede and Hofstede's studies (2005) about 'power distance'.

Along the Hofstedes' lines and complementary to this last point, a gender problem is also clearly present in Latin America, in what is known as a 'macho culture' that illustrates the relationships between men and women in organisations. It is hypothesised (Meentzen and Gomáriz, 2003) that this gender segregation excludes women from the macho 'mafias' where knowledge is shared more easily and, consequently, they receive less information in quality and quantity. This same phenomenon is also part of the explanation why women in Latin American organisations get into trouble when they are promoted to higher management levels.

The Latin American culture is also characterised by massive – both active and unconscious – resistance to any kind of formalisation and standardisation (by not registering formally, not playing by the rules, being late, and ignoring deadlines). Informal practices in informal organisations (De Soto et al., 1986) and informal practices in formal organisations are almost universal.

Going back to the Latin American history, there are two old phenomena that continue to have a strong influence on today's ideology and culture – colonialism and Catholicism. Even before the European invasion, societies were marked by imperialist domination. The Inca, Maya and Aztec empires (amongst others) grew by means of conquest and slavery. When European empires arrived, they imposed their domination scheme over the previous ones. At the beginning of the nineteenth century this colonial scheme was replaced by British domination, and at the end of the nineteenth century was progressively replaced by the US domination that continues until today.

This long lasting foreign domination marks the Latin American character, creating the feeling that everyone and everything coming from those dominant countries is superior. It also marks, among many other characteristics, the way in which the theories are adopted and implanted from the industrialised countries.

There is also a particular kind of Catholicism that Spanish and Portuguese conquerors brought to Latin America, which responded to their colonial interests. This biased version of Catholicism has influenced the way of thinking, increasing the tendency to submit to superior forces, obedience, guilt, sin, expiation and, especially, the acceptance of punishment. This culture can be considered a *punitive culture*, where subordinates' behaviours are directed to avoid punishments and to obtain rewards by submission and over-adaptation to bosses' wishes and demands.

WHAT CHARACTERISES LATIN AMERICAN ORGANISATIONAL CULTURES

In accordance with what characterises the general Latin American culture, it is also necessary to understand some characteristics of the Latin American organisational culture as it is highly relevant for understanding the many ways information and knowledge flux are distorted and blocked.

'Mafia' Values

Because of the strong Latin American family and small group values, sense of loyalty to the in-group usually has priority over other ethics and loyalty (Hofstede and Hofstede, 2005; Trompenaars and Hampden-Turner, 1998). This can lead organisational in-groups to behave like 'mafias', where inner ethics are strongly respected and are far more important than general socially accepted or declared values.

The individual's loyalty to his/her in-groups (Gómez et al., 2000) is based on his/her needs for acceptance and survival, creating permanent conflicts between declared organisational values (the stated organisational Vision and Mission) and everyday organisational behaviour. As a consequence, despite the organisation's pretended allegiance to accepted Western values, management practices and formal procedures, there is a big distance between what is declared (espoused theory) and what is actually happening in real life practice (theory-in-use) (Sbarcea, 2001).

Is not a surprise, then, that hiding critical information from other co-workers (Cabrera and Cabrera, 2002) is discreetly but widely practised and ethically justified, if this behaviour protects individual or in-group interests. It can also produce an important flow of information by informal channels in the form of *gossip*, when information is shared with formally unauthorised persons, but with whom the individual feels the moral urge or the convenience to share that information.

Hiding information is a result of the dilemma between loyalty to the organisation (or the formal part of the organisation) versus loyalty to the in-group, as this is what the individuals' survival depends on. This means some information cannot flow through the formally established channels because of the resistance of individuals to betray their in-group. In this way, sharing information is avoided, delayed or manipulated before transmission and these behaviours are morally justifiable. These practices are severely damaging to the formal organisational KM system, as extensive and important pieces of information and knowledge are not introduced into the formal system and flow secretively between in-group members.

Newly arrived managers think they have full control of knowledge in their organisations but what they control is only the visible part of organisational knowledge, and not the vital invisible part.

Organisational Feudalism

The strong loyalty within the in-group creates strong barriers to in-group/out-group dynamics and impedes knowledge dissemination. As a result, if two people need to interact because of organisational reasons, but are part of two different in-groups, the actual possibility for real and open collaboration and knowledge cross-pollination is severely limited. This distrust continues even though they are aware that it is damaging to the task and future of the organisation.

Similar to what has been suggested about Russia and China and the Arab World (see Michailova and Hutchings, 2006; Weir and Hutchings, 2005), organisational cultures in Latin America tend to be highly compartmentalised, generating *organisational feudalism*. Dominant individuals or groups tend to define and protect their own territory, leaving general organisational interests in second place. Individuals and/or small group interests are preferred over the general long-range interest of the full organisation and, consequently, knowledge dissemination across these borders is mostly declarative, despite the existence of formal procedures or software for KM (Boisot and Child, 1999; Briggs, 2005; Turner and Makhija, 2006). Knowledge and knowledge retention are used as weapons in the internal fight for power between different in-groups, which leads to dysfunctional relationships throughout the organisation.

Anti-empowerment Culture

The cultural distance, submissive behaviour, rivalry and distrust between organisational layers based on cultural, social, gender and race motivations, have severely damaged both top-down and bottom-up communication, creating biases in how knowledge is disseminated between organisational layers and departments.

This neat hierarchical order implies that both bosses and subordinates tend to accept that bosses have the legitimate right to possess and retain information, and it is illegitimate for subordinates to ask for this information to be shared. Knowledge sharing is a mandatory condition for empowerment, thus in this kind of context, every effort to empower subordinates is highly limited and will only occur in very specific situations, where there is no cultural distance between a boss and his/her subordinate.

Communication between an expatriate Western manager and a Westernised Latin American subordinate will appear to be efficient, as the native subordinate will behave 'appropriately' in front of the expatriate. However if the expatriate sees how the local interacts with his/her own native subordinates, he/she will be confused by the inconsistent behaviour. This will cause the expatriate to question the native subordinate as he/she will be doubtful of the validity of agreements made with the subordinates. In this case, the subordinates will tend to show a full agreement ('reverence') although they do not understand or are confused by the interaction, or disagree with the orders received.

Punitive Culture and Management by Objectives

The old recipe for managing is known as Management by Objectives (MBO) (see Drucker, 1954) and is almost universally accepted and practised in all Latin American countries and organisations. What some managers are not aware of is that any managerial formula, inserted in a different cultural context, acquires different connotations and implies side effects probably not present in the original theory. When inserted in a highly hierarchical and punitive culture like Latin America, MBO can induce very destructive practices as objectives tend to be irrational and inflexible, degenerating into menacing challenges and severe punishment as a consequence of failure.

Some Latin American managers tend to reduce their roles to that of a rewards-system administrator, granting rewards in cases of success or inflicting punishments in cases of failures. As a logical consequence, the end of the period report is a stressful moment where executives are obsessed with achieving the goals or pretending they have accomplished them (Kohn, 1992, 1999). Another problematic consequence of this system is that it creates a tendency to submission, reinforcing the cultural tendency for submissive behaviour in relationships with authority that inhibits organisational learning, knowledge sharing and creativity. As a result, disagreements between a boss and his/her subordinates are infrequent or are superficial as subordinates are afraid to disagree with their bosses. Subordinates fear that any disagreement could be considered as a rebellion against the boss's authority and a menace to their egos, and dread the dire consequences.

As an inevitable consequence, a logical but pathological reaction is the subordinate's need to falsify data and pretend that targets have been accomplished. Errors are not considered as opportunities for learning but as menacing situations where face is lost and the person is in danger of being fired. Thus, organisational mistakes are hidden from management (as far as it is possible) so that they cannot be corrected, usually until it is too late and mistakes have exploded beyond control and created a crisis. This phenomenon creates an important problem for building a shared meaning between native workers and expatriate Western managers. While the expatriate asks for pure data and clear information for feedback and corrective purposes, the native worker may interpret that as an intimidating and punitive demand. In other words, while the Westerner is asking for openness, the native feels the urge for self-protection and distance. This situation can be worsened if the Westerner is unaware of these cultural differences.

Culture of Pseudo KM

As is typical in any highly hierarchical and punitive culture, knowledge retention is a key source of power. Hence, despite the fact that knowledge dissemination is formally encouraged, claimed and proclaimed, it is actively resisted and sabotaged in actual behaviour. Even in the more formalised organisations that have formal procedures for knowledge dissemination and retention, the quantity and quality of knowledge that flows are only a small fraction of what is managed informally or not shared outside the in-groups.

In the context of executive unemployment and imminent personnel reductions, the value and relevance of not sharing information is extremely high. Consequently, some key knowledge is not codified or incorporated into the company's knowledge base, but is hidden and used as a source of power and a weapon in internal rivalry. This creates a higher bargaining value.

Some of this information is even used, in a corrupted fashion, to create parallel businesses that are suppliers of the same organisation. Among the many manifestations of corruption (Bamrud, 2002; Boehm, 2005; Pei, 2006), using inside information for personal profit is a practice not uncommon in Latin America's private and state sectors. Some executives create companies (supposedly owned by different persons) and facilitate them to become a provider for the company they work for. For these illegal schemes to work, it is critical for them to hide information and knowledge, ensuring that other executives do not have access to them.

Informality

As mentioned above, informality is pervasive in societies and organisations (De Soto et al., 1986; Ghersi, 1997; Harriss-White, 2003). Estimates suggest that the informal economy sector in Latin America accounts for up to 60 per cent of the total economy in some countries (Romero, 2006; Universidad de los Trabajadores de América Latina, 2006). This characteristic is highly relevant to Latin American organisational behaviour because most formal efforts to manage knowledge require codification, formalisation and reduction in ambiguity.

But this informality goes far beyond the informal economy, as it is a pervading attitude. Even inside formal organisations and local branches of transnational corporations, Latin American executives tend to behave informally. For example, formal companies can sell a part of their production to formal or informal distribution channels without invoices (what is called 'to sell underground' or 'to sell in-the-dark'). This attitude includes the tendency to not register activities into the formal system. There are frequent reports of executives actively resisting presenting reports and registering data, because they consider it a waste of valuable time.

KNOWLEDGE MANAGEMENT IN LATIN AMERICAN ORGANISATIONS

Evidently, there is no typical Latin American organisation. As an example, the situation in local branches of transnational corporations is clearly different from that of local corporations (mainly family owned corporations) and more distant from the medium, small and micro organisations (almost always family-owned) and big state-owned companies and organisations.

Local branches of transnational corporations, local corporations, state-owned companies and organisations make up approximately 5 per cent of all organisational units, while the other 95 per cent are medium, small and micro organisations. For the sake of simplicity, the first 5 per cent of organisations will be called the 'modern' (larger) units and the other 95 per cent will be called the 'traditional' (smaller) units. Although it is evident that there is immense heterogeneity within these categories, some generalisations are reasonable.

Knowledge Management in the 'Modern' Units

The 'modern' units claim and pretend to play by the rules of modern management. All of them have state-of-the-art computer-based information systems, enterprise resource planning and modern data bases and can use data warehousing and mining tools. Most of their management hold MBA degrees from prestigious North American and European business schools or from prestigious Latin American business schools (that usually abide by North American standards and frequently have US accreditation). They adopt the latest concepts of the US and European management academy and frequently hire consultants in order to meet these global standards.

In the most prestigious local branches of transnational corporations and local corporations, most of the local higher management tend to be white, US-educated or educated in local expensive universities, English–Spanish bilingual speakers, who come from the local upper class and are loyal followers of the global rules. Cultural considerations must be practised, especially in relationships with personnel in lower organisational positions, who are not normally part of the same cultural groups (De Long and Fahey, 2000). Expatriate managers from North America and Europe notice the power asymmetry, social distance, submission and other cultural peculiarities while their local counterparts seem to be blind to these phenomena.

Transnational companies obviously share procedural (bureaucratic, routine), managerial and technical knowledge with their local branches in Latin America, but what really happens in these local branches is mediated by local cultural factors.

In these 'modern' units, knowledge is formally and professionally managed and they experience the same kind of resistance that Western organisations face when trying to manage knowledge, for instance, the difficulties of encoding implicit knowledge or the unwillingness of executives to register explicit knowledge into the organisational knowledge pool.

Knowledge Management in the 'Traditional' Units

On the other hand, the 'traditional' units are a heterogeneous set of organisations, with different sizes and characteristics. They are the medium, small and micro companies that account for roughly 95 per cent of all organisation units in Latin America.

Contrary to what occurs in the 'modern' units, integrated computer-based information systems are almost absent, despite the pervasive and growing presence of stand-alone personal computers with Microsoft Windows and Office and other business applications and local area networks. Managers with an internationally accredited MBA are scarce and they are far less interested in the new concepts of business administration.

In these units, face-to-face contact and informal ways of sharing information prevail. They are very hierarchical organisations, with a high power distance, although the cultural distance between owners, managers and white- and blue-collar workers is less important than in the modern units. They rarely have a KM programme and usually are not even aware of this concept. Knowledge is intuitively, informally and unconsciously managed. In spite of this, they are able to manage knowledge quite successfully. As knowledge is managed in a highly informal and implicit way, knowledge hoarding is almost absolute, especially by those with status, privilege and power.

Except in a few Latin American countries (for example Chile, Costa Rica and Uruguay) or in some specific areas in other countries (for example Northern Mexico, some parts of Brazil and Argentina), the 'traditional' units and their informal and conservative practices show a tendency not only to prevail but to prosper.

CONCLUSIONS

The Latin American culture, like any other culture, has many limitations. Fortunately, it also has many good points that, if correctly exploited, could generate an accelerated development for its organisations.

Cabrera and Cabrera (2002) noted that less individualistic cultures are more open to knowledge sharing and less assertive cultures are easier to transform. They have a tendency to prefer face-to-face contact, social interchanges and the sharing of food, alcohol and dancing in any possible situation. This helps in the diffusion of tacit knowledge and building of trust. This trust is a necessary condition for knowledge to be disseminated. The above mentioned circumstances produce larger in-groups and, under the correct catalyst, these in-groups are more permeable to interchange with out-groups.

Informality also has a positive side. It trains executives and organisations to be flexible and opportunistic, generating highly adaptive organisations and a fertile ground for what Nonaka and Takeuchi (1995) describe as 'creative chaos'. These characteristics create opportunities for programmes that develop KM in Latin America. Its success is dependent on the cultural conditions described and the many complex peculiarities that the modern and the traditional units possess.

This chapter concludes with some practical recommendations for Western managers managing a Latin American company or a local branch of a transnational corporation:

- Be aware of the multi-culturality of Latin American societies. Beyond race and social origin, people have peculiar levels of cultural *mestizaje*. This makes them interpret things in peculiar and unexpected ways, for instance the phrases, slogans, orders and, especially, the principles that the Western manager is trying to enforce.
- Despite the fact that some managers seem to be totally Westernised, they tend to behave differently towards the foreign boss and native subordinate.
- Latin Americans tend to show agreement with figures of authority, especially if they are Westerners and White Anglo-Saxon Protestants, but this does not mean they are persuaded to abide by the explicit rules.
- There will be immense opportunities for foreign managers if they are aware of the above-mentioned barriers and are able to overcome them successfully.

REFERENCES

Arellano, R. and D. Burgos (2003), *Lima ciudad de los Reyes, de los Chávez, los Quispe*, Lima: EPENSA.

Bamrud, J. (2002), 'Latin Business Chronicle: Fighting Corruption', 19 June, 2006, http://www.latinbusinesschronicle.com/reports/reports/corruption.htm

Boehm, F. (2005), 'Corrupción y Captura en la Regulación de los Servicios Públicos', *Revista de Economía Institucional*, **7**(13), 245–63.

Boisot, M. and J. Child (1999), 'Organisations as Adaptive Systems in Complex Environments', *Organisation Science*, **10**(3), 237–52.

Briggs, J. (2005), 'The Use of Indigenous Knowledge in Development: Problems and Challenges', *Progress in Development Studies*, **5**(2), 99–114.

Cabrera, A. and E.F. Cabrera (2002), 'Knowledge Sharing Dilemmas', *Organisation Studies*, **23**(5), 687–710.

Carreón, H. (2000), 'Shattered Identities: "Malinchismo" as a Dissociative Identity Disorder Caused by Ritual Racial Abuse', 19 June, 2006, http://www.aztlan.net/identity.htm

Casado-González, J.M. (2003), 'Decálogo Etiológico de las Esquizofrenias Empresariales', *Harvard-Deusto Business Review*, **119**, 56–68.

De Long, D.W. and L. Fahey (2000), 'Diagnosing Cultural Barriers to Knowledge Management', *Academy of Management Executive*, **14**(4), 113–27.

De Soto, H., E. Ghersi and M. Ghibellini (1986), *El Otro Sendero (The Other Path)*, Lima, Peru: Editorial El Barranco.

Domínguez, F.A. (2004), '¿Nuevo malinchismo?', 26 May, 2006, http://www.espaciosdigital.com/articulos/verarticulo.asp?ID=83

Drucker, P.F. (1954), *The Practice of Management*, New York: Harper & Row.

Frankl, V. (1997), *Man's Search for Meaning*, New York: Pocket Books.

Ghersi, E. (1997), 'The Informal Economy in Latin America', *Cato Journal*, **17**(1), 99–108.

Gómez, C., B.L. Kirkman and D.L. Shapiro (2000), 'The Impact of Collectivism and In-group/Out-group Membership on the Evaluation Generosity of Team Members', *Academy of Management Journal*, **43**(6), 1097–106.

Harriss-White, B. (2003), 'La Desigualdad en el Trabajo en la Economía Informal: Cuestiones Esenciales y Ejemplos', *Revista Internacional del Trabajo*, **122**(4), 507–18.

Hofstede, G. and G.J. Hofstede (2005), *Cultures and Organisations: Software of the Mind*, 2nd edn, New York: McGraw-Hill.

International Labour Organisation (2004), 'América Latina y el Caribe', in *Tendencias Mundiales del Empleo*, Geneva: OIT.

ITIM International (2003), 'Geert Hofstede Cultural Dimensions', 26 May, 2006, http://www.geert-hofstede.com/

Kohn, A. (1992), *No Contest*, Boston, MA: Houghton Mifflin.

Kohn, A. (1999), *Punished by Rewards*, Boston, MA: Houghton Mifflin.

Lanyon, A. (2000), *Malinche's Conquest*, Sydney, Australia: Allen & Unwin Pty.

Meentzen, A. and E. Gomáriz (2003), *Democracia de Género, Una Propuesta Inclusiva*, El Salvador: Fundación Heirich Böll.

Messinger-Cypess, S. (1991), *La Malinche in Mexican Literature*, Austin, TX: University of Texas Press.

Michailova, S. and K. Hutchings (2006), 'National Cultural Influences on Knowledge Sharing in China and Russia', *Journal of Management Studies*, **43**(3), 383–405.

Nonaka, I. and H. Takeuchi (1995), *The Knowledge-Creating Company: How Japanese Companies Create the Dynamics of Innovation*, New York: Oxford University Press.

Passuth, L. (2004), *El Dios de la Lluvia Llora Sobre México*, Mexico: Muchnik.

Pei, M. (2006), 'The Dark Side of China's Rise', *Foreign Policy*, **153**, 32–40.

Romero, R. (2006), 'Economía Informal', 26 May, 2006, http://www.utal.org/economia/informal.htm

Romero, R. and A. Nolacea-Harris (eds) (2005), *Feminism, Nation and Myth: La Malinche*, Houston, TX: Arte Publico Press.

Sbarcea, K. (2001), 'The Mystery of Knowledge Management', *Management*, **48**(10), 33–6.

Tenorio, E. (2006), 'Debraye Hostil Sobre Cultura y Emancipacion Indigena y

Ejemplos Sobre Eepredación de la Cultura Mexicana', 26 May, 2006, http://www.gratisweb.com/bordodexochiaca/Casino1.htm
Trompenaars, F. and C. Hampden-Turner (1998), *Riding the Waves of Culture: Understanding Diversity in Global Business*, 2nd edn, New York: McGraw-Hill.
Turner, K.L. and M.V. Makhija (2006), 'The Role of Organisational Controls in Managing Knowledge', *Academy of Management Review*, **31**(1), 197–217.
Universidad de los Trabajadores de América Latina (2006), 26 May, 2006, http://www.utal.org/alatinaycaribe.htm
Weir, D. and K. Hutchings (2005), 'Cultural Embeddedness of Knowledge Sharing in China and the Arab World', *Knowledge and Process Management*, **12**(2), 89–98.
Wikipedia (2006a), 'Kapo', 26 May, 2006, http://en.wikipedia.org/wiki/Kapo
Wikipedia (2006b), 'Stockholm Syndrome', 26 May, 2006 http://en.wikipedia.org/wiki/Stockholm_syndrome
Wikipedia (2006c), 'Dissociative Identity Disorder', 26 May, 2006, http://en.wikipedia.org/wiki/Dissociative_Identity_Disorder
Wikipedia (2006d), 'Mestizo', 26 May, 2006, http://en.wikipedia.org/wiki/Mestiza

PART FIVE

Conclusion

11. Conclusion: towards a cross-cultural and institutional framework

Kavoos Mohannak and Kate Hutchings

The previous chapters presented a broad range of issues in managing knowledge and provided a view of the totality and complexity of the various dimensions of knowledge management (KM), especially from cultural and institutional perspectives. Each author presented a large range of issues on the KM landscape and discussed how cultural and institutional influences impact on KM. Thus, it would be helpful to come up with some general concluding remarks. This chapter draws some conclusions and proposes a framework within which KM can be synthesised from a cultural and institutional perspective.

The theme of this book focused on the concept of KM from cultural and institutional perspectives and particularly in developing economies. The reason was that cultural diversity, as evidenced in the case studies, has a definite impact on the work-related values and attitudes of employees and their support and understanding of KM. In this regard, it is possible to postulate that if cultural diversity impacts on the work-related attitudes and values of employees, it will also influence the degree to which employees value knowledge and the manner in which they participate and support KM within the enterprise.

Surely, one of the common themes which arose from the case studies is that a manger in a cross-cultural environment must address the cultural diversity of the workforce on KM. It is therefore of the utmost importance that an understanding must be developed of the impact of cultural diversity on work-related attitudes and values and thus ultimately also of the impact of cultural diversity on KM. Effective and efficient KM will depend, to a large degree, on the ability of management and other stakeholders to create an environment in which cultural diversities or employees are taken into account when KM processes are designed and implemented.

Throughout this book, we were also concerned with the transformation of societies, especially through the application of knowledge. The accumulation and efficient use of knowledge, whether it is technical, industrial or managerial in nature, has played a central role in each of these transformations. Whether it is the role of KM development in the expansion of Taiwan's electronics and manufacturing industries; or the role of tacit knowledge transfer in the economic and social transformation of former socialist societies; or the way in which Polish ex-socialist firms acquired dynamic capability – having knowledge is the key factor in each leap forward. Institutional changes and changes in relations between institutions are important in understanding this context. In a rapidly changing environment, the performance of socio-economic systems is increasingly determined by their institutional adjustment capacity. To ensure a well-balanced adjustment process, it is important to understand the determinants of institutional change, which is deeply embedded in cultural practices. The abilities to learn and foster personal experiences constitute the human side of the 'culture of knowledge' and are key elements of knowledge societies and institutional adjustment. As a result, all KM activities need to be people-centred.

Although KM is often seen as a technological issue, in practice it is widely understood that technology is a relatively small part of any successful KM programme. This is because a tool cannot be utilised without the corresponding cultural and organisational practices. In the case studies we observe that without understanding the people, the processes and the culture, knowledge cannot be managed satisfactorily if they are not incorporated into the equation. In effect, information technology is necessary for KM in any complex environment, but it is not sufficient.

We are living in an era where the present and future will essentially be determined by our ability to use knowledge wisely, a precious global resource that is the embodiment of human intellectual capital and technology. As we begin to expand our understanding of knowledge as an essential asset, we realise that in many ways, our future is limited only by our imagination and ability to leverage the human mind. As Spender (Chapter 2) rightfully argued 'social institutions act as important constraints over the application of managerial imagination ... institutions create the complexities of contemporary society in which individual freedoms are both offered and protected from the imaginings of others'.

The country case studies included in this book show that some activities and institutions in the KM process are more directly steered by local cultures. In India for example, culture continues to affect sharing or managing knowledge especially at individual and micro levels. This was investigated by looking at the differences based on religion, caste, language and region. This supports the idea that the cultural backgrounds of people in developing countries often reduce the effectiveness of certain activities, which is not the case in developed countries (Chen et al., 2006). This was evident from the case of Latin America as well, where its culture is characterised by both active and unconscious resistance to any kind of formalisation and standardisation.

Calderón-Moncloa (Chapter 10) also found that in Latin America, there exists a socially accepted high 'power distance', which derives from huge socio-economic, racial and educational asymmetries. This proves that informal practices and organisations are almost universal. In these societies, similar to Russia, China and the Arab World, organisational cultures tend to be highly compartmentalised, generating what the author called 'organisational feudalism'. In fact, it appears that knowledge retention in these societies is a key source of power. As a result, although knowledge dissemination is formally encouraged, it is actively resisted. Consequently, some key knowledge is not codified or incorporated into the company's knowledge base, but it is hidden and used as a source of power.

Similarly, in transition societies such as China, Russia and former socialist economies, knowledge sharing may be extensive if an in-group relationship exists between the respective members. In fact, as discussed by Hutchings and Michailova (Chapter 5), the distinction between in-groups and out-groups influences relationships to a high degree in the transition economies. Networks and communication in these countries are based largely on collectivist relationships, which involve highly frequent exchanges and operate at both workplace and private levels. Furthermore, as shown, relationship building is tied to the development of trust and shared context. In these societies, although implicit communication styles are used, much knowledge is still tacit. In this regard, the ability of an organisation to harness tacit knowledge as a source of learning is influenced greatly by social and institutional factors (Lam, 2000).

From an institutional perspective, it is also possible to observe from the case studies that elements of a complex web of socio-technical interactions tie the firm and its environment together. For example, as examined in the case of Poland, local firms particularly faced with intense international competition had to rapidly adapt to the radical changes in the external environment and renew competencies. As a result, specific institutional arrangements emerged that enabled and restricted strategic and organisational options at both macro and micro levels. Further, the analysis by Kaminska-Labbé and Thomas (Chapter 4) shows how firms' capabilities are embedded in social power bonds, which manifested themselves throughout the privatisation process. Their analysis definitely enriched our understanding of how firms acquire capability, especially in high-velocity markets which demand the rapid creation of situation-specific new knowledge.

Mauritius (Chapter 8) provided yet a different story. In this case, KM was accumulated from entrepreneurial organisations and the government created effective institutional arrangements for knowledge sharing and development. The case also argued that human resources can develop capabilities and become capable but there is a need for relationship building, discipline, mutual respect and the right learning environment, which is an essential ingredient for capacity development. Another important lesson from this case is that a country should invest significantly in education if it aims to become a knowledge society.

The observations above suggest that various activities within knowledge processes can be influenced by local culture and institutions. In fact, institutional relationships may sometimes increase inequality and a KM culture must be inclusive. At the enterprise level, businesses operate in institutional environments, where knowledge and intellectual capital are key factors in economic development and competitiveness. As observed from the previous cases, this is only possible through the empowerment of individuals. It is of utmost importance to bear in mind that different people manage knowledge differently. Once enterprises realise and embrace this fact, the knowledge of the employee will truly become the knowledge and the most valuable asset of the enterprise.

Based on previous analysis, several main differences also emerge between Western and developing economies. It appears that while collectivism prevails in the developing countries, individualism prevails in developed and Western countries. However, in the developing and transition economies, transfer of individual (tacit) knowledge is extensive and this knowledge increases in utility when it becomes available to others in the organisation. These observations are consistent with the existing KM literature and cross-cultural management (for example Hofstede, 2001; Nonaka and Takeuchi, 1995). Davenport and Prusak (1998) also maintained that the Western culture organisations reward and raise the status of people who own knowledge. Hence people believe that knowledge is their special right and privilege, which should be preserved at all costs. However, less individualistic cultures are more open to knowledge sharing and less assertive cultures are easier to transform (Cabrera and Cabrera, 2002).

In developing countries, culture uncertainty or chaos is regarded as a phenomenon that can be employed to the advantage of KM in the enterprise. For example, in Latin America and former socialist countries, the authors demonstrated that informality trains executives and organisations to be flexible and opportunistic, generating highly adaptive organisations, a fertile ground for what Nonaka and Takeuchi (1995) call 'creative chaos'. In this way, organisations stimulate the knowledge creation process by deliberately introducing tension and chaos, for example by inducing breakdowns of set routines or habitual frameworks, and evoking a sense of crisis (Nonaka and Takeuchi, 1995). However, from a Western perspective, the use of uncertainty or chaos to create knowledge and support KM is avoided.

From the cases, we also observed that knowledge creation, appropriation and application are linked with education. For example, the Moslem societies in the Middle East and the contemporary Mauritian society increasingly rely on education to prepare for the knowledge society and to harness and maximise potential benefits. 'Knowing how to know' becomes ever more important, with education playing a major role in shaping mental frameworks and creating mental flexibility. This is particularly important for individuals from developing countries, who wish achieve more and ensure a better education with fewer resources. The developing countries are also struggling to protect their national cultural identity, which is threatened by the predominance of Western cultural, information and media products. The protest against the ongoing process of commercialisation of knowledge and information is actually a protest against the exploitation of indigenous knowledge and culture, which is the heritage of the developing countries' national culture and institutions.

From a theoretical point of view, knowledge is an internal cognitive structure of human beings. It cannot be managed, but the processes that support the creation and exchange of knowledge can be the subject of management, in particular the processes which involve many knowledge actors.

These observations suggest the need for a more aggregated analytical approach, in order to untangle the increasingly complex process, to help develop a comprehensive understanding of knowledge processes for the creation, transfer and deployment of this unique asset. Knowledge production and exchange is no longer primarily an individual process, but is more of a participative and collaborative process. Knowledge production and exchange is no longer dependent on primarily hierarchically structured and controlled institutions, but is open to everyone. Everyone has the opportunity to participate actively in the process of producing and exchanging knowledge. What counts in open communicative networks is not status or position in hierarchies, but competence and the willingness to share knowledge.

The role of knowledge in a cross-cultural and institutional perspective is therefore not confined by an organisation's boundaries. Instead, it evolves around networks of common practices, experiences and traditions. In most cases, KM is the result of recursive multi-dimensional and holistic processes. Intercultural exchange and multicultural settings can stimulate and enrich conditions for KM. The so-called 'relational approach' should be an emerging emphasis for cross-boundary and cross-cultural exchanges in knowledge and learning processes.

A consideration for a KM framework is to address different approaches to KM, which can be systematised with a view to developing a holistic and relational framework. In practice, the framework has to provide a coherent and general language that enables the various KM styles within different cultural and institutional settings to be understood. As discussed, KM can be viewed as consisting of several dimensions where cultural and institutional factors influence organisational knowledge processes. To understand and manage knowledge in organisations, we need to understand what knowledge is, how it is used, what its management consists of, and how we can improve organisational knowledge processes. We have to develop a set of integrated constructs that can be used to discuss knowledge from cross-cultural and institutional perspectives. As we have seen in the previous chapters, both macro and micro level issues need to be considered. At the macro level, contextual, cultural and institutional factors reflect on the organisational priorities and practices. The first dimension, therefore, is *contextual*. At the micro and individual levels, the second dimension reflects the *participants*, and the employees' behaviour determines actual KM activities. Lastly, at the organisation level, the third dimension reflects the *processes* created and integrates KM initiatives for creating, coding and sharing knowledge.

The objective of any cross-cultural and institutional KM framework is to endow an enterprise with a robust KM environment. That is, the technological, social and cultural settings and physical surroundings allow knowledge to be shared effectively throughout the enterprise. The aim of the suggested framework is to create an awareness of the impact of cultural diversity on KM, within the complex and dynamic environment of the institutional context within a country.

Based on these assumptions, any cross-cultural and institutional framework for understanding the KM style should include at least three dimensions: contextual factors, the participants and the KM process (see Figure 11.1).

The contextual factors (macro-level environment) (that is the context and macro environment within which KM is practised). This set of factors relates to institutions within a particular socio-cultural context and implies that the knowledge transfer and sharing is not taking place in a vacuum but must be seen as part of a wider environment. This can be described in terms of the structure and dynamism of the cultural, political and social institutions. Previous cases have clearly shown that KM is influenced by a series of macro level factors. These macro level factors include the national contextual factors, which are composed of combined economic, cultural, social and political factors. As observed in the case studies, each society has its own ethos and set of institutional and social values that underpin the culture of KM and sharing. In fact KM can occur in many different constellations, ranging from deliberate management (for example Taiwan) to institutional and social responses to emerging economic situations (for example former socialist countries).

It is the importance of these macro level issues and the cumulative impact of their interaction that has led to the growing interest in the cross-cultural and institutional issue in KM literature (for example Zhu, 2004). In other words, the cultural and institutional view implies that sets of institutional actors play

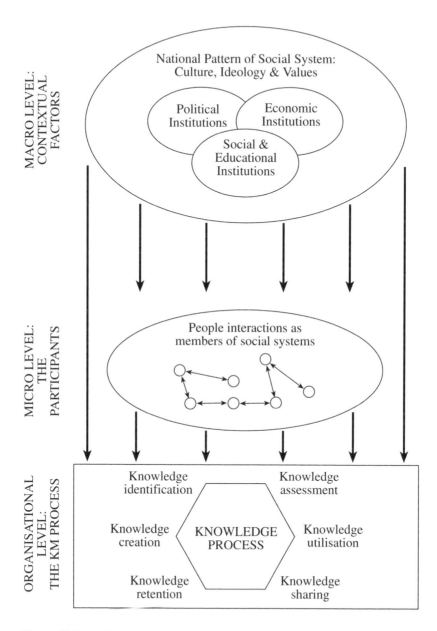

Figure 11.1   Relationships between macro, micro and organisational dimensions in KM

important roles, especially in influencing knowledge sharing and transfer. In fact, the influence of these factors is evident in the KM style of developed and developing countries.

The participants (micro-level factors) (that is the employees, who are culturally diverse in nature). At the micro level, the participants as employees are characterised by their level of knowledge, social backgrounds and culture. These individuals may influence communication and interaction in regard to knowledge exchange within organisations and are concerned with the relationships of individuals in terms of adaptations, contact pattern and communication mechanisms. The importance of these characteristics is demonstrated by the fact that knowledge interaction is an avenue for linking different participants and enabling them to share and transfer knowledge.

Furthermore, the role of the employee as the primary creator, codifier and carrier of knowledge is to accept and carry out his/her responsibility in creating, coding and sharing individual knowledge. The participants are responsible for sharing and transferring this knowledge in order to become an asset to the enterprise and, as a result, to contribute to its competitiveness within the global knowledge economy. As shown in the case studies, the complexity and dynamics of individual employees should be taken into account when KM is introduced in the enterprise. This situation becomes even more challenging when the employees have different cultural backgrounds and nationalities, as is the situation within the context of the multinational enterprise. It is thus clear that KM is a highly 'personalised' area of management science, which cannot be isolated from the individual employee, who is to a large degree responsible for its continued existence within the enterprise.

The KM process (that is knowledge creation, codification and sharing which takes place through knowledge conversion). At the organisation level, the KM functions consist of KM processes such as knowledge generation, codification, transfer and sharing. As observed in the case studies, organisations must be conducive to KM processes and employees must support KM principles for KM to be effective and efficient. There is no single process which can encompass all instances of knowledge generation, adaptation and transfer. There are, for example, many possible mechanisms ranging from personalised individual tacit knowledge sharing to strategic KM systems.

The role of the enterprise, therefore, is to provide the context for KM. The enterprise must form an environment which can be regarded as conducive to the creation, codification, transfer and ultimately the use of knowledge. The challenge for these enterprises resides in the fact that conditions and environments for knowledge creation, codification and transfer should remain stable and intact, regardless of changes occurring in both internal and external environments.

However, as maintained by Kuhlen (2003), the KM process should be addressed in a dynamic and communicative view, which emphasises the ongoing growth and renewal of knowledge and information in a continual process of exchange and communication. In this view, information is not just the result of a particular distribution or retrieval process but is also the result of communication processes, which are interactive and collaborative in the production of new knowledge. Kuhlen (2003) emphasises that knowledge and information in all areas and applications are increasingly produced, distributed and used collaboratively. In this view, an important part of the process takes place in the form of an exchange between different actors, such as individuals. Accordingly, there should be a focus on interaction between different actors within the enterprises. Hence, the KM process should not be seen as the product of only one actor, but as the result of an interplay between actors; in other words as a product of networked or linked actors. In this situation, new ideas can emerge if knowledge and contacts generated through communication are combined. As seen in previous cases, a rare exchange is one which takes place between individuals who share tacit knowledge.

In conclusion, the creation of a KM culture does not allow for a standard procedure to be followed at all times and in every situation. Truly innovative outcomes can only be achieved through a case-by-case approach. This is strongly influenced by ethical postures and views, configurations of culture, innovation and knowledge, which are always dynamic, flexible and contextual.

REFERENCES

Cabrera, A. and E.F. Cabrera (2002), 'Knowledge Sharing Dilemmas', *Organisation Studies*, **23**(5), 687–710.

Chen, Y.N., H.M. Chen, W. Huang and R.K.H. Ching (2006), 'E-Government Strategies in Developed and Developing Countries: An Implementation Framework and Case Study', *Journal of Global Information Management*, **14**(1), 23–46.

Davenport, T. and L. Prusak (1998), *Working Knowledge: How Organisations Manage what They Know*, Cambridge, MA: Harvard Business Press.

Kuhlen, R. (2003), 'Change of Paradigm in Knowledge Management: Framework for the Collaborative Production and Exchange of Knowledge', in H.-C. Hobohm (ed.), *Collected Papers from the 69th IFLA Conference on Knowledge Management*, Berlin: IFLA Publications, pp. 45–66.

Hofstede, G. (2001), *Culture's Consequences: Comparing Values, Behaviors, Institutions and Organisations Across Nations*, Thousand Oaks, CA: Sage Publications.

Lam, A. (2000), 'Tacit Knowledge, Organisational Learning and Societal Institutions: An Integrated Framework', *Organisation Studies*, **21**(3), 487–513.

Nonaka, I. and H. Takeuchi (1995), *The Knowledge-creating Company*, New York: Oxford University Press.

Zhu, Z. (2004), 'Knowledge Management: Towards a Universal Concept or Cross-cultural Contexts?', *Knowledge Management Research and Practice*, **2**, 76–9.

Index